CN00661989

THE
ROYAL MARINES
ON THE WESTERN FRONT

THE
ROYAL MARINES
ON THE WESTERN FRONT

DANIEL J McLEAN

Pen & Sword
MILITARY

AN IMPRINT OF PEN & SWORD BOOKS LTD.
YORKSHIRE – PHILADELPHIA

First published in Great Britain in 2021 by
PEN AND SWORD MILITARY
An imprint of
Pen & Sword Books Limited
Yorkshire – Philadelphia

ISBN 978 1 52676 386 0

Typeset in Times New Roman 10.5/13 by
SJmagic DESIGN SERVICES, India.
Printed and bound in the UK by CPI Group (UK) Ltd, Croydon, CRO 4YY

Pen & Sword Books Limited incorporates the imprints of Atlas, Archaeology,
Aviation, Discovery, Family History, Fiction, History, Maritime, Military,
Military Classics, Politics, Select, Transport, True Crime, Air World, Frontline
Publishing, Leo Cooper, Remember When, Seaforth Publishing, The Praetorian
Press, Wharncliffe Local History, Wharncliffe Transport, Wharncliffe True Crime
and White Owl.

For a complete list of Pen & Sword titles please contact
PEN & SWORD BOOKS LIMITED
47 Church Street, Barnsley, South Yorkshire S70 2AS, United Kingdom
E-mail: enquiries@pen-and-sword.co.uk
Website: www.pen-and-sword.co.uk

Or
PEN AND SWORD BOOKS
1950 Lawrence Rd, Havertown, PA 19083, USA
E-mail: Uspen-and-sword@casematepublishers.com
Website: www.penandswordbooks.com

Contents

Introduction

On 28 October 1664, an important day in British military history, the Duke of York and Albany's Maritime Regiment of Foot was formed in London at the home of the Honourable Artillery Company. Resplendent in their yellow coats, they were an immediately impressive sight, but none could surely have foreseen the extraordinarily professional, versatile and tenacious force into which they would develop. Today few military units can boast of such a widely-held and well-deserved reputation, yet much of their history remains a mystery to even the seasoned scholar of military history. Their development of commando warfare in the early 1940s certainly raised their profile to the level it retains today, but prior to that they had already developed a courageous and enviable record that had planted them firmly in the history of the British Empire.

As Lord High Admiral and brother of King Charles II, the Duke of York and Albany had an influential position both at court and in the defence of the realm, and so it was logical that he should be chosen to establish the new regiment which was largely recruited from the Trained Bands of London. The King's Order in Council decreed:

At the Court of Whitehall the 28th October 1664
Present

The King's Most Excellent Majesty
His Royal Highness ye Duke of York   *Earle of Middleton*
Lord Chancellor   *Lord Bishop of London*
Lord Treasurer   *Lord Ashley*
Duke of Albemarle   *Mr Vice Chamberlain*
Duke of Ormond   *Mr Secretary Morice*
Earle of Anglesey   *Mr Chancellor of ye Duchy*
Earle of Lauderdaill   *Sir Edward Nicholas*

Upon a Report from the Lords the Committee for the Affairs of His Majesty's Navy Royal and Admiralty of this Kingdome

> *this read at the Board, His Majesty was pleased to Order and direct that twelve hundred Land Soldiers be forthwith raised in readiness to be distributed to his Majesty's Fleets prepared for Sea Service, which said twelve hundred men are to be put under One Colonel, One Lieutenant Colonel and One Sergeant Major and to be divided into Six Companies. Each Company to consist of two hundred Soldiers; and to have one Captain, One Lieutenant, One Ensign, One Drummer, Four Sergeants and Four Corporals, and all the Soldiers aforesaid to be armed with good Firelocks. All which Arms, Drums and Colours are forthwith to be prepared and furnished out of His Majesty's stores. The care of all which is recommended to the Duke of Albermarle his Grace, Lord of His Majesty's Forces.[1]*

Soon known as the 'Admiral's Regiment', the small force of 1,200 grew swiftly, and forty years after its establishment received its most famous battle honour – Gibraltar. While the rock itself was largely captured by sailors of Admiral Byng's squadron, the marines played a vital part in the action and their sole occupation and defence of the rock during the siege of 1704-5 confirmed their reputation in the minds of the British people. The significance of the action is clear from the single battle honour that graces the globe and laurel cap badge of the Royal Marines even today.

After a further fifty years, on 5 April 1755, an Order in Council placed the marines under the control of the Admiralty and named them His Majesty's Marine Force, comprising fifty companies in three divisions at the naval ports of Portsmouth, Plymouth and Chatham: 5,000 men in total.[2] Their duties became further established during the subsequent naval conflicts of the eighteenth century as the provision of landing parties, of sharpshooters in battle and the maintenance of discipline onboard His Majesty's ships, but was again to diversify with the turn of the new century. Bomb vessels, mounting large mortars capable of firing explosive shells, had developed to a point where specialist personnel were required to operate the weapons in addition to the seamen capable of handling the ship and so initially they were served by men and officers of the Royal Regiment of Artillery. However, disagreements over whether army officers could be subject to naval orders and discipline meant that the arrangement quickly became untenable. Consequently, in 1804, the Marine Artillery Companies were formed and before long had become known as the 'blue marines' as a result of their blue artillery uniforms, compared to the red coats of their infantry counterparts.

In the same period, in 1802, King George III had renamed the Marine Force the Royal Marines, largely through the encouragement of Admiral John Jervis,

INTRODUCTION

First Earl St Vincent, whose admiration for the marines was the result of many years' service alongside them at sea. The order read:

> *In order to mark his approbation of the very meritorious conduct of the Marines during the late war, [the King] has been graciously pleased to direct that in future the corps shall be called the Royal Marines.*[3]

The expansion of the British Empire inevitably brought with it an ever-greater increase in the size of the Royal Navy, and thus the number of marines required for service at sea. However, they were also used for a variety of peace-keeping duties ashore, such as in Northern Ireland, in Newcastle in 1831 and during the general strike of 1842. The need for a larger force necessitated a greater administrative and logistical organisation and so in 1855 the Royal Marines Light Infantry (amended slightly to Royal Marine Light Infantry in 1862) was formed to fulfil these needs. The Royal Navy had begun to formalise its doctrine of naval brigades and the RMLI played the traditional part of light infantry, landing first and scouting ahead of the main force of conventional infantry and artillery, provided at that time by sailors.

In 1862 the Marine Artillery Companies were reformed as the Royal Marine Artillery (RMA) and the force assumed the form which it was to hold for the next sixty years. The RMLI was primarily based in the three establishments of Forton Barracks, Gosport, Stonehouse Barracks, Plymouth and the Royal Marine Barracks at Chatham. A fourth division at Woolwich closed with the dockyard in 1869 but had already become largely obsolete after the opening of the Royal Marines Depot at Deal in Kent, adjacent to the historic anchorage of the Downs and in the shelter of the Goodwin Sands. This was to remain the corps depot until 1991 and the home of the Royal Marine Band Service until 1996.

Forton Barracks occupied a site on the road from Gosport to Fareham that had seen military occupation since it housed French and American prisoners of war in the middle of the eighteenth century, but the barracks that were to become home to the RMLI were completed in 1807. For forty years they were occupied by a large number of different army battalions, none of which remained for longer than two years, until purchased by the Admiralty and, after £40,000 of improvements[4] had been completed, the Portsmouth Division of the RMLI took possession of their new home in March 1848. Subsequent decades of the nineteenth century saw the construction of a theatre, a school, a gymnasium and one of the largest parade grounds in the country.

Stonehouse Barracks may have housed marines based in Plymouth since 1756, from when the earliest surviving buildings date, but the principal period of construction was between 1779 and 1785. The site was periodically expanded up to the early 1870s and remained the home of the Plymouth Division of the RMLI up to the abolition of the divisional system in the 1940s. Today it is home to 3 Commando Brigade, but after a long and illustrious history it is scheduled for disposal by the Ministry of Defence by 2023. The Royal Marine Barracks at Chatham was first occupied in September 1779 and for the majority of its career was home to just over 1,000 men and officers. The Melville Hospital for Seamen was built adjacent to the site in 1827 but was purchased by the Admiralty and converted into extra accommodation in the opening years of the twentieth century. The barracks closed in 1950 and lay empty for several years, though some military, naval and educational uses were considered.[5] The establishment was finally demolished between 1959 and 1960.

The original Marine Artillery Companies had also been based in Chatham, but in 1824 they were provided with their own home for the first time when a series of storehouses in the Portsmouth Gunwharf were converted into barracks. This was to be their primary establishment for thirty-four years until 1858 when they moved to Fort Cumberland, a fortification first constructed over a century before in order to protect Portsmouth from a landward assault via Langstone Harbour. Though the fort was rearmed with modern rifled Armstrong guns shortly after the RMA's arrival, they soon outgrew its facilities and so a purpose-built establishment was created a short distance to the west at Eastney, looking south towards the Isle of Wight across the Solent. Eastney Barracks was designed by the Assistant Director of the Admiralty Works Department, William Scamp, and was described by Pevsner as: '…the best and most complete barracks of the post-Crimean War period'[6]. It certainly remains an extremely impressive complex, though now converted into housing. For several years after closure it continued to house the Royal Marines Museum, but that too has now closed, to be amalgamated with the National Museum of the Royal Navy in the dockyard, close by HMS *Victory* and the *Mary Rose*.

In 1914 the Royal Marines remained a far cry from the commando force of modern experience. It was certainly an efficient and impressive weapon, or indeed selection of weapons, within the Royal Navy's armoury, but it had never engaged in prolonged warfare ashore, certainly not on the scale that was to come. Nor, however, had any other arm of the British armed forces, and the Royal Marine Light Infantry and Royal Marine Artillery were to more than acquit themselves over the subsequent four years of conflict. Perhaps the best way to give an impression of the corps and its public perception early in the war is through this excerpt of an article written for the *Mexborough and Swinton Times*, a local newspaper in South Yorkshire, by E. Charles Vivian and published on 21 August 1915:

INTRODUCTION

Somebody once went to Eastney Barracks, one of the four Divisions whence the Royal Marines go out to the ships of the fleet & to work of every kind in every part of the world: that somebody was shown around the various shops & drill grounds & appliances with which a Marine becomes familiar in the course of his training, & finally that somebody turned to the man who had acted as his guide:- 'But nobody ever hears of the Marines', he said. 'What do you do?' 'Oh, nothing,' his guide answered, rather wearily. The reproof took effect, & the visitor apologised. For the Marines do everything, & the man who sets out to compile a record of what they do is as venturesome an individual as he who sets out to compile the history of the corps. In the first case, one might set down every form of military and naval activity, & in the second case, one might set to work to write the histories of the Navy & Army, omitting only the military work on the Indian frontier.

Ordinary regiments have their colours, on which are inscribed the actions & campaigns in which the owners of the colours distinguish themselves: the Marines adopt as their badge the globe, this stating simply that no colours (though the Royal Marines Light Infantry have them) could contain their world-wide distinction, & their motto – Per Mare Per Terram – backs the tacit statement. The word 'Gibraltar', at which place they put up their long and memorable defence, & a laurel wreath which commemorates their gallantry in the taking of Belleisle, complete the badge. Such a list of distinctions as regiments place on their colours would, in the case of the Marines be a recital of practically every campaign, & nearly every action, in which the British Navy and Army have taken part.

...On entering the barracks one is struck by the atmosphere of the pace in which these men are trained; outside the barrack gate are jerry-built houses, little shops & all that one would expect in this suburb of a naval town; inside is cleanliness, solidity & neat efficiency – one passes into a world that is better ordered, better managed, & of more healthy atmosphere than the civilian world outside. From the magnificent mess room of the officers' mess to the great central kitchen in which the men's meals are prepared, one gathers a sense of things done in the best possible way, & that sense persists in surveying the training of the men, the provisions for their comfort, the range of sport & recreation provided for their spare time – for every detail of their lives in

the period of training. From this period they pass equipped, mentally & physically, to take their place in the ships of the Fleet, with the Armies in France & the Dardanelles, in German South-West Africa, or on anti-aircraft service in the United Kingdom. For the Marines are ubiquitous & in every respect of this present campaign they have their share.

...On land, the Marines are used for manning coast defences & certain naval bases, for manning siege & heavy artillery in France, Belgium & South Africa; for contributing to the strength of colonial expeditionary forces, in manning anti-aircraft guns where needed, in working all the motor transport used in connection with their duties, & as an infantry brigade now forming part of the Royal Naval Division in the Dardanelles.

The corps is the most self-contained, the most self-supporting of any branch of the services; even the clothing & boots worn by the men are manufactured by & under the auspices of the authorities at the Barracks; trained as both sailors & soldiers, Marines comprise shoemakers, tailors & mechanics of every kind; on a foundation of infantry training they build a knowledge of every gun in use in both Navy & Army, &, if the camels used in the Egyptian campaign may be counted, there have also been mounted Marines. The colloquialism, 'Tell that to the Marines', is in the nature of a compliment to the corps, in reality, though it may appear as ridicule on the surface; its origin lay in the fact that a Marine is so well instructed & so intelligent that, if he will believe a thing, it must be true, & if it were not true the teller would meet his just reward... it is safe to say that there is more scope for intelligence in the Royal Marines than in any branch of either Navy or Army.

Given average intelligence & the desire to learn, the man in the Marines has more chance of fitting himself for & taking promotion than any other man....Yet another point with regard to this diversity of training is the fitness of the men for almost any kind of employment on their return to civil life. Infantry, cavalry, or artillery, on putting off uniform, are still soldiers by habit: the Marine, having been everything & done everything, is able to take up any form of civilian work as easy as he turned from the use of a big gun to the repair of a field telephone or the running of a motor-car.

...And then, a last conclusion, there is the spirit in which the men of the corps are trained, & the resulting spirit of the

men themselves. One may see things in the classes training at gun-laying, where every man knows that the score on his card must be good for the credit of the corps of which he is a member; in the squads swinging out to drill, made up of finely-developed bronzed healthy-looking men, from which the best is asked & by whom the best is given, for the credit of the corps: in the care, the individual instruction, the study of best methods, with which every instructor devotes himself to his task, for the credit of the corps; in the disciplined efficiency evident at every turn, by reason of which the Royal Marines consider themselves – & with justice – the finest body of men in the British forces. It is a corps of great traditions; of unequalled distinctions. It is 'nobody's-child', soldiers trained for sea service, & sailors ashore, capable of doing the work of both. The lack of official parentage has given rise to self-reliance & self-sufficiency, so that whatever arises to be done, the Marine can do it. In their work & their manner of doing it, as in the matter or pre-eminence in sport, the Marines yield their place to none; the man who joins this corps is not only fitting himself for service with the best trained body of men that the Navy & Army possess, but he is also educating himself in ways that will be useful for the rest of his life.[7]

Administration and Training

The scale and duration of the war inevitably had a great effect on the structure and overall administration of the Royal Marines, as with all branches of the armed forces. When war was declared in August 1914 there were 18,260 serving members, comprising 13,425 in the RMLI, 3,393 in the RMA and 1,442 in the Royal Marine Bands. The RMLI were split between the four port divisions of Portsmouth (Forton Barracks in Gosport), Plymouth (Stonehouse Barracks), Chatham and Deal, with the RMA headquartered at its historic home of Eastney Barracks near Portsmouth.

Though the corps was very nearly at its voted strength of 19,000, it suffered particularly from a shortage of officers. Admiral Fisher's Selborne-Fisher scheme, through which all officers of the naval service were to be recruited and trained together, had seriously reduced the number passing into the marines until 1912. The effect was so marked that limited specialist officer recruiting resumed,[8] with forty-seven appointed as probationary second lieutenants in that year and the same number in 1913. Even so, at the declaration of war the RMLI found itself short by thirty-nine officers and the RMA by nineteen, even when the fifty-nine trainee officers, at various stages of training, were included. The Reserve of Officers was immediately mobilised,[9] yet a shortage remained and indeed grew as the battalions increased in size with the first flush of wartime recruiting. Consequently, the first batch of forty temporary officers arrived at Eastney on 20 September 1914 and after a few brief weeks of training were sent to join battalions in their home ports. Many of these came from the Officer Training Corps of the public schools and universities, but as the war progressed an increasing number of permanent commissions were also given to senior NCOs of the corps, including those recalled from retirement. Regardless of background, permanent commissions were only offered up to the usual peacetime limit of numbers so as to avoid the creation of a cohort of unemployed officers after peace returned. Later in the war a significant number of temporary officers were recruited from the army's Officer Cadet Battalions. They received only a brief acquaintance with corps history and tradition before being sent to the 1st Reserve Battalion at Blandford for drafting.

It was still the case in wartime that some officer candidates were accepted for permanent commissions, so naturally it was necessary for these individuals to receive significantly more training, in spite of the pressing need for leadership at the front line. Both RMA and RMLI candidates underwent an intensive three months' course of infantry and general military training at the Deal depot, after which further courses in gunnery at HMS *Excellent* and electronics at HMS *Vernon* followed. Successful candidates then crossed Portsmouth harbour to the Royal Marines school of musketry, established at Browndown Camp in Gosport in 1916, under the command of Lieutenant Colonel F.E. Chichester, assisted by the staff of the Portsmouth Division RMLI, on loan from Forton Barracks.[10] Such an establishment was made necessary by the overwhelming of the army facilities at Hythe as the armed forces continued to expand.

Until this moment in its history the Royal Marines had never allowed short service engagements for other ranks and all marines signed on for twelve years of service. They were eligible to join from the age of 17 (though their period of engagement only began at their 18th birthday), with the exception of buglers who could join from 14. After their twelve years of service many would immediately sign on for a further nine in order to reach the immediately pensionable point of twenty-one years. However, the rapid expansion of the corps and the temporary nature of any conflict meant that short service engagements were offered for the first time in September 1914. These men received a programme of six weeks' basic training at Deal, after which they joined the newly-established training camp of the Royal Naval Division at Blandford in Dorset. Opened in November 1914 (Nelson Battalion were the first to arrive, on the 27th), the RMLI moved in at the end of January 1915 and established their headquarters at the village of Shillingstone and it was from here that they departed by train for Devonport on their way to Gallipoli only a week or so later, on 6 February 1915.[11]

Blandford Camp, on the exposed and wind-swept downs of central Dorset, was considered ideal for military training, but the accommodation that it provided could hardly be described as luxurious. Wooden huts, in groups of sixteen, each one accommodating twelve, fourteen or sixteen men, were meagrely warmed by coke stoves, the men sleeping on thin straw palliasses laid on wooden boards which in turn rested on trestles. Though only a short distance from the market town of Blandford itself, the camp was designed to be self-contained. It included both Methodist and Anglican churches, a YMCA and a post office, as well as the necessary junior rates', petty officers' and chief petty officers' messes and a wardroom for the officers. A somewhat satirical postcard, available in the camp at the time, described life there in this way:

'What a Happy Place is Blandford'
'What a happy place is Blandford' is a song that's rather new,
But I fancy that its topic should appeal to all of you,
For if anyone should ask you where your happiest mem'ries link,
You would answer in a chorus 'Oh, in Blandford,' I don't think!

Oh what a happy place is Blandford,
Envied by all soldiers near and far,
Oh my heart always inclines
To the good old A1 Lines,
Oh what a merry lot they are.

We've a rather mixed collection in the Blandford RND,
For we've got 5000 sailors who have never seen the sea,
And we've got a naval transport of 500 horse-marines,
The express design of Winston to supply the Turks with beans.

Oh what a happy place is Blandford,
Such a jolly place to war,
But if you've ever been to sea,
Gad, you'd love the RND,
Oh what a lucky lot you are.

Oh, they feed like lords at Blandford, on delicious bully beef.
They don't know what it died of, but suppose it died of grief,
For thinking of the men who've got to eat its tawny flesh,
But it's better than tinned salmon when the salmon isn't fresh.

Now of all the many units in this variegated camp,
There's one that stands out clearly of a different sort of stamp.
For of all this khaki navy in this wonderfull'st shows
There's none will stand comparing with the Blandford medicos.

Oh what a happy place is Blandford,
There's no unit nearly on a par.
And we've got the best CO,
That this camp will only know,
Oh what a lucky lot we are.[12]

Blandford remained the home of the Royal Naval Division for the vast majority of the war, until they transferred to more substantial barracks in Aldershot in the middle of 1918, and the camp was handed over to the newly-formed Royal Air Force. It exists today as the home of the Royal Corps of Signals.

It was already the case that marines serving on foreign stations could have their service extended by up to two years, under the conditions of the Royal Marines Mutiny Acts 1847,[13] but that provision was clearly inadequate and so the Royal Marine Act of 1914 extended that to those serving at home, and when it was replaced two years later by the Royal Marine Act 1916 the wording was altered to allow retention until the end of the war, whenever that might be. The Act of 1914 stated:

> *Section Five of the Royal Marines Act, 1847, which enables the term of service for a Marine to be prolonged if the term expires whilst he is serving on a foreign station, shall during the continuance of the present war apply, and shall be deemed always to have applied, wherever a Marine may be or may have been serving at the expiration of his term of service, with a substitution of a reference to the Admiralty for the reference to the Commanding Officer of the foreign station.*[14]

After their transfer to France and the reorganisation of the RMLI into the 1st and 2nd Battalions the War Office, having assumed authority over the training and administration of the RND, directed that reserve battalions be established at Blandford in June 1916. Lieutenant Colonel J.B. Finlayson took command of the 1st Reserve Battalion Royal Marine Light Infantry (1/R Bn RMLI), with a staff of experienced officers, many of whom had been promoted from the ranks, as company commanders. Recruits received from Deal were here subjected to a six to eight-week package of musketry, bayonet drill and bombing identical to that undertaken by the army, before being transferred to 63 Infantry Division Base Depot in France, thence on to a regular battalion. Until the introduction of conscription in 1916 these recruits had been obtained through the corps' own efforts across the country, but under the new system they were drawn from both naval conscripts and those of the army pool at Reading. Until 1917 only recruits rated A.1 at their medical were accepted for the RMLI, but at that point those classed as B.1 and C.1 were allowed and, after a short period of training at Deal, replaced men of the higher category in shore battery duties.

Those men detailed for the RMA brigades serving ashore, rather than at sea, undertook the same basic infantry training at Eastney as their sea-going counterparts, after which they trained at Fort Cumberland, just a mile along the shore. Here Major G.E. Barnes, under the authority of Commandant Sir George Aston, trained the officers and men of the Royal Marine Artillery (RMA) brigades in their respective items of ordnance, while Lieutenant Barkley instructed the drivers and mechanics in the various lorries, tractors, mobile workshops and other vehicles necessary for the brigades' deployment. It was also from here that battery crews accompanied the first guns ready for service in France until their own were delivered at a later date.

Pay for the Royal Marines had always been a complicated affair, as rates of pay and allowances varied depending on whether an individual was serving ashore or at sea. The separation allowance caused particular consternation as when a man was serving ashore he received the army rate, but when at sea he received the navy's rate which was considerably lower, yet the separation from one's family was the same. The provision of suitable uniforms and equipment was a further issue at the beginning of the war. Financial provision had not been made to equip the Royal Marines for long periods of service ashore, and so no khaki service dress was available for issue and '07 Pattern webbing was also in short supply. The Royal Marine Brigade therefore sailed for Belgium in their blue serge tunics, and it wasn't until their return that service dress was available. It had also been the case up to this point that annual issues of clothing were made and that any further replacements required were charged to the individual, but the conditions of wartime meant that this system quickly became unworkable, and instead replacement items of uniform were issued free of charge by order of company commanders.

The administration of the 63rd Royal Naval Division by the War Office also necessitated changes in the way that men joining the division were received and administered. During the Gallipoli campaign the division's reinforcement camp had naturally been located in Malta, the home of the Royal Navy's Mediterranean Fleet. Here, under the command of Lieutenant Colonel G.J. Mullins RMLI, it had efficiently supplied some of the most hard-hit units of the campaign, but transfer to the Western Front meant that a certain amount of conformity to the army norm was expected. The reinforcement camp was thus transformed into the Infantry Base Depot of the 63rd Division, though it remained something of an anomaly as it also administered the new arrivals of the Royal Marine Artillery into theatre, as well as those of the Royal Marine Light Infantry.

It was initially established on 10 June 1916 at Étaples, the largest single concentration of British troops on the Western Front, which housed over 100,000 men of many different units at its height in 1917. Lieutenant Colonel Mullins remained in command, as Deputy Assistant Adjutant General, and on 31 October 1916 the depot was moved to Beau Marais on the eastern outskirts of Calais for ease of access to the principal port receiving troop ships from Dover. Again, the independence of the 63rd Division was apparent as other divisional depots were amalgamated as the war progressed, but that of the RND, with its peculiar (to the War Office) practices and traditions, remained. The only other divisions to retain such a privilege were those of the Guards and the dominion troops. The divisional depot remained something of a steady presence in the otherwise ever-changing life of the RMLI and RMA in France, and indeed the majority of adjutants and quartermasters were taken from the officers of those units rather than from the many RNVR officers who were the majority in the division.

Chapter 1

Belgium, 1914

Ostend

In 1912 the First Sea Lord, Admiral Prince Louis of Battenberg, had drawn up plans for the formation of a Royal Marines 'Flying Column' in case of conflict.[1] The principal effect of this order was that fifty per cent of the 3rd and 4th Reserve Fleets were to be manned by the Royal Fleet Reserve so that a larger number of regular marines would be free to join the column when required. Consequently, on 2 August 1914, with war seemingly imminent, the Admiralty issued the order for the column to form for the first time. Initial responses were slow, though the Royal Marine Artillery and Chatham Division RMLI produced their required battalions in good time. Eventually four battalions were formed – RMA under Lieutenant Colonel G.M. Campbell, Chatham under Lieutenant Colonel C. McN. Parsons, Portsmouth under Lieutenant Colonel F. W. Luard, and Plymouth, under Lieutenant Colonel G.E. Matthews CB.

Though men had been found, officers remained in short supply, and so the adjutants and third quartermasters of each division were attached to their respective battalions, and the whole column came under the command of Major General Edwin McCausland RMLI, a veteran of Egypt in the 1880s and colonel commandant of his own division before promotion in 1910 (the Royal Marines used that rank in place of brigadier general until 1913[2]).

In addition to struggling for numbers, the Royal Marine Brigade, as it was now named, also struggled to equip its battalions with 1902 Pattern Service Dress, and instead of khaki uniforms they retained their Royal Marine blues, complete with Brodrick Cap, for their service overseas. The Brodrick was in fact retained by the Royal Marines right up until the amalgamation of the RMLI and RMA in 1923, long after it was disposed of by the army, and was never nearly as unpopular with marines as it was with soldiers, perhaps because of its similarity to a sailor's cap with which they were all familiar.

With a small number of 12-pounder guns and Maxim machine guns the battalions assembled at Portsmouth on 7 August: the RMA and Chatham

1

Battalion were accommodated at the vast and imposing Eastney Barracks, the Portsmouth Battalion at their home barracks of Forton, Gosport, and the Plymouth Battalion at Browndown Camp on Stokes Bay. Such concentration made the deficiencies starkly apparent – the brigade remained short of nearly half of its required officers, yet was hugely overborne with NCOs, a large number of whom were found to be too old for active service abroad. It was perhaps a temporary relief, then, when the Admiralty ordered the dispersal of the brigade staff on 20 August and the battalions returned to continue training at their respective headquarters. At 7pm on the 25th, however, orders were received from the Adjutant General Royal Marines, General Sir William Nicholls KCB RMA, that the brigade was to sail for Ostend that very night. No new brigade staff had been appointed and no details were given as to the type of service to be expected, so a rather baffled Chatham Division was heavily-loaded as it marched to Sheerness to embark in the cruisers *HMS Euryalus* and *Aboukir* (tragically sunk less than a month later by the German submarine *U9*[3]), under the command of Admiral Arthur Christian of the 7th Cruiser Squadron. They were joined by a new brigade commander, Brigadier General Sir George Aston KCB RMA, a much-respected commander who had fought in Sudan and South Africa, but who would be invalided home less than a month later.

The Chatham Battalion landed at Ostend at 3.30am on 27 August, soon to be joined later that morning by the Portsmouth and RMA Battalions in *HMS Prince of Wales, Formidable, Irresistible* and *Venerable*, and by the Plymouth Battalion in *HMS Prince George, Caesar, Goliath* and *Vengeance* on the following morning. A new brigade staff still needed to be appointed, so Aston chose Captain Sketchley, adjutant of the Portsmouth Battalion, as his brigade major, but the lack of detail and organisation from the Admiralty almost proved disastrous when airships and aircraft of the RNAS arrived in support unannounced and were almost fired upon by the anxious and ill-informed marines. This airborne support was commanded by Commander Charles Samson, a great pioneer of naval aviation who had performed the first take-off of an aircraft from a ship at sea in 1912[4] and also, shortly after his arrival in Belgium, introduced armoured vehicles to the British armed forces for the very first time, after witnessing their success at the hands of the Belgian Army.

General Aston deemed that there was not enough time for a full reconnaissance of the town, as German cavalry patrols had been seen in the area as early as the 24th, and so a 7-mile long line of defensive outposts was established around the town from the Bassin de Chasse in the north to Mariakerke in the south, with Maxim guns dug in to cover all major roads out of the town and cyclist patrols (with fifty bicycles provided by the local population) extending into the surrounding countryside to determine the extent of German activity.

At 1pm on 28 August General Aston reported to the Admiralty that Ostend was strongly held and that Bruges and Dixmuide were both clear of enemy troops. The local population were worried, however: news reached them on that same day of the terrible German actions at Louvain where the mediaeval library had been burned, 248 civilians killed and the remaining population of 10,000 expelled. Brussels had largely escaped such horrors as the Belgian government had elected not to attempt to defend the city and some citizens of Ostend advocated the same course of action, but Aston continued to strengthen his defences over the succeeding two days.

The naval support available from the 7th Cruiser Squadron was negligible: the shallow coastal waters forced the larger ships to remain offshore and the high sand dunes meant that the smaller destroyers were incapable of providing any supporting fire inland because of a lack of target visibility. In addition to this their exposed station laid them open to attack by German submarines known to be operating in the North Sea. Admiral Christian was decidedly unsettled. On the 30th the broken remnants of the Belgian 4th Division, which had withdrawn from Namur with the French, passed through the town on the way to Antwerp. The Admiralty could not have known at the time, but the German Army believed that the Royal Marine Brigade could well be the advance party of a much larger force, but without that knowledge, and with the continued threat to the naval support, orders were received for the brigade to return to England at 4am on the 31st. For twelve hours all ranks laboured to load all stores and equipment with only one small crane. Each battalion sailed for its home port, and the Admiralty signalled that 'The whole operation has been carried out in such a way as to be a credit to the Marine Corps.'[5]

The Royal Marines' first deployment of the war was, therefore, one which did not see them immediately engaging with the enemy, though the army's II Corps had lost 7,000 men at the Battle of Le Cateau only the day before they arrived. However, the defence of Ostend certainly demonstrated the corps' flexibility and its ability to take on a large defensive task with no notice and little matériel support, an experience which was to prove extremely useful thereafter.

Armoured Cars

Upon return to England the brigade underwent a substantial reorganisation designed to make best use of the men available in light of the experiences of Ostend. The RMA Battalion was withdrawn from the brigade and its platoons absorbed into the Howitzer and Anti-Aircraft Brigades already established at Portsmouth. The three remaining battalions formed a new brigade with the fourth battalion being provided theoretically by the RMLI Depot at Deal (under the command of Lieutenant Colonel R.D. Beith), though each other port was required to provide a company and a platoon in order to achieve this. Each battalion now numbered 750, and General Aston remained in command despite the removal of the artillery, while the brigade, now 3 Brigade of the Royal Naval Division, settled down to consolidate its training at Freedown, near Walmer in Kent, on 12 September 1914.

Two days earlier the manpower problem had been further compounded by the selection of 150 men, along with Major Armstrong, Captain Graham and Lieutenants Coode and Lathbury, along with 50 men from the RMA under Lieutenant Williams, to man the armoured cars of the RNAS in Dunkirk. These vehicles, under the command of Commander Samson, were not in fact all armoured, but were all armed with a water-cooled Vickers machine gun. This was before the introduction of the Silver Ghost chassis-based model that began professional production the following month and which was to become so familiar over the succeeding two decades. Instead Samson commanded a mixed selection of acquired Rolls Royce and Mercedes vehicles, some of which he had fitted with ship's boiler plates as a rudimentary form of armour.[6] Each column usually comprised nine cars, manned by a mixture of RNAS and RM personnel, whose role remained largely undefined but who roamed widely and so made contact on several occasions with German cavalry patrols, whose swift departure from the scene made identification largely impossible. Even so, their speed gave the impression of a much larger force and on several occasions provided the allies with intelligence of enemy movements, though they could do little to stop them.

The squadron was based at the RNAS aerodrome of St Pol, west of Dunkirk (though today part of the port), and operated as far inland as Arras and Douai, where on 1 October 1914 they arrived to find the town being heavily shelled and the French defenders taking cover from snipers in the houses leading away from the Valenciennes Gate. Lieutenant Coode, deciding to assist, reversed his car up the street, firing his gun at the enemy positions as they went. Upon reaching the station it was clear that they could make no further progress, so Lieutenant Coode consolidated their gains with a half company of marines, along with fifty assorted French troops led gallantly by Private McMullan of the Portsmouth Battalion, but ultimately Douai was to fall into enemy hands.

On 3 October a convoy of 150 buses transported the squadron from Morbecque, where it had moved from St Pol, to Antwerp via Dunkirk and Bruges in order to join the Royal Marine Brigade on the 5th. Captain Graham's section had been detailed to escort Winston Churchill, as First Lord of the Admiralty, into Antwerp, but the orders arrived too late and they had to be content with escorting him out of the town upon his departure.

As October wore on the sections engaged in more and more varied work. Some of the guns were dismounted to be used by the RM battalions, but half-way through the month Major Armstrong returned to England with half of the company. On the 16th Captain Graham was sent by Commander Samson with three cars and twenty men to Major General Thompson Capper, commanding the 7th Infantry Division. They were employed in locating the German cavalry on the Menin-Roulers road, losing two men in such an engagement on the 18th when they unexpectedly came into contact with the enemy at only 50 yards. Thankfully the cars were being reversed up the road in order to effect a quick withdrawal if required, as indeed it was. Lieutenant Lathbury had, somewhat unusually, attached his section to the 3rd Dragoon Guards in 6 Cavalry Brigade and fought alongside them throughout the first half of the First Battle of Ypres, but all remaining RM members of the squadron were returned to their battalions in England on 3 November and so the Royal Marines' excursion into armoured life came to an end.

Dunkirk and Antwerp

After their return from Ostend the infantry battalions in Walmer might fairly have been expecting a period of time in which to train their many new and inexperienced members and to work up to being the efficient fighting force expected, but in fact they were to receive less than a week. Only six days later, at midnight on 18 September, orders were received from Churchill that the Royal Marine Brigade was to embark at Dover the following morning, accompanied by the Oxfordshire Yeomanry Hussars, elements of the RNAS and a small detachment of Royal Engineers. General Aston was reminded by the First Lord of the Admiralty that German forces could overwhelm his brigade if they so chose, but that he was again to give the impression that he was the advance guard of a much larger force, and that he would have achieved his aim if he provoked them into responding accordingly.[7] Consequently, recruits' drill rifles were exchanged for live weapons overnight and on the morning of the 19th the brigade and its companions embarked in the *City of Edinburgh* and *Lake Michigan*, bound for Dunkirk.

Upon arrival transport had been arranged in the form of ninety civilian London buses, purchased and shipped to France by the Royal Naval Division, as well as fifty private motor cars driven by their owners, all of whom were given (perhaps surprisingly) temporary commissions as second lieutenants in the Royal Marine Light Infantry. The buses, of the 'B Type', were taken into service along with their drivers, who drove them to Dover or Southampton, stopping at Chatham or Eastney to be issued with uniform and kit. More of this

5

extraordinary company, transporting troops in buses that sometimes retained their advertisements, will be given elsewhere.

On 25 September General Aston was invalided back to England and replaced by Colonel Archibald Paris, who was soon to be promoted to major general in order to command the entire Royal Naval Division, a task which he fulfilled so popularly and whole-heartedly until seriously injured in June 1917, after also having been appointed a Knight Commander of the Order of the Bath (KCB) in the 1916 New Year's Honours List. Paris decided to leave the brigade's many recruits at Dunkirk for further training under Lieutenant Colonel Godfrey while he took the Deal, Chatham and Plymouth Battalions on to his newly-established headquarters at Cassel and sent the Portsmouth Battalion to replace French forces at Lille. It was clear, however, that the German Army was closing on Antwerp and the loss of the port would put the French channel ports in peril: St Nazaire was proving to be an unsatisfactory disembarkation point for the British Expeditionary Force and could not alone be relied upon to provide for them. That, as well as the large oil reserves and concentration of shipping at Antwerp, meant that immediate action was required. On 30 September the outer ring of the port's defences were broken through and it appeared that the Belgian government was preparing to withdraw its field army.

Winston Churchill's rather extraordinary personal visit, which was hardly a holiday, took place on 3 October. Arriving slightly incongruously in the uniform of Trinity House, and meeting in secret with King Albert of the Belgians and Baron de Broqueville (Prime Minister), Churchill agreed four principal points:

1. That the Belgian Army would endeavour to continue to defend Antwerp for at least a further ten days.
2. That within three days of the meeting the British government would confirm whether it could provide a relief force and, if so when it would be ready to deploy.
3. That if the British could not provide such a force then Belgium was to be free to abandon the defence of Antwerp.
4. That if the Belgian field army had to be withdrawn then the British government would send a force to Ghent in order to protect their withdrawal.

Following his meeting, Churchill inspected the defences. An eyewitness described the extraordinary scene:

'It was a chilly day and he [had changed into] a long black overcoat with broad astrakhan collar and his usual black top hat and swung his silver-topped walking stick. In his customary manner, he completely ignored the enemy fire from howitzers, rifles and machine guns and astonished the Belgian troops by taking complete charge of the situation, criticizing the siting of guns and trenches and emphasizing his points by waving his stick or thumping the ground with it.

He then climbed back into his car, waiting impatiently to be driven to the next section of the front line. Later, when the reinforcing Royal Marines arrived and were settled in, Winston came along to inspect them, dressed suitably for this more maritime occasion. He was "enveloped in a cloak, and on his head wore a yachtsman's cap," observed an accompanying journalist. "He was tranquilly smoking a large cigar and looking at the progress of the battle under a rain of shrapnel which I can only call fearful."[8]

Consequently, the Royal Marines were again sent into action. Colonel Paris had received his orders early in the day and by 8.30am the brigade was entrained in cattle trucks with Maxim guns mounted to repel possible attack en route. Travelling via Dunkirk and Bruges they arrived at Vieux Dieux, several miles east of Antwerp, at 11pm and went into billets at 4am for a few hours' rest. At first light the brigade, along with the 7th Belgian Infantry Regiment, moved along the Lier road to relieve the exhausted and depleted 21st Belgian Infantry Regiment, occupying wide and shallow trenches that afforded little protection against shelling, if any. They immediately set about improving the defences and each battalion sent a company to occupy advanced posts towards the river in order to prevent the enemy from crossing. The Deal company, on the left of the position, was commanded by Major Pryce-Browne, but he was killed during the morning. He had only recently rejoined the corps, having resigned his commission with the intention of seeking ordination. At the same time No.3 Company of the Plymouth Battalion occupied the town of Lier itself (King Albert of the Belgians' headquarters until a few weeks earlier), holding the bridge over the River Nete and in such a strategically important position attack was inevitable. When it came, 200 of the enemy were killed or wounded by the marines before they brought up artillery and forced the Plymouth company to withdraw.

On the afternoon of 4 October the Belgian army abandoned Fort Kessel in the face of overwhelmingly heavy German shelling and during the following night the lighter enemy artillery moved up to the river bank, forcing the remaining Royal Marine advanced posts to retire. As they huddled in the trenches, bayonets kept down out of sight so as not to reflect the light of burning Lier, the defence of Antwerp must have begun to seem impossible. At dawn on the 5th the enemy crossed the river, but a gallant counter-attack by the 7th Belgian Infantry, 2nd Chasseurs and the Portsmouth Battalion RMLI forced them back, where they remained during the subsequent day and night. The comparative quiet of that night allowed 1 and 2 Brigades of the Royal Naval Division, manned by sailors rather than marines, to arrive in Antwerp unobserved and Colonel Paris was given command of the division with the temporary rank of major general. Major Sketchley, Brigade Major of the Royal Marine Brigade, was appointed GSO2 and Colonel A.E. Marchant CB was sent from England to take Paris's place as brigade commander. Conveniently, the enemy did not attack again until the divisional reorganisation was complete, but the blow when it came was a heavy one. The substantial British reinforcements expected under the command of General Rawlinson had not arrived, prompting Churchill to offer to resign from the Admiralty in order to command the defence himself. This offer was not well received by the Prime Minister, who remarked privately:

> 'Winston is an ex-Lieutenant of Hussars, and would if his proposal had been accepted, have been in command of two distinguished major generals, not to mention brigadiers, colonels etc: while the Navy were only contributing its little brigades.'[9]

At dawn on the 6th the Belgian troops on the brigade's right were overwhelmed, losing the villages of Boomlaar and Hulst and while the former was recovered by a counter-attack at 8.30am, the German capture of Hulst left a huge hole in the Royal Marines' right flank. General Paris sent the First Naval Brigade to assist the Belgians, but they had already withdrawn to the village of Donk, well behind burning Lier, and after several more hours' heavy shelling the Royal Marine Brigade was also forced to withdraw. The new line, four miles away, stretched between the villages of Vremde and Boshoek and was being hurriedly prepared by Belgian army engineers. The Germans took advantage of the situation to follow closely, and at dusk, as the Marines consolidated their new defensive line, the enemy could be heard communicating by means of bird calls, somewhat eerily after the heavy day's artillery bombardment.

The new trenches could not stand for long, however, as they ran along a well-defined metalled road and so were an easily-ranged target for the German artillery. Realising this, the Belgians began to withdraw to the city's inner defences two hours before dawn on the 7th, leaving General Paris with no option but to do the same, only to see the trenches obliterated by shelling shortly after they were evacuated. The Naval Brigades joined the Belgians in the forts and trenches of the city's last line of defences, while the Royal Marines withdrew to a cinema film factory at Chateau Rouge, Waes Donk, near Fort Mortsel. Throughout the day the shelling continued, and the burning oil tanks of the American Petroleum Company provided a horrible backdrop for the British and Belgian troops forlornly holding the defences. Even so, the British trenches were seemingly well-defended, with the inundated flood-plain to their left and the line of the River Scheldt held by the Belgians on their right. It was to the latter that the enemy therefore turned his attentions and after a fierce fight gained a foothold across the river, building a light bridge during the night.

As the British 7th Infantry and 3rd Cavalry Brigades had been unable to join the Royal Naval Division, at 7am on the 8th General Paris informed General Rawlinson that he would almost certainly have to withdraw once night fell as the Belgian garrison troops were fading fast; indeed the Chatham Battalion had just been forced to take over a section of the redoubt line from its exhausted defenders. The tension was only further heightened by Belgian General Dossin's mistaken report that Forts 1, 2 and 4 had already fallen to the Germans, causing panic amongst his own men. At 5pm the decision to withdraw had to be made – to wait any longer would severely risk the British troops being closed up in the city and forced to surrender. The decision was telephoned directly through to Churchill in Whitehall and General Paris gave his orders. The First Royal Naval Brigade was to leave the city by the Malines Gate, crossing the city pontoon bridge and proceeding to Zwyndrecht where they would rendezvous with the Second Royal Naval and Royal Marines Brigades who would simultaneously leave by the Burght pontoon bridge.

The Chatham and Deal Battalions led the withdrawal, beginning at 7.30, followed by the Second Royal Naval Brigade and Drake Battalion. After a hard march through crowds of refugees, burning buildings, dead horses and fallen tram-wires they arrived at St-Gillaes-Waes, where they entrained for Ostend, and so to England. The Plymouth Battalion, acting as rearguard to the column, made the same journey but under even more trying conditions, as the only train left at St-Gillaes-Waes was already half-filled with refugees, and after reaching Blankenbergh they were forced to march the last sixteen miles into Ostend.

The Portsmouth Battalion had the most terrible time of all. Detailed to follow the First Royal Naval Brigade, miscommunication meant that that unit did not set off until 10.30pm, three hours later than intended, and then lost its way in the heavy shell-fire of the rapidly crumbling city. General Paris's orders had instructed them to cross the river at 10pm, but the confused state of affairs meant that they did not accomplish that task until just before dawn, seeing the bridge destroyed immediately behind them once the enemy realised what was happening. Even now, having escaped the city, their ordeal was far from over. By 5pm on 9 October the battalion halted in the village of St Nicholas, having had no rest or food for twenty-four hours. Just as they were attempting to requisition rations news arrived that the Germans were in the next village, Lokeren, only five miles away, so Colonel Luard (in command) was forced to march his troops a further eight miles north where they reached the small village station of Kemzeke.

They had telephoned ahead to stop one of the refugee trains on its way to Ostend. The 400 marines, as well as 600 sailors who had become detached from the First Royal Naval Brigade, crammed into the train of open wagons that was already heavily loaded with terrified Belgian civilians fleeing the German advance. At 8pm they departed Kemzeke towards Ostend in the hope that their withdrawal from Antwerp was complete, but only twenty minutes later the train was fired upon from both sides. The Germans had clearly not only overtaken them, but knew that the train was carrying them as well as the civilian refugees. A mile or so further on the train suddenly stopped. In the silence Colonel Luard sent men to investigate, who reported that the driver and fireman of the engine had disappeared into the night, leaving the train stranded in the middle of a rapidly-developing battlefield. Two Royal Navy stokers therefore set about getting the train moving again but ten minutes later, at almost exactly 10pm, they realised that the enemy had diverted the train into a siding and derailed several of the wagons.

Rifle fire broke out from all sides in the darkness as Colonel Luard attempted to detrain and form up his men in the midst of screaming women and children as the ambush intensified – Major French and Lieutenant Gowney RM, along with several RN officers, led a section of marines to drive back the enemy, killing six and injuring many more. They too received casualties, as did the civilians, and Surgeon Lieutenant Greig RN was captured while attending to injured refugees. Confusion reigned. While Colonel Luard continued to attempt to extract his men from the train under fire some were simply too exhausted to move, while others climbed down from the wrong side of the train in the darkness and walked straight into the hands of the enemy.

In total, three quarters of the marines and all but twelve of the 600 sailors were captured, including Lieutenant Crossman who had been injured in the fighting. Colonel Luard and the remaining 100 formed up at the front of the train and, under covering fire from Major French and his party, continued on foot towards Ostend. Eight miles further on, after forty miles in total, the broken remnant of the Portsmouth Battalion RMLI reached the station of Selsaete at dawn on 10 October, having had no food or clean water for 48 hours. They fell into the first train to Bruges and finally rejoined the division at Ostend. Major French and Lieutenant Gowney were both awarded the DSO for their extraordinary conduct in the action.

By the time the brigade embarked for England on the 12th, 23 men had been killed, 103 wounded and 311 were missing, most of whom were to spend the next four years of war either as German prisoners of war or interned in the Netherlands. Sailing for England, each battalion returned to its own headquarters, but Forton Barracks was a forlorn and empty place compared to a month earlier.

Public perception of the defence of Antwerp varied considerably. The popular image of 'plucky little Belgium' did not quite counter-balance the unequal fight in which the Royal Naval Division had been placed by the government. On 13 October 1914, the day that the RMLI returned home, a scathing column in the *Morning Post* (reprinted in the *Daily Mail* on the following day) made the situation plain to its readers:

Some little time ago we ventured to warn the Government of the danger of any amateur or civilian interference with the military and naval operations on which the fate of the British Empire depends. The affair of Antwerp shows that this warning was not only necessary but that it was unheeded. And the time has come, in our judgment, for more plain and definite speaking...

What has to be said, then, is that the attempt to relieve Antwerp by a small force of Marines and Naval Volunteers was a costly blunder, for which Mr Churchill must be held responsible on the present evidence.

...When, therefore, it became obvious that the German attack could not be adequately met, the proper course was for the Belgian Army to retire from the position and retreat to a position of more safety... A more futile scheme was devised: at the last moment a mixed force of Marines and Naval Volunteers, with a few heavy guns, were thrown into the city. By that time the outer sector of the fortifications had already been breached; the city lay at the mercy of the great howitzers; the line of retreat was most seriously threatened; and it was pressingly important that the Belgian Field Army should retire without delay. The force thrown into the city by the Admiralty consisted partly of our admirable Marines – as fine a force of its kind as there is in the world – but largely of odds and ends thrown together, and Volunteers who were undergoing training for quite different sorts of work. These men were rushed across and thrown into the trenches when the position had already been lost...

But the worst of the whole affair was not the loss of our fine Marines and brave Volunteers, ill as we can spare them for a rushed undertaking. The most serious result of the diversion was that it encouraged the Belgian authorities to prolong a

*defence which, on clear evidence, they had before been forced
to recognise as hopeless, and to delay in a position from
which it became hourly more difficult to extricate their army...
The despatch of the British Force, then, did not extricate the
Belgian Army, but on the contrary, tended to delay it until
its extrication had become more difficult and dangerous; the
movement, in short, was within an ace of bringing the Belgian
Army to destruction.*

Many may have agreed with the newspapers' condemnation of Churchill's
decision to send in the Royal Naval Division, but it is not a conclusion which
should be accepted without reservation. The First Lord of the Admiralty
may have been a somewhat forceful personality, but he did not expect nor
intend the RND to complete the defence of Antwerp successfully without
substantial further assistance. Indeed, there is no evidence that the intention
was ever to successfully defend the city indefinitely at all, but simply to
harass the enemy and to allow the Belgian Field Army to withdraw without
being utterly destroyed. The decision to deploy the RND was indeed made at
Churchill's suggestion, but not without the approval of Cabinet, including Lord
Kitchener, and while in hindsight a good number of political commentators
saw Antwerp as a prophecy of Churchill's later failure at Gallipoli, it was a
failure (if at all) of the British government as a body, not of Churchill as an
individual, as well as because of the lack of support from other allied forces.
The Foreign Secretary, Lord Grey, wrote angrily on the 11th, after hearing
that the French high command had complained that British efforts at Antwerp
had not been co-ordinated with their own plans, that '...*the object was not
achieved partly because General Joffre did not fulfil the expectation of sending
a sufficient French force in time to co-operate with the British force for the
relief of Antwerp.*'[10] Of all those who might have regretted the fall of Antwerp,
it was Albert, King of the Belgians, who wrote defensively to General Paris in
March 1918, saying:

> *You are wrong in considering the Royal Naval Division Expedition
> as a forlorn hope. In my opinion it rendered great service to us
> and those who deprecate it simply do not understand the history
> of the War in its early days. Only one man of all your people had
> the prevision of what the loss of Antwerp would entail and that
> man was Mr. Churchill....*
>
> *Delaying an enemy is often of far greater service than the
> defeat of the enemy, and in the case of Antwerp the delay the Royal
> Naval Division caused to the enemy was of inestimable service*

to us. These three days allowed the French and British Armies to move North West. Otherwise our whole army might have been captured and the Northern French Ports secured by the enemy.

Moreover, the advent of the Royal Naval Division inspired our troops, and owing to your arrival, and holding out for three days, great quantities of supplies were enabled to be destroyed. You kept a large army employed, and I repeat the Royal Naval Division rendered a service we shall never forget.[11]

Whatever the cause of his predicament, General Paris could do nothing but immediately set to work rebuilding his division, and a draft of 600 'Kitchener' recruits, as well as new temporary officers, helped to fill numbers. Three months of intensive training followed, first at battalion headquarters and later at Shillingstone, near the divisional headquarters at Blandford, in Dorset. It was from there in February 1915 that the Royal Naval Division departed for its gallant but almost disastrous service in Gallipoli, about which much has been written elsewhere.

Chapter 2

France 1916

On 29 April 1916 the Royal Naval Division underwent a change that was significant in administration, if not in daily practice. After a year and a half of service under the orders of the Admiralty it was transferred to the authority of the War Office. Internal reorganisation had already been effected and on 27 July 1915 the Chatham and Deal Battalions had been amalgamated into the 1st Battalion Royal Marine Light Infantry, with the Portsmouth and Plymouth Battalions combining to form the 2nd Battalion. This was due to the terrible losses that had already forced the reduction of each battalion to only three companies, or two in the case of Plymouth. Even those that remained were under strength.

By May of 1916 the depleted battalions had finally been withdrawn from Gallipoli and were resting at Mudros, the base of the Royal Navy's Eastern Mediterranean Squadron and headquarters of Admiral Arthur Christian who had transported the Royal Marines to Ostend in the early days of the war. They had suffered terribly over the preceding year, with only 13 of the division's original 131 officers who had landed in 1915 not being killed, injured or otherwise invalided home, but it was at Mudros at 3pm on 7 May that General Paris received news that his shattered division was not to sail to England as it might have expected, but to France. The Royal Naval Division had fought boldly and bravely at Gallipoli, but more was to be demanded of them and so within an hour and a half from the receipt of the order the 2/RMLI, under Lieutenant Colonel A.R.H. Hutchison, was embarked in HTS *Briton* ready to sail for Marseille. The 1/RMLI, under Lieutenant Colonel E.J. Stroud, sailed in the SS *Aragon* a week later, along with the Cyclist Company under the indomitable Major French who had served so bravely at Antwerp. The men themselves did not have any idea where they were bound, but of course hoped for home.

Private Horace Bruckshaw of the 2/RMLI wrote in his diary, *'No one seems to know where we are going but all sorts of pleasant rumours are afloat – and otherwise. Anyhow we are in for a pretty long trip it is plain to see... Roll on England.'*[1] It was not until the day before they disembarked that he and the others were sure of their destination. Upon arrival at Marseille, still in their KD shorts from Gallipoli, they entrained for Pont-Remy on the Somme before marching the six miles to Longpré, just north-west of Amiens, arriving at 6pm on 17 May to go into billets. Here they settled into the IV Corps training area for two months of retraining and reorganisation as many, if not most, members of the two battalions had no experience of the kind of warfare they were to soon experience.

Upon arrival in France, machine-gun companies and trench mortar batteries had been formed for each battalion from a mixture of RM and RNVR personnel, armed with Lewis guns for the first time in place of the long-suffering Maxims that had accompanied the division since the beginning of the war. Brand new Mk III Short Magazine Lee-Enfield rifles and Brodie helmets were issued to each man on 20 May and the now necessary gas helmets six days later. With steel helmets and long trousers, they were now altogether more adequately equipped for their new task.

Shortly afterwards the Divisional Train was reformed under Lieutenant Colonel A. Liddell ASC, and Divisional Engineers (247, 248 and 249 Field Companies and the divisional Signal Company) and Field Ambulances (148, 149 and 150) were attached. Major French's successful cyclist company was eventually disbanded in June as being of no further use and finally the division obtained its own artillery for the very first time when 223 and 317 brigades RFA (along with their attendant ammunition column) were attached under the command of Brigadier General A.H. de Rougemont. On 16 July the transfer of the division to the army chain of command was completed, and it was renamed the 63rd (Royal Naval) Division, with 1, 2 and 3 brigades becoming 188, 189 and 199 respectively.

The original 63rd Division, a Northumbrian territorial division, had been earlier disbanded, but the new one had enough of an identity of its own already. An independent Infantry Base Depot was consequently established at Calais under Lieutenant Colonel G.J.H. Mullins RMLI, which also served the RMA units in France, examined elsewhere in this book. Suddenly the 63rd Royal Naval Division began to very much resemble any other of the British Army on the continent, but it was the subtle differences in routine and tradition which continued to cause problems, not least in Whitehall, as well as remaining a source of great pride for its members. RN and RM ranks were retained and, while the War Office assumed responsibility for recruitment, training and discipline, the Admiralty continued to appoint its own officers and to issue pay and allowances. After a short while the naval ratings of the division began to wear their rate badges on their left arm and the equivalent army rank on the right. Officers often wore both stripes on their cuffs and pips on their shoulders. Many in the War Office were desirous that the 63rd should

15

conform to the usual army routines, eliminating its naval traditions, and it was only through the distinct support of Sir Edward Carson, First Lord of the Admiralty, that they were able to continue – and continue they proudly did.[2]

From Longpré the 1st Battalion was to be the first of the RMLI to see action in France. On 28 May 1916 both battalions entrained for the front at Pont-Remy and on 3 June the 1/RMLI was inspected by General Sir Charles Monro, in command of the First Army, at Maisnil. This deployment and inspection was completed under Colonel Stroud in the temporary absence of the brigade commander. For the subsequent two weeks the battalion was tentatively introduced to the trench warfare of the Western Front by attaching each company in turn to battalions of the 47th Division operating in the line between Lens and Vimy Ridge. This proved to be a very different experience from that of Gallipoli, which had been bad enough: Bruckshaw wrote, '*We were jolly glad to get out of it safely, and I am not anxious to spend another hour like that one. No, thanks.*'[3] After a short period of time holding the line between Bajoles and Maistre the 1/RMLI were withdrawn to Frévillers for a further three weeks' training.

On 14 July they again entered the firing line, relieving the 24th Battalion London Regiment in the Angres II sub-sector, and two days later Colonel Stroud resumed his command of the now rapidly improving battalion. On the following day General Paris assumed command of the whole Angres-Souchez sector and from that point until 29 September the two RMLI battalions relieved each other in turn in Angres II, becoming intimately acquainted with the muddy trench routine required, entertaining themselves with great rat hunts and trench mortar duels with the enemy. The dust and flies of Gallipoli became almost a distant memory. Casualties were taken as a result of shelling, snipers and illness, but it was a broken ankle which was to send Colonel Stroud back to England, sustained when inspecting trenches on 11 August. The lives of the Royal Marines were quieter at this stage of the war than many, however, as the Battle of the Somme continued to rage to the south, but they were not to be entirely spared that ordeal.

Arrival on the Somme and the Battle of the Ancre

On 4 October 1916 the 63rd Royal Naval Division, including both battalions of the RMLI, marched to Ligny-Saint-Flochel for an overnight train to Acheux-en-Amiénois. This was the first time that the whole division had moved together since 190 Brigade, newly-trained, had joined them in July. From Acheux it was a comparatively short march east to Mailly-Maillet for the 1/RMLI and to Englebelmer for the 2/RMLI, both within range of the German guns on the front line, and their experience of the Somme began. The former were under canvas, as they were to be so many times over the next two years in that village, but at Englebelmer they were put into billets, which by this time were almost exclusively the cellars of the largely ruined village. Gone were the days of billeting officers politely asking for rooms from the local population; shelter was taken wherever it was available. The battle had now been proceeding with its infamously high casualty rate for three months and the allied advance south of the River Ancre left a German salient centred around the village of Beaumont Hamel.

Thiepval had finally fallen during the last week of September and other advances during October meant that the enemy no longer held their commanding elevated positions from which to control the Ancre valley, so it became increasingly clear that an allied attack on that and the Beaumont Hamel salient stood a better chance of success than at any prior moment. Upon their arrival, therefore, the 63rd Division were warned to prepare for attack, as the line from Serre in the north down to the river was to be attempted in a single sweep in a few short weeks' time. Taking over the Serre-Beaumont Hamel section of the front, the two battalions alternated between the line and rest in the villages of Forceville and Hédauville, both immediately to the west of Englebelmer, and so just a little further from the shelling. Here, in the safety of the open Picardy countryside, they conducted intense training in battalion attacks, musketry, bombing and a host of other skills necessary for the successful prosecution of the attack. It was during this period of alternating duty and training that one of the greatest tragedies fell upon the division.

At about 1.55pm on 12 October General Paris and his staff were visiting 190 Brigade (made up of army battalions though a part of the 63rd Division), when a German 15cm shell (known to the British as a 'Five-Nine') fell directly between the general and Major Sketchley, still serving as his General Staff Officer (Grade 2) (GSO2), in the trench known as Sixth Avenue. Sketchley was killed outright and so one of the longest serving officers of the division fell. Appointed adjutant of the Portsmouth Battalion at Forton Barracks on the outbreak of war, he had served continually as brigade major and then divisional GSO2 ever since. Major Ernest Sketchley DSO was buried in the Forceville Communal Cemetery with a firing party of 200 provided by the 1/RMLI. General Paris was severely injured by the blast, receiving wounds to his shoulder, back and, most seriously, to his left leg. Thankfully his ADC, Lieutenant B. Nicholson RNVR, was only knocked over by the force of the explosion and was able to render swift first aid, enough to see the general evacuated to the 3rd Casualty Clearing Station at Puchevillers though the leg had to be amputated shortly after. He survived and lived until 1937, though clearly had to relinquish his divisional command.

The loss of General Paris was of greater impact to the division than simply sentiment. Under his leadership and the support of the Admiralty the distinctive nature of the 63rd had been maintained, pulling the men together as a coherent whole bound by common traditions, history and even vocabulary, but that was to become more of a struggle than ever before. Paris was replaced by Major General Cameron Shute CMG DSO, late of the Welsh Regiment and Rifle Brigade, a man seemingly determined to stamp out the naval traditions of the division he had inherited. He had an unwavering belief in the efficacy of military efficiency as he saw it that would not be deterred. As General Blumberg wrote in his account of the situation, Shute was *'...a very able soldier, but at first matters did not go altogether smoothly, as the methods of the R.N.D. were peculiar to themselves and somewhat puzzling to newcomers.'* At times like this, protected by naval seniority, the Naval Discipline Act, and the patronage of the First Lord of the Admiralty, it was perhaps inevitable that a certain mischievousness should come to the fore, as it soon did in the form of Sub Lieutenant Clifford Codner, a former miner who had been rapidly promoted and then commissioned into the Hawke Battalion of the RND in 1915.

In accordance with naval tradition Codner had requested 'leave to grow', that is, permission to grow a beard. Shute, known by now to the division as 'Schultz the Hun', was inspecting the trenches early in his command and was dismayed by the sight of an officer with a beard, which would have run entirely contrary to army discipline, and demanded that it be shaved off. Codner knew, however, that he was entirely within the limits of the King's Regulations and so, perhaps still rather boldly, he stood his ground and defied the divisional commander's order. Hurried signals followed between Divisional HQ and the Admiralty with the inevitable conclusion that Shute was forced to withdraw his order, much to the delight of the division's officers, so much so that Lieutenant A.P. Herbert (later Member of Parliament for Oxford University) composed a widely distributed poem entitled 'The Battle of Codson's Beard', with names amended for publication:

'The Battle of Codson's Beard'

I'll tell you a yarn of a sailor-man, with a face more fierce than fair,
Who got round that on the Navy's plan by hiding it all with hair;
He was one of a hard old sailor-breed, and had lived his life at sea,
But he took to the beach at the nation's need, and fought with the
    R.N.D.

Now Brigadier-General Blank's Brigade was tidy and neat and trim,
And the sight of a beard on his parade was a bit too much for him:
'What is that,' said he, with a frightful oath, 'of all that is wild
    and weird?'
And the Staff replied, 'A curious growth, but it looks very like a beard.'

18

And the General said, 'I have seen six wars, and many a ghastly sight,
Fellows with locks that gave one shocks, and buttons none too
*   bright,*
But never a man in my Brigade with a face all fringed with fur;
And you'll toddle away and shave today. But Codson said, 'You err.'

'For I don't go much on wars, as such, and living with rats and worms,
And you ought to be glad of a sailor lad on any old kind of terms;
While this old beard of which you're skeered, it stands for a lot to me,
For the great North gales, and the sharks and whales, and the
*   smell of the good grey sea.'*

New Generals crowded to the spot and urged him to behave,
But Codson said, 'You talk a lot, but can you make me shave?
For the Navy allows a beard at the bows, and a beard is the sign
*   for me,*
That the world may know wherever I go, I belong to the King's Navee.'

They gave him posts in distant parts, where few might see his
*   face,*
Town-Major jobs that, break men's hearts, and billets at the Base;
But whenever he knew a fight was due, he hurried there by train,
And when he'd done for every Hun—they sent him back again.

Then up and spake an old sailor, 'It seems you can't 'ave 'eared,
begging your pardon, General Blank, the reason of this same beard:
It's a kind of a sart of a camyflarge, and that I take to mean
A thing as 'ides some other thing wot oughtn't to be seen.

'And I've brought you this 'ere photergraph of what 'e used to be
Before 'e stuck that fluffy muck about 'is phyzogmy.'
The General looked and, fainting, cried, 'The situation's grave!
The beard was bad, but, KAMERAD! he simply must not shave!'

And now, when the thin lines bulge and sag, and man goes down
*   to man,*
A great black beard like a pirate's flag flies ever in the van;
And I've fought in many a warmish spot, where death was the
*   least men feared,*
But I never knew anything quite so hot as the Battle of Codson's
*   Beard.*[4]

Just at the moment at which the division was training most intently for action the authority of its commander was being undermined, yet this also helped to reinforce the camaraderie of 188 and 189 Brigades, united as they were by their unique naval identity among all the units on the front.

Heavy rain meant that the mud of the Somme was at its characteristic worst in October 1916 and the shelling had reduced the trenches in many places to a series of craters, the combination of which increased the rate of casualties from both enemy action and illness. In the middle of the month it was decided to shift the division south from Serre and instead they held a 1,200-yard front facing the village of Beaucourt-sur-Ancre, with the right hand divisional boundary marked by the river itself where the trenches ended in the boggy ground of the valley before rising again towards Thiepval on the other side. On the 17th the 1/RMLI marched to bivouacs at Hedauville, then on to similar accommodation at Englebelmer, where they were joined by the 2/RMLI on the following day. Though within easy reach of enemy artillery they were at least out of sight and some took advantage of the rolling Somme downs to catch hares with which to supplement their rations.

While the 1/RMLI alternated with the Howe Battalion in the front line, reconnaissance of the Beaucourt section and training at Englebelmer continued, and on the 28th the 2/RMLI were inspected there by the Commander-in-Chief, Sir Douglas Haig. A young officer of the battalion, Second Lieutenant Louis Stokes (described later in this book), wrote to his parents that when Haig asked him if there were any problems he reported that the men's bivouacs were not waterproof, but the C-in-C simply said 'Hmm' and walked away. A debate followed between Stokes's servant and the battalion sergeant major concerning Haig's competence.[5] However, as uncomfortable as these arrangements were, the marines were at least spared the monumental task, dictated by Shute, of straightening the line of the newly-inherited trenches and digging new assembly trenches on the ridge leading down to the river in a single night on the 20th. This was achieved through the employment of two shifts of 500 men each, but such movement could not but attract the notice of the enemy. Subsequently, during the night Lieutenant Commander Arthur Asquith, supervising the work, was temporarily buried by a German trench mortar which also ruptured both of his eardrums. Much to his own annoyance he was invalided home as a result, but as he was the Prime Minister's son, and since his brother Raymond had been killed in action only five weeks earlier, some have suggested that little excuse was required for him to be removed from the front line.

The assembly trenches did at least offer some shelter from the enemy, as they were located at the point where the British line turned sharply down a reverse slope away from the German trenches, but of course General Shute was far from happy. Inspecting the new works, one of his staff officers found evidence of bad latrine routine, and Shute resumed his tirade against the practices and, as he saw it, ill-discipline of the division. Lieutenant Herbert saw his opportunity for further ridicule, and wrote another poem which is unusual in that it names the senior officer at whom it is targeted, particularly considering the tone of the final two lines:

> *The General inspecting the trenches*
> *Exclaimed with a horrified shout*
> *'I refuse to command a division*
> *Which leaves its excreta about.'*
>
> *But nobody took any notice*
> *No one was prepared to refute,*
> *That the presence of shit was congenial*
> *Compared to the presence of Shute.*
>
> *And certain responsible critics*
> *Made haste to reply to his words*
> *Observing that his staff advisors*
> *Consisted entirely of turds.*
>
> *For shit may be shot at odd corners*
> *And paper supplied there to suit,*
> *But a shit would be shot without mourners*
> *If somebody shot that shit Shute.*[6]

As might be expected, it was immediately popular in the division, and there will have been many wry smiles as it spread far along the line, sung to the tune of 'Wrap me up in my Tarpaulin Jacket'.

As October turned into November so the rain turned into sleet and snow and an issue of cardigans on the 7th was most welcome, if still inadequate, as the battalions had no greatcoats. On 11 November, two days before the planned attack, the 1/RMLI relieved Nelson Battalion in the left of the line, up against what is now the edge of the Newfoundland Memorial Park, while the 2/RMLI went again into bivouacs at Englebelmer for a final night's rest. On the following afternoon, after a church parade at 2pm, they moved into their battle positions in the second line immediately behind their fellow marines. In the intervening twenty-four hours the 1/RMLI had already sustained thirty casualties, including Captain Clarke, and the state of the trenches in the wet weather did nothing further to improve morale in the face of an impending attack. Both Battalion HQs spent the night in the same dug-out, being entertained by stories from their cook, Sergeant Jerry Dunn, who gave them hot cocoa just before 3am, at which point they began their crawl out of the assembly trenches to wait for dawn in no man's land. Sergeant Meatyard, Signal Sergeant of 2/RMLI, recorded the experience at that point:

> *About 3am on the morning of the 13th certain platoons crawled out in No Man's Land and got close up to the Germans' barbed wire – there lying flat and still, patiently waiting for zero. At 5.45am we were ready and waiting, the morning light just beginning to show itself. All watches had been synchronised. At five minutes to six the CO announced five minutes to go. What a time it seemed going. There was not a sound to be heard. The question was (and our success depended on it) – was Fritz in the know – as it was nothing new for him to get wind of an attack and the time it was coming off – but this time he was apparently taken by surprise. Each morning at dawn for the last few days our guns had been giving him pepper, and no infantry attack took place...* *I expect he got fed up with these false alarms.*[7]

The attack, on Friday 13 November, was to be preceded by a 'rolling barrage' in which the divisional artillery would lay a curtain of shells in front of the advancing battalions, periodically moving forward by steps in order to protect them as they approached their objectives. The shelling would force the enemy to remain in their deep dug-outs (of which there were many in the sector), and if the allied troops kept close up behind the barrage they could theoretically deal with survivors as they emerged from below ground once the shelling had lifted. In order to assist in this the advance was made in waves, with each wave of men leap-frogging past the one in front in order to ensure that each captured German line was fully secured as the advance continued ahead.

The plan issued to the division contained four objectives: the first, named the 'Dotted Green Line', was the third German trench line which ran immediately in front of the slightly sunken station road linking Beaumont Hamel to the north-west with Beaucourt railway station down by the river. The second objective, the 'Green Line', was a heavily defended ridge that rose up beyond the station road, and which presented a rather more formidable task. The third, or 'Yellow Line', ran parallel to the Green Line up a slight valley between the ridge and the village of Beaucourt itself, and the final or 'Red Line' objective was situated on the far side of the village, where a new defensive line was to be established in the wake of a successful attack.

The first wave comprised 188 Brigade – the 1/RMLI and the Howe, Hawke and Hood Battalions of the RND. The second wave was 189 Brigade, with

2/RMLI on the left, followed by the Anson, Nelson and Drake Battalions stretching down the hill towards the river on the right. Finally, the third wave was 190 Brigade as divisional reserve, made up of the 10/RDF, 4th Bedfords, 7th Royal Fusiliers (7/RF) and the 1st Honourable Artillery Company (1/HAC). In light of the heavy losses in other attacks of the Somme it had been decreed that each battalion second-in-command, with several other officers and NCOs, including two company sergeant majors, would remain at the transport lines in order to replace casualties as required. James Macbean Ross, battalion medical officer to the 2/RMLI for much of the war, described such an attack:

> *Dawn is just breaking and a thick mist envelops everything. The companies are all waiting in their 'jumping off' trenches for 'zero' time to arrive. The Commanding Officer, Adjutant and medical officer are in a trench a short distance behind. 'Zero' time arrives. Bang–bang bang–bang bang–bang go the field guns; Crrrr-ump-crrrr-ump go the howitzers; shrapnel bursts overhead and machine gun bullets whizz past. The Artillery have formed a barrage under cover of which the infantry advance on the enemy trenches. The barrage slowly creeps forward, our men unconcernedly follow it. Up go the Boche's S.O.S rockets until the scene resembles a Crystal Palace Brock's benefit night. The enemy artillery quickly reply to the frantic signals of their infantry and their barrage opens. Many of our men fall, some dead, others wounded. The remainder push on and are in the Hun's front line directly our barrage has passed over it. The bombing of dug-outs and hand to hand fighting ensues. Many of our men fall, but few of them before doing all, or even more than all, of what is expected of them.*[8]

Suddenly, in the early morning light, the barrage began and at 6am the first wave advanced in an orderly fashion into the dark of a misty morning in the Ancre valley. The 1/RMLI, under Lieutenant Colonel Cartwright, were hard up against the left of the line and advanced in four waves, with a platoon of each company in each. Immediately a heavy bombardment began in response from the German guns, falling particularly on the 1/RMLI on the left. The ground there was particularly muddy and pock-marked with shell holes, and the resultant slow advance meant that every single company commander (Captains Loxley, Hoare, Browne and Sullivan) had been killed before the battalion had reached the first German line. General Blumberg estimated that fifty per cent of the battalion became casualties in the same period. Elements of the first and second waves of the 1/RMLI managed the reach the Dotted Green Line of the third German trench in spite of heavy losses, while the third and fourth waves consolidated their hold on the first two trenches behind them. The enemy were still fighting for every inch of that line and so when the 2/RMLI began the second wave of the attack they expected a quiet time up to the first objective, only to see intense hand-to-hand fighting continuing as they emerged from the mist. Even so, they successfully assisted in the capture of the Dotted Green Line and then, with the 51st Division on their left and Anson Battalion on their right, advanced onwards towards the station road.

At exactly 7.30am the barrage lifted from the Green Line to the Yellow, and as elements of the 1/RMLI advanced again the commanding officers of both battalions, Lieutenant Colonels Hutchison and Cartwright moved their joint headquarters up to the recently captured second German trench, while the Green Line ahead was still being cleared by 190 Brigade. Sergeant Meatyard, gave a calm and detailed account of that operation:

> Receiving a certain codeword, the CO, Adjutant and our headquarter staff went over amidst not many shells but plenty of spitting bullets and arrived at a German trench which under previous arrangements was now the advanced telephone station. From here I received orders to lay a wire to a certain position ahead and with Private Peach proceeded to lay the wire forward, unreeling as we went along. Almost everything had been hit with shell and it was one continual mass of debris and mud, and pools, some half filled with water and many badly wounded men lying helpless. Eventually reaching the position I connected up and got through to headquarters (Brigade).
>
> Many around me were getting sniped and as the Commanding Officer came along I gave him the tip to keep very low, which he did. The Adjutant, Captain Farquarson, was wounded here, and was wounded again whilst going back; Captain Muntz, Adjutant of 1/RMLI was also sniped here, being shot in the head (from which he afterwards died), The German trench we were now in was in a chronic state, once you took a step you had a job to get your leg out, the mud being so deep and sticky. Wounded Germans and our own men were lying about all over the place; what had been dug-outs were now partly closed by the muddy landslides that had taken place as a result of our gunfire and choked the entrances. The telephone was working well and I was in communication with Brigade. German prisoners were now coming in in large numbers holding up their hands and saying 'Finny'.[9]

By 9.15am the battalions in the centre and right of the division had largely strengthened their hold on the Green Line and were anxious to push on, but General Shute held them back until the depleted RMLI and RDF battalions on the left had made good their advance on the first objective. Fifteen minutes later a ten-minute barrage allowed all remaining units of 188 Brigade to move up and regroup on the Green Line, with Lieutenant Colonel Cartwright personally rallying the men of his own 1/RMLI as well as those separated from their own battalions. Waving his cap and shouting 'Come on Royal Marines', he led his battalion forward, with enfilading fire coming from a redoubt to the right (undamaged by the artillery barrage) and from German trenches to the left, as yet uncaptured by the 4th Gordon Highlanders of the 51st Division. Elements of the division continued to push towards the Yellow Line until 5pm, led by Lieutenant Colonel Freyberg, who received the Victoria Cross for his actions.

Darkness fell, but the action did not stop. Overnight Lieutenant Colonels Hutchison and Cartwright continued to push forwards with the remnants of their respective battalions, and for this both were awarded the Distinguished Service Order, with Sergeant Meatyard receiving the Military Medal. On the morning of the 14th tanks were called up to dispose of the enemy strongpoint that was still giving trouble to the right flank. Beaucourt itself was captured by 10.30am that morning, with several hundred more German prisoners being taken. It was on that morning that Sergeant Meatyard himself was hit by shrapnel, and later explained:

When I woke up I found myself in a dug-out, head and arm bound up. Hadn't the slightest idea how I got there. One of the stretcher bearers of the Howe Battalion had bound me up. After a while I thought I could walk and with the assistance of one of the staff I was taken to the rear. With two other walking wounded we toddled off all together. An incident I remember was, as we passed a battery of artillery, one of the crew came up with a basin of hot cocoa and asked us to partake of it. It was a godsend, and showed the kindness one can get at the hands of a soldier... [At the dressing station] they soon got to work. I had several pieces of shell extracted from my arm and the head wound dressed – I can't recommend the razor that was used to get the hair off!

When the 1/RMLI went into action on the early morning of 13 November they numbered 480. By the end of the battle only 138 remained alive and uninjured; 47 were known to have been killed, 210 were wounded and 85 were missing.

Of his 23 officers Lieutenant Colonel Cartwright was left with only two, Captain Nourse and Lieutenant Van Praagh, 9 having been killed and 12 injured.

In the 2nd Battalion Lieutenant Colonel Hutchison was left with only one uninjured officer, Lieutenant Campbell. Even now the remnants of the RMLI had to remain in the line under heavy shell-fire until relieved by the 37th Division on the 15th, the 2/RMLI at noon and the 1/RMLI at 2pm. From there, exhausted and depleted, yet victorious, they marched back to Englebelmer and thence on to Hedauville. Today the Ancre British Cemetery, nestled at the foot of the slope down to the railway line and the river, is filled with gravestones bearing the Globe and Laurel of the Royal Marines and the anchor of the Royal Naval Battalions. Others lie buried in many different cemeteries in the surrounding fields and villages, and of course many more lie still unknown on the battlefield.

There was no time to mourn and the war continued: on the very next day the 2/RMLI received Captain H.B. Inman as its new adjutant and a draft of fourteen subalterns, freshly trained at Gosport, to replace those killed and injured. After only a few days of training and reorganisation the battalion relieved the 7th Sherwood Foresters in the Saint-Pierre-Divion sector, immediately across the river from the scene of devastation only a few days earlier, and there they were relieved by the 1/RMLI on the 25th. Such was the immediacy of the Ancre.

Chapter 3

France and Belgium 1917

On 11 January 1917 the division moved again to its old haunt on the Ancre. Here 188 Brigade, including 1/RMLI occupied the line immediately north of the river, opposite Beaucourt that they had fought so hard to reach, and the 2/RMLI in 189 Brigade were the next to the south, across the river in the area of the small village of Saint-Pierre-Divion. The reserve battalion of this sector had the privilege of occupying the Saint-Pierre-Divion Tunnel: 200 yards long and 50 feet deep, it was an extraordinary example of the extent to which the German army had established itself in these positions before the British assaults of 1916. Many rooms led off the central passage, including an officers' mess and a hospital, and the complex had originally included an upper storey, but upon capturing the complex in November the 36th Division had deemed that uninhabitable and had blocked it off.

The British Army now held the upper hand on the Somme, and the division was keen to capitalise on its recent successes. Consequently, on 3 February, 188 Brigade was ordered to advance to Puisieux and, if possible, to capture the useful spur which ran across in front of the village of Miraumont. The attack took place at night, with 189 Brigade supporting with their Lewis guns by keeping the enemy opposite their own position (in the village of Grandcourt) under cover and therefore unable to provide enfilading fire. In a short time the attack was a success and on the morning of the 4th the 1/RMLI withstood a vicious counter-attack to maintain their newly-held position.

The following morning a curious incident occurred which was to be the first indication of much greater movement to come. Major Miller, temporarily commanding 2/RMLI in the absence of Lieutenant Colonel Hutchison, reported to brigade that there was a fire in the German trench in front of Grandcourt known as OG1. This burned furiously for four hours and as it was such an unusual sight Miller decided that the battalion would investigate when it was dark enough to approach unseen. At midnight an officer's patrol under Captain Inman slowly approached, but as they got closer could see no sign of the enemy at all, in fact the trench was entirely deserted right down to the river on the left. Returning to report to Major Miller, it was clear that an easy gain was available, and so the deserted trench was occupied by a platoon with a Lewis gun at 3pm on the 6th, reinforced by a second platoon an hour and a quarter later.

The task now turned to examining the extent of the German withdrawal: officers' patrols into Grandcourt in the night were fired upon, but one managed to reach the cemetery on the far eastern side of the village by working round by the south, and in the early morning further attempts to enter the village were unopposed. Consequently, B Company under Captain Inman and C Company under Captain Cutcher occupied the village and dug in to the east, having gained two miles of ground from the previous British line in one night. Captain Inman was awarded the Military Cross for his actions of the preceding twenty-four hours. Little did they know on that first morning that all along the front the German withdrawal to the Hindenburg Line had begun.

The Actions at Miraumont, February 1917

The spur running in front of the village of Miraumont had been largely captured by 2/RMLI and the rest of 189 Brigade, but not entirely, and so it fell to their counterparts in 188 Brigade to complete that task. On the night of 14/15th the 1/RMLI relieved the 10th Royal Dublin Fusiliers (RDF) in the Puisieux trenches next to Grandcourt and at 10pm on the 16th they lined up to await the start of a dawn attack. The trenches from which they were to advance had suffered seven months of battering by the artillery of both sides by this point and resembled little more than a loose collection of ditches and potholes – many ration parties and returning patrols had become entirely lost because the line was so indistinguishable. The marines' objective lay about half a mile ahead and was a sunken road running across their front from Baillescourt Farm, and included two enemy strongpoints, one known as 'The Pimple'. The 1/RMLI were to be on the left of the attack (with two companies of the 2nd Battalion providing a protective left flank for the duration), with Howe Battalion attacking on their right. The weather had begun to warm and, while that on its own might have provided a small amount of comfort, the thaw which ensued made the front line even more uninhabitable than before.

Zero hour approached at 5.45am, and the advance began in an orderly fashion, with all companies reaching their objectives, though the RMLI encountered considerably more opposition than the sailors of Howe. Major Ozanne, leading D Company, captured the Pimple at 6.40, not least through the efforts of Sergeant W.G. Scott, who bravely skirted the stronghold's defences to bomb it through the rear entrance, for which he was awarded the DCM.

Captain Pearson commanded A Company and though their advance, and that of B Company under Major Wellesley, had been entirely as ordered, the tape laid for them to follow had followed a diagonal course rather than going straight at the enemy, and it was presumed that the compass of the RE officer who had laid it had been affected by the sheer weight of metal in the ground after so much shelling. This mistake turned out to be fortuitous however, as their original objective was still heavily defended with wire, whereas C Company's front, where they ended up, was much less strongly held and Pearson's men advanced along the length of the trench instead of assaulting its front, achieving the same aim and capturing sixty prisoners in the process. Captain Pearson was also awarded the MC for his bravery during the attack: as he advanced, rifle in hand, he saw a German machine gun being set up to his left and so calmly stopped amid the gunfire, raised his weapon, and shot one of the enemy soldiers of its crew. Joined by Lieutenant Sanderson, they killed five before the machine-gun crew gave up in their attempt. Had they been successful they could easily have swept the sunken road with machine-gun fire, where the victorious marines were regrouping to consolidate their gains.

Battalion headquarters was established in the sunken road, though the heavy casualties incurred in the attack left Lieutenant Colonel Cartwright with only 200 men along a 1,000-yard line, so two platoons of Hood Battalion were sent up to reinforce the road at dusk. A comparatively quiet night in the new line followed, but at 7.30am on the 18th the enemy bombarded the road with artillery, leading many to expect a counter-attack. Fortuitously the fog prevented such an action until 10.30am, when Captain Pearson spotted two battalions of enemy troops advancing from 300 yards away. At this moment the military machine swung into action and fortunately everything worked as it should: the telephone line to battalion and brigade headquarters was working and an SOS message brought down shrapnel shells on the enemy within two minutes, causing them to turn and flee, first on the left and then also on the right. Major Ozanne gleefully reported to battalion HQ 'Boche bolting like rabbits', and Lieutenant Colonel Cartwright, thinking that he in turn was passing on the message to a brigade signalman repeated the phrase, only to be horrified to realise that he was speaking directly to the brigadier at the other end of the telephone! Rephrasing the message as 'Enemy retiring hastily, Sir, helped by our fire', Cartwright hoped that his momentary lapse might go unnoticed, but in fact it was Ozanne's original message which was passed up to Corps and Army level, where it was received with great delight.

Overnight they were relieved by 2/RMLI, but the continued thaw and subsequent mud meant that the last company couldn't get into the line until after dawn, though their movements were thankfully covered by yet another misty morning. One more attempted counter-attack was again driven off by shrapnel, but in practice the attack was complete and a success. The commander-in-chief sent a message directly to Brigadier General Prentice in command of 188 Brigade, saying 'Many congratulations on success of your operations on 17th.'[1] Major Ozanne was awarded the DSO, principally for his dealings with the counter-attacks, but also for his courage and determination throughout the consolidation of the sunken road. Twelve NCOs and men were also awarded the MM.

Though a success, Miraumont was another costly operation for the Royal Marine Light Infantry: when the attack began the 1/RMLI comprised 16 officers and 500 men, but two days later only 3 officers beyond Lieutenant Colonel Cartwright (Captain Pearson, Lieutenant Hall and Second Lieutenant Champness) remained uninjured, and barely 100 men. Captain Huskisson, the adjutant, hurriedly had as many men buried as possible, each marked by a wooden cross and a bottle containing their name and number. These were later replaced by zinc plaques attached to the crosses, and the place became known as Royal Marine Cemetery.

Gavrelle and Arleux

The 63rd Royal Naval Division played a minor role in the Battle of Vimy Ridge and came away comparatively unscathed, but it was in the last week of April that they were again to see heavy action in their own right. The Battle of Arras had begun on 9 April, and after two weeks of fighting the allied line had advanced to a line marked by the villages of Arleux, Oppy and Gavrelle, immediately east of Bailleul, behind which the German defences were only half finished. If British troops could break the line here they would have a commanding position from which to assault the Arras plain beyond.

On 23 April 189 and 190 Brigades captured the village of Gavrelle in a startling attack conspicuous for its gallantry, not least by two of its battalion commanders, Commander Arthur Asquith, who had successfully petitioned to return to his old Hood Battalion after Lieutenant Colonel Freyberg VC had been appointed to command 58 Brigade, and the extraordinarily young Commander Walter Sterndale-Bennett, who was later to die of his wounds at Passchendaele in November aged 24. Both RMLI battalions were now together in 188 Brigade, and so spent the 23rd in reserve, but their time was to come during the following week.

A second allied attack was planned on Gavrelle for the 28th with two objectives. Firstly, the capture of the high ground marked by a windmill to the north-east of the village. German positions here threatened the British hold on Gavrelle as well as preventing further advance towards Arras.

In addition to this the attack would support that of the Canadian Corps and 2nd Division attacking immediately to the north at Arleux and Oppy Wood (the 'Arleux Loop' trench system), and also the efforts of the 37th Division attacking Greenland Hill to the south. This operation would take place in three stages. Firstly, the 1/RMLI would form a defensive flank to their left, advancing alongside the 2nd Division to some unfinished German trenches behind the enemy front line. Once that was complete the 2nd Division would advance to their next objective before the 1/RMLI joined them at that point. At the same time the 2/RMLI were to advance east to the windmill, capturing it and the German trenches to the south, while Anson Battalion protected their right flank.

Thirty-six hours before the attack, on the night of 26/27th, Major Huskisson took a small party to occupy an isolated trench half-way between Gavrelle and Oppy from which to assess the enemy's position. Creeping silently through the mud, this was achieved by 3am and he subsequently found that the German trenches were still heavily wired, but runners were unable to get back to inform the battalion because of heavy shelling. Zero Hour for both battalions was 4.30am on the 28th. As the whistles sounded at 2pm the 1/RMLI, with the Essex Regiment on their left, advanced to find the wire uncut by the British artillery, as Major Huskisson had seen, and machine-gun fire enfilading from 'Railway Post' on the right. They were forced to regroup in a series of shell holes in front of the enemy positions and, though one officer with approximately thirty men did penetrate the German wire, they were taken prisoner as soon as their ammunition was expended.

A great loss to the battalion was that of their commanding officer, Lieutenant Colonel Cartwright: away from his HQ, he was shot in the stomach as he left the British front line to redirect a Lewis gun team and died of his wounds two days later on the 30th. At this moment the battalion simply could not make any further progress, in spite of tenacious bombing attacks by two companies of the 1/HAC, under Lieutenant Reginald Haine, supporting them from 190 Brigade who were otherwise in reserve. In addition to that, the enemy had seemed to be expecting an attack at this point, almost certainly because the British position was on a forward slope, allowing all movements to be visible. Of the four company commanders from the 1/RMLI, only Major Huskisson survived the action.

The 2/RMLI were initially more successful in their attack, but they also suffered greatly. They advanced quickly to their first objective but did so with an unsupported right flank as Anson Battalion came under extremely heavy fire. Even so, at 7.45am Lieutenant Colonel Hutchison was able to report to Brigade HQ that his battalion had captured their first line and were quickly closing on the second. However, the wire here too was largely undamaged, so A, C and D Companies all had to pass through a narrow opening before fanning out to attack another close German trench, all the while being enfiladed by rifle fire from both sides. During this same time Lieutenant Newling, a young platoon commander of B Company (commanded by Major Eagles), had advanced towards and then took the strongly-defended windmill, capturing 100 German soldiers whom he sent back to the British line unarmed and unescorted. The other platoons of B Company were unable to reinforce his position as they were held up by sustained and accurate enemy machine-gun fire, so Lieutenant Newling and his platoon held the windmill alone all day, repelling three sustained counter-attacks, and for this he was awarded the Military Cross.

The rest of the company held the former German front line, but it wasn't until after dark that they were able to relieve the windmill. It was a further twenty-four hours before the RMLI battalions were relieved by the 31st Division, but the capture of Gavrelle windmill provided the British line with a secure foothold against enemy action for quite some months afterwards. Several other awards for gallantry and bravery were made: Second Lieutenant E.A. Godfrey received the MC for commanding the trench mortar battery in action under fire for sixty hours without a rest and Corporal T. Salt and Acting Corporal W.A. Watts both received the DCM for their actions with the same unit. Private Glyndwyer Davies received the DCM for a most extraordinary action in which he advanced to an enemy strongpoint entirely alone with his rifle, demanded its occupants' surrender and brought fifty prisoners back to the British line. A number of Military Medals were also awarded.

The highest number of casualties of any day in the history of the Royal Marine Light Infantry was recorded on 28 April 1917 with an unusually high proportion of fatalities amongst them. They included Private Horace Bruckshaw, whose diaries were referred to earlier in this book and who died near the windmill, and Lieutenant Edgar Platt, a platoon commander of 1/RMLI. As far as is known he was the youngest British officer to die in the war, at only 17. The son of a Cambridge clergyman, he had attended St Faith's Prep School where he was in the year below Louis Stokes, an RMLI officer killed at the Ancre in November 1916. Passing on to the well-known Christ's Hospital school in Sussex, it was while there that a girl gave him a white feather, indicating cowardice, during the school holidays. Although only aged 15, he determined to join up. In April 1915 he joined the RMLI, giving a false date of birth, and served as part of Major French's cyclist company, but by September had been offered a commission, still at the age of 16. After active service during the Easter Rising in Ireland, he joined 1/RMLI in France as they returned from Gallipoli, where he served at the Ancre and Miraumont.

Perhaps his real age was known – it appeared in his obituary in *The Times* that August, in which Major Ozanne is quoted as saying:

> *He trained under me at Plymouth and from the first proved himself a leader and a cheerful, uncomplaining sportsman. For one so young, he showed remarkable strength of character, and his memory will live long in the hearts of very many. It was impossible to think of fear when he was about, and I am sure he went like a hero, facing the enemy to the last.*[2]

Edgar Platt's body was not recovered and his name appears on the Arras Memorial to the Missing.

The brigade remained in the sector while resting away from the front line. Lieutenant Colonel Hutchison was promoted to brigadier general in command of 190 Brigade, leaving both RMLI battalions in need of new commanders after the death of Lieutenant Colonel Cartwright. To that end Major Ozanne took charge of the first battalion and Major Miller of the second, both being promoted to temporary lieutenant colonel. It seems extraordinary today, but during this period of rest after heavy fighting a divisional horse show was arranged for 14 June, at which 1/RMLI won the prize for best battalion transport, having to show in good order one water cart, one cooker, one limbered wagon with a pair of horses, one limbered wagon with a pair of mules and two pack animals under a mounted NCO. They also won the individual prize for best limbered wagon. Shortly afterwards they were also inspected by their Colonel in Chief, Admiral Lord Charles Beresford, in recognition of their recent courage in action. Later that summer the divisional commander, Major General Lawrie, presented four solid silver bugles as prizes for inter-battalion competitions in cross-country, boxing, football and bayonet fighting – the RMLI won all of the first three, the fourth going to 1/HAC. Pride in the division and its distinct identity remained, even in the face of death.

The Second Battle of Passchendaele

By the autumn of 1917 the RMLI's time on the Somme was over, for now at least. On the night of 2 October both battalions entrained at Tinques for the journey north, but with different destinations. The 1/RMLI were bound for Poperinghe, the 2/RMLI for Houpoutre, but it was clear that they were both destined for the tremendous battle raging for control of the Belgian village of Passchendaele.

The Third Battle of Ypres had begun in the midst of a warm, dry summer, but by the autumn the rain had been falling for weeks. General Gough wanted to bring it to an end as it was clear that the German-held Belgian ports could not be reached before the spring, but Field Marshal Haig insisted that the capture of the Passchendaele ridge was vital to the security of the front for the winter. After the arrival of the 63rd Division they completed almost three weeks of training, which some deemed excessive, but on the 23rd 188 Brigade was on the move and preparing to fight. The 1/RMLI moved to the canal bank 1,000 yards north of Ypres before relieving the 11th Royal Scots in the front line the following night. The infamous, clinging, sucking Flanders mud was much in evidence to them from this first moment in the salient, and the trenches they inherited hardly warranted the name, being instead a conveniently located series of shell holes.

The divisional pioneers, the 14th Worcesters, struggled to complete any works before they filled with water, and completed assembly trenches were barely of any more use than the craters that surrounded them. This was the hellish mire that lives on in the British folk memory of the war as a whole. At the same time, the 2/RMLI went into the support line at Irish Farm, relieving troops of the 9th Division, though they were hardly more comfortable there and twenty-four hours later, on the night of the 25/26th, they moved again, into position for the expected attack. The brigade's left boundary, to the north, was the Lekkerboterbeek stream, and the right boundary was approximately 1,500 yards to the south-east. The 1/RMLI was to occupy 900 yards of that front, though with only 16 officers and 597 other ranks, and Howe Battalion would be advancing with them on their right. By 2am on the 26th they were in position, with their first objective ahead of them in the muddy darkness. That line was a series of German blockhouses in front of the Paddebeek stream, named Berks Houses, Bray Farm, Banff House, Varlet Farm and Source Trench. At 5.40am the rolling barrage commenced, and the battalion advanced close behind in three lines, with separate objectives. In the most treacherous of conditions (it had been raining for six hours by this time) Berks Houses, Banff House and Bray Farm were quickly overwhelmed, in spite of constant enemy fire from the left, with Captain Van Praagh (the adjutant) and Second Lieutenant Williamson both winning the MC in the process.

So far the marines' attack was progressing entirely as hoped and expected, which is extraordinary considering the condition of the ground that they had covered. Once the battalion had established itself on the far side of its objective the next stage began, as the 2/RMLI passed through them at 6.30am and formed up behind a stationary barrage ready to cross the Paddebeek towards the second objective. At exactly 7.36 the barrage moved ahead and the battalion moved off behind it. A Company quickly made progress and crossed the stream under Lieutenant Peter Ligertwood, who had provided each platoon with a small red flag, blessed by the chaplain, as a rallying point. After the war the three of these flags which survived became hallowed relics in the officers' messes of the RMLI battalions, but Lieutenant Ligertwood died of his wounds, only withdrawing from the front after being wounded for a fourth time, and not before pointing out the next objective and ordering his men towards it. Thus, he inspired A Company to push on in a valiant attempt to follow the orders of their dying commander.

The mud and the shelling made it intensely difficult to recognise any of the objectives, and enemy counter-attacks in the afternoon hampered further advances, particularly for Howe Battalion on the right, who were reinforced by C Company of Hood but could still do no more than maintain their position. By dusk A Company of 2/RMLI were forced by constant shelling and machine-gun fire to withdraw back behind the Paddebeek, where all positions were consolidated overnight and maintained during the following day, the 27th. At 5pm both battalions were relieved by 190 Brigade and withdrew to Irish Farm: between them they had lost 661 other ranks as casualties, including Company Sergeant Major W.W. Love, a well-regarded SNCO who had been orderly room sergeant of the Portsmouth Battalion (then 2/RMLI after amalgamation) since Gallipoli, and had recently been promoted to company sergeant major. Just before 188 Brigade were relieved General Prentice, in command, received this message from the Army Commander, General Gough:

> *Please convey to all ranks engaged in today's operations my very great appreciation of their gallant efforts; they have my sincere sympathy, as no troops could have had to face worse conditions of mud than they had to face owing to the sudden downpour of rain this morning. No troops could have done more than our men did today, and given a fair chance, I have every confidence in their complete success every time.*[3]

It took two further attacks by the division, with a total of nearly 3,500 casualties, to capture the line before the 63rd handed over to the 1st Division. Shortly after this action Brigadier General J.F. Coleridge (Indian Army) relieved General Prentice in command of 188 Brigade: the son of an RMLI officer, he was to successfully lead the brigade until the end of the war. Transferring from 189 Brigade, his place there was taken by the ever-popular Commander Arthur Asquith, a naval officer unusually promoted to the military rank of brigadier general for the appointment, but certainly a man whom 189 Brigade would follow anywhere.

Welsh Ridge

As a cold winter settled in, November 1917 saw the successful British action at Cambrai, with the Flesquières Salient created by the new front line. Between the 15th and the 20th the 63rd Royal Naval Division took over a wide 6,000-yard front from the 31st and 62nd divisions which included the strategically and observationally important Welsh Ridge, running south-west, perpendicular to the defences of the Hindenburg Line. The enemy knew that they were coming and the division's morale was boosted by the capture of a German communication which stated that the 63rd were about to arrive and a determined resistance was to be expected! When they did take over the sector it was found to be very thinly manned, partially because of its size, and so the first few weeks were largely engaged in augmenting the defences in the hope of a somewhat quiet winter. The breadth of the sector required each brigade to have two battalions in the line with one in support, and after Christmas 1917 188 Brigade had Howe Battalion and the 1/RMLI in the line (the latter being the right battalion of the division), with 2/RMLI in support.

The early morning bombardment by the enemy's artillery had been slowly increasing since Christmas Day, indicating that an attack may be imminent and it was at this moment, on 30 December, that the enemy delivered a powerful attack against the whole divisional front, wearing white suits to camouflage themselves against the winter snow. Their ruse had allowed them to advance right up to the British wire unseen behind their own rolling barrage. Both the 7/RF and 5th Shropshire Light Infantry (5/KSLI) on the left of the line were overwhelmed, but the 1/RMLI held on, repelling the attack with grim determination. At that moment Howe, also on the left, fell back too, allowing the enemy to occupy Welsh Support Trench until they were again driven out by a fierce counter-attack by the Anson Battalion later that night, for which their commanding officer, Lieutenant Commander Buckle, was awarded the DSO, and which Sir Douglas Haig described as an 'admirably executed counter-attack'.[4] The suddenness of the assault had been almost overwhelming and fighting continued for most of the next day, but the enemy's attack was finally defeated largely due to the continued actions of the division's machine-gun companies and trench-mortar batteries. Sadly, the commanders of both such sections in 188 Brigade, Lieutenant Campbell RNVR and Lieutenant Westby RMLI, were killed in the action, but the 63rd had successfully held back an estimated fifteen battalions of the German Army attempting to take the strategically vital position of Welsh Ridge.

Chapter 4

France and Belgium 1918

The first two and a half months of 1918 began comparatively quietly for the 63rd Royal Naval Division, for they were not involved in any major actions, remaining in the vicinity of Flesquières; but casualties continued. On 1 February the commanding officer of 2/RMLI, Lieutenant Colonel G.L. Parry was hit by a sniper in an exposed area of trench while on his rounds and died the following day. Known affectionately as 'Old Bill', his death was a terrible blow to the battalion. The lack of hygiene prevalent in trench life meant that diarrhoea was prevalent amongst the battalion, and a committee of officers was formed to consider the epidemic which threatened to weaken their operational effectiveness.[1]

On 1 March the Royal Naval Division Machine Gun Battalion officially came into existence, with its distinctive cap badge of crossed machine guns above the letters 'RND'. As the month continued there were some signs to experienced hands that the enemy were contemplating an offensive – increased artillery bombardment, and in the third week several days of gas attacks, from which Hawke Battalion particularly suffered being reduced to a strength of approximately 150 men. Few, if any, could have known the scale of what German High Command had planned, but if Germany was to win the war then they would have to make a significant breakthrough before the American troops, now massing in France, could enter the fray.

Three and a half million men had now been quietly positioned opposite the British front from Arras to La Fère, with more than twice as many divisions on the front line as the allies had. And so it was on 21 March that the German 'Spring Offensive' began, with massive attacks on the Fifth Army and immediate substantial losses of ground for the British Army. Ludendorff's intention had been to punch a hole in the British line with the newly created and fast-moving *Sturmabteilung* – storm troops – and the gap that they created would then be widened by heavier infantry before reserve forces completed the assault. The RMLI remained part of V Corps of the Third Army, immediately to the left of the principal enemy thrust, and so they too were dragged into the action.

The Spring Offensive

At 4.45am on 21 March the world changed for 188 Brigade as 6,000 German guns opened fire on a 40-mile front in one of the largest single bombardments ever seen. Aimed principally at support lines in order to cut off communication, it was followed up by an attack of mustard gas with which to soften the defence of the front line before the first storm troopers appeared through the fog at 5.15am. The front-line battalions engaged in desperate hand-to-hand fighting and at 6am four guns were sent up to the intermediate line by the Machine Gun Battalion, with the rest following with the divisional reserve at 9am. The situation was rapidly worsening. By 2pm the RMLI battalions in the centre were exposed on three sides, with the brigade to their left and the corps to their right both having retreated, so Corps HQ informed them that if counter-attacks were not successful they too would have to withdraw overnight. Consequently, such orders were issued at 9.45pm.

The 1/RMLI passed through the ranks of the 2/RMLI, who covered their withdrawal to Chapel Wood, but the enemy appeared not to have noticed the evacuation until 3.30am, and so it was completed in an orderly and unhampered fashion. It was at this point that the offensive resumed with a heavy bombardment of HE and gas shells which, combined with thick fog, hampered any attempts at communication. Consequently, Lieutenant Colonel Farquharson of 2/RMLI attempted to lead a support company forward to assist those in the firing line but was hit by shell fragments and soon died of his wounds. He had served in the battalion since Gallipoli where he had been adjutant during the evacuation. Chaos now reigned in Chapel Wood: Lieutenant Collier was killed, the commanding officer was close to death and the second in command, Major Coode, and Captain Wrangham were both injured, so Lieutenant Commander Coote of Anson Battalion assumed command.

On the 22nd the enemy's rapid advance threatened to outflank V Corps altogether, and after a heavy attack on the village of Havrincourt at 3.30 that afternoon orders were issued to withdraw further: 188 and 190 Brigades occupying the Metz Switch, with 189 Brigade going straight into reserve in the third trench system. But at 10pm a further report was received, this time indicating that the village of Fins, to the rear right of the division, was already occupied by the enemy and so further movement was required if they were to maintain a defensive line at all.

At 2.30am on the 23rd Divisional HQ moved back to the village of Beaulencourt, and at 7am issued orders that 188 and 190 Brigades were to withdraw to the 'Green Line' which ran for 6,000 yards east of Ytres and Bertincourt, with 189 Brigade remaining to man the third system until they had done so. The RMLI battalions therefore proceeded directly west, crossing the

Canal du Nord and arriving at the Green Line at midday, in company with the 47th and 17th Divisions on the right and left. At 1pm 188 Brigade's rearguard passed through the third system and 189 Brigade also began to pull back. As they did so Lieutenant T. Buckley of 2/RMLI was busy demolishing as many buildings and destroying as many stores and ammunition dumps as he could. He was one of the very last to withdraw behind the Green Line and received the MC for his actions. The Green Line itself was largely incomplete and hardly in a state to hold up a successfully advancing enemy force. The trenches in front of Bertincourt ran immediately east of a high railway embankment; they were no more than three feet deep and there was no wire in place, all of which combined to make them an easy target for artillery with no cover afforded to the defenders. Consequently 188 Brigade, arriving first, worked frantically to improve the defences that they were to occupy as 190 Brigade continued to arrive, doing so by 2pm.

At 4pm a heavy bombardment of the embankment was begun by the enemy, who had clearly seen the work that was progressing. At 10.15pm 189 Brigade had also completed their withdrawal to the Green Line, and from left to right the defences were held by the Oxfordshire and Buckinghamshire Light Infantry (Ox & Bucks) (on the right of the 2nd Division), 1/RMLI, 2/RMLI, Hood, Drake, 4th Battalion of the Bedfordshire Regiment (4/Beds) and the 1st Artist Rifles (1/Artists), with 7/RF, Hawke and Anson in reserve. The hour or so thereafter seemed to pass strangely, with the fires of Lieutenant Buckley's work illuminating the ground ahead, and the stillness punctuated by the exploding of the small arms ammunition left behind.

The stillness did not last. At 11.30pm the 47th Division on the right began to fall back further with little or no warning, and so a company of Anson Battalion were sent to provide a protective flank against enemy action from that direction, but the incessant fog prevented this from being communicated to Brigade HQ for a further two hours. At midnight Divisional HQ heard almost simultaneously that the enemy were in Bus and Léchelle, but that they were being held by Hawke and the 7/RF, leaving 190 Brigade in an extremely precarious position. Counter-attacks by the 17th Division were promised by Corps HQ, but these did not appear, and at 4.23am on the morning of 24 March an extremely heavy barrage of HE and smoke shells was put down by the enemy on Bertincourt, immediately behind the Green Line, in an attempt to prevent the RND from withdrawing, while their infantry simultaneously attacked from the front. It was inevitable then that vicious hand-to-hand fighting must ensue, during which both sides sustained considerable casualties, and the 2/RMLI was forced to send a support company to reinforce Anson on the right flank to prevent the enemy from breaking through. This could not last, and it was with relief that orders were received just before 8am to withdraw further, back through the shelled remnants of Bertincourt to the 'Red Line', which ran between Rocquigny and Barastre, where the RMLI and 188 Brigade were to occupy positions in front of Villers-au-Flos and Rocquigny itself, while Divisional HQ removed towards Bazentin le Grand. Extricating itself from the ongoing fighting was a near impossible task, not least because communication was still entirely hampered by the fog, and so perhaps inevitably the forward companies of each battalion were in a short time surrounded and taken prisoner, while the support companies managed with great difficulty to get away. All along the line the coloured flares used for communication by the storm troopers could be seen arching through the air, ominously signalling their continuous advance.

The British withdrawal was now widespread along the front, but 188 Brigade proceeded to the Red Line without much attention once they had managed to get clear of Bertincourt itself. Upon arrival Major Clutterbuck took charge of the remainders of both RMLI battalions and twelve guns of the RND Machine Gun Battalion did much to slow the enemy south of Lesboeufs under the command of Lieutenant Anderson RNVR. It seemed for a moment that the enemy's advance might be slowed, as counter-attacks by the 17th Division and a group of tanks appeared to have pushed them back as far as Bus and Léchelle, but at 2pm the Divisional HQ arrived at Beaulencourt and, reviewing the situation, concluded that a further withdrawal was necessary: they had no contact with Corps HQ, nor with the divisions on both sides of them, so to hesitate any longer could cause them to be disastrously outflanked. Consequently, he gave orders for another move, this time to a line between Martinpuich and Bazentin-le-Petit, a further six miles to the rear. The march began at 3pm, with three parallel columns of almost ironic orderliness, one of each brigade accompanied by its own artillery for use as required, with the most depleted, 189 Brigade, in the centre.

Two hours later the division was resting by High Wood, east of their intended destination, when orders were received from V Corps to establish a defensive position between their location and Eaucourt l'Abbaye, but this was not received by 188 Brigade, including the RMLI, who continued on to Martinpuich as originally planned where their guns and transport became entangled in the chaotic traffic at the point where several roads converge in the village. This confusion allowed the enemy to capture the east corner of High Wood and the useful higher ground to the north, taking some of the British guns in the process. While establishing their position 189 Brigade came under a sudden and sustained attack from the storm troopers, whose coloured flares brought down six bombs and strafing machine-gun fire from their attendant aircraft. In the face of such stiff opposition the brigade still succeeded in defending itself, while 190 Brigade established themselves in reserve at Courcelette. Eventually 188 Brigade, receiving the orders intended for the afternoon, joined the line at High Wood in the early hours of the morning. General Coleridge, the divisional commander, was at his newly-relocated headquarters in Albert, considering the enemy's disposition and his next move. The 24th March had been a terrible day of constant retreat in the face of the enemy that could not continue indefinitely.

But the German advance was relentless and at 5.30am on the 25th they again attacked and pierced the 47th Division on the right of the 63rd, the 17th on the left coming under heavy fire three hours later. By 9.30am the line of the 17th Division was broken and they were in retreat, leaving both flanks of the Royal Naval Division exposed. The 500-strong remnant of 190 Brigade joined 188 Brigade in an attempt to defend Martinpuich, but there was little to be done against such overwhelming numbers while the momentum of the battle continued. By mid-afternoon though, a valiant attempt had been made to secure the right flank, but the situation could no longer be sustained and the order was given to withdraw to Thiepval, approximately two miles to the west.

First went 189 Brigade, while the combined forces of 188 and 190 brigades provided cover. In the early evening General Coleridge held a conference of his commanding officers and adjutants on the top of Thiepval Ridge, from where much of the situation could be considered. It was there that Brigade Major Thompson was wounded and Lieutenant Colonel Kirkpatrick, commanding Anson, was killed, both by HE shells. The brigades expected to remain in their comparatively strong positions on the ridge overnight, presumably prior to withdrawing across the Ancre the next day, but in the event further orders were received from V Corps to do just that at 12.45am on the 26th, and the operation was completed successfully by 6am, 188 Brigade again acting as rearguard. This left them in a naturally strong defensive position: the Ancre at this point was winding, with wide marshy edges, and the embankment of the Arras-Albert railway provided a ready-made parapet.

While the divisional artillery withdrew to Englebelmer one 18-pounder gun was retained by the river as a further incentive against the enemy attempting to cross. The division had now been fighting almost continually for five days; they were exhausted and increasingly ill-equipped, though the transport officers of both RMLI battalions did extraordinary work in reaching their companies wherever they happened to be in the ever-evolving battle. The fact that they were now on familiar ground may have been comforting in the sense that they knew the area well, but it was also a crushing disappointment to be retreating over fields that had been so hard-won a year and a half earlier, with the loss of so many of their own men who still lay buried on every side.

Almost as soon as the last man had crossed the Ancre and the bridges blown the message came through that the Germans appeared to be intending to attack from the south-east, threatening to cut off the division's battalions at the front from their headquarters in Albert. A German officer, conducting a reconnaissance of the 2/RMLI, was captured carrying maps and orders stating that Englebelmer and the low ridge upon which it is situated must be captured at all costs, so as to command the northern approaches to Amiens. Such a development would be disastrous, so the defence of the 63rd Division, the 47th to its south and the 17th in the north became vital in the prevention of widespread defeat and capture. Thankfully the 17th held, driving off a stiff attack from the north-east, and it was at this point that the division was finally relieved after its greatest feat of endurance of the war so far.

During the afternoon the 12th Division arrived from the west, with 53 Brigade relieving 190 Brigade, who withdrew to Englebelmer to grasp what little rest they could in the face of continuous enemy aggression, while 188 and 189 brigades were relieved at 7pm, the 1/RMLI by a battalion of the Queen's Own (Royal West Kent) Regiment (retiring to Martinsart), and the 2/RMLI by a battalion of the Royal East Kent Regiment (The Buffs). They too marched to Englebelmer at first, but the perceived danger of attack there meant that they were quickly diverted to join their fellow battalion at Martinsart. The situation demanded every effort and there was no time for prolonged rest.

Haig issued his famous 'Backs to the wall' communication,[2] so 188 and 189 brigades were put under the control of the 12th Division. After darkness fell rations and ammunition were issued in Martinsart, but while that was underway, at 8pm the enemy again began to shell the village. Though there were many cellars in the ruined village in which to take cover, the defensive preparations were delayed by three hours until the shelling stopped at 11pm. Only an hour later, shots were heard and troops began to fall back through the village, evidently under attack from enemy infantry. German troops had advanced further west at several points down the Ancre valley, and in the 63rd Division's sector had penetrated right to the western edge of Aveluy Wood, much to their surprise. Very soon afterwards, early on the 28th, news indeed came that up to 2,000 enemy troops were advancing on Englebelmer, with many having crossed the river under cover of darkness during the divisional hand-over, surprising Brigadier General de Pree of 189 Brigade and his brigade major as they rode towards the village, though they narrowly escaped.

General Coleridge ordered his battalions to stand to in anticipation: Anson and 2/RMLI advanced upon the enemy, reaching them just before 3am and attacking with such ferocity that the superior force retreated in disarray towards Aveluy Wood and the river. Fifty prisoners and thirteen machine guns were captured in that extraordinary and unexpected action. Shortly after 4am they marched exhausted into Mailly Maillet, thence on to billets in Forceville. There, finally, they had four days to recover from the most extraordinary action in which they had been involved. Kit was cleaned (and replaced where necessary and possible), they were inspected by the brigade commander and had their first church parade for a long time, no doubt with much to consider.

During the action 37 had been killed, almost 200 were wounded in hospital, and more than 550 were missing, of whom half were later known to have been captured.

Aveluy Wood

It was a policy repeated by many commanding officers of the RMLI during the war that reorganisation and retraining were the vital step immediately after action in restoring and maintaining fighting efficiency. Thus the four days at Forceville were not ones of languid recovery, but of military routine, and on the 2nd both battalions marched to Toutencourt for the night, then back to the familiarity of Englebelmer on the 3rd. Out of billets and back in bivouacs they were shelled on a number of occasions, as if they needed reminders of the enemy's closeness and it was here that eight replacement officers arrived to join them. The stretched capability of the RMLI's recruiting and training capacity was in evidence: only one of the new men was a Royal Marines officer, with two of the others being sent from the Queen's Own Royal West Kent Regiment and five from the Middlesex Regiment.

On the night of the 3rd their period of 'rest' was over and they marched into support lines behind 190 Brigade east of Aveluy Wood, though the proximity of the enemy meant that the support line was somewhat improvised. The line here was complex and hard to maintain with confidence. Consequently, when the 7/RF were attacked at 9am on the 5th help was required and A Company of 1/RMLI was sent up under Captain Campbell to assist at 1.30pm, followed by B Company and Battalion HQ at 3pm. Lieutenant Colonel Fletcher, in command, led patrols in the wood himself to establish the extent of the line and two gaps were discovered. Lieutenants Proffitt and Bailey were both awarded the MC for their actions in closing these gaps in the face of enemy action, as was Captain Campbell for his exemplary work in establishing a defensive right flank to the 7/RF, linking up with the left of the 24th (County of London) Battalion (24/Londons). The wood was secured, but its density and the convoluted nature of the line meant that such a situation might change at very short notice.

In the early hours of 6 April the 2/RMLI moved into support north-west of the wood as it came under renewed attack by the enemy. As the situation again became confused the two battalions organised a counter-attack. Captain Newling, who had won an MC at Gavrelle Windmill, acted most courageously in personally ensuring contact was maintained with the 4/Bedfords on the left, before returning to the counter-attack which had by now begun. He found it being held up by German machine guns, so he led men of his own company to capture the position, allowing the counter-attack to succeed and earning a bar to his MC in the process; fifty-six prisoners and ten machine guns were also captured. The line was more securely established now and the remaining elements of the 7/RF withdrew. Late in the afternoon of the 7th, as dusk fell, the RMLI were themselves relieved by Anson and, apart from one more short, quiet stretch, their time at Aveluy Wood was at an end.

It had been a long, hard fortnight for the RMLI, and in recognition Lieutenant Colonel Fletcher received the DSO, while Brigadier Generals Hutchison and Coleridge were both made CB. All members of the battalions had acted in exemplary fashion and a great deal of other awards were also made, as the 63rd Royal Naval Division had played a central part in halting the greatest single German offensive since the beginning of the war, during which they had captured 1,200 square miles of territory, but inherited a line far less defensible than that from which they had advanced. As their progress slowed, so their determination and enthusiasm wavered while that of the British hardened, and the front was not to remain in its new position for long.

The remaining days of April 1918 comprised three weeks of intensive organisation and training for the Royal Marines, while at the same time occupying the reserve line near Toutencourt. The problem remained of how to bring both battalions up to strength again after their many losses through casualties and capture. The Reserve Battalion and depot in England struggled to supply their needs, not least because of the demands placed upon them by the manning of the 3/RMLI in the Aegean and the recent creation of the 4/RMLI, not to mention the RMA. Sentiment cannot dictate the demands of war and so, reluctantly, the decision was taken to amalgamate the first and second battalions as 1/RMLI under Lieutenant Colonel Fletcher, with Major Lawrie as second in command and Captain West as adjutant. On the 23rd the 2/Royal Irish arrived to take the place of the 2/RMLI in the brigade, and on the 29th the amalgamation was officially complete, bringing to an end three years of service.

It was at this same time, however, that the atmosphere had begun to change: the retreat of the Spring Offensive had ended and training for advance was at hand. On the night of 7 May 188 Brigade took over the left sector in front of the village of Hamel, still in the Ancre valley, and they were suffused with the new offensive spirit. On the night of the 18th C Company and Hawke battalion waited behind a heavy artillery and trench mortar barrage before advancing on the enemy's outposts in the dark. Finding them abandoned, they advanced further until turned back by machine-gun fire from the railway embankment, destroying all enemy positions as they returned to their own line. On the night of the 24th an even bigger raid commenced, with platoons attacking along the whole divisional front and inflicting a great deal of damage. Though the RMLI were not in the line at the time, the 63rd distinguished itself in many places.

Training continued when in reserve, but on 10 June one of the final links with Gallipoli and earlier was lost when Brigadier General Hutchison was promoted and appointed Assistant Adjutant General Royal Marines, the professional head of the corps, thus necessitating a move to the Admiralty. It was a move much deserved, but one which marked the end of a long and distinguished career in the field. However, the division soldiered on, and soon its renewed vigour was to be rewarded.

The Hundred Days' Offensive

Marshal Foch's 'great offensive' began in July with Mangin's perhaps unexpected victory near Soissons, and as it continued the German attacks around Rheims failed and they began to withdraw beyond the Marne, a place of many memories for both the French and the British. The British Fourth Army rose to the task in heroically turning back the enemy before Amiens in what Ludendorff called '…the Black Day of the German Army', and suddenly Lieutenant Colonel Fletcher's commitment to immediate reorganisation and retraining after action was vindicated as the brigade once again moved forwards with optimism and renewed aggression. As Blumberg noted, '…the division went forward sure of their superiority to the enemy.'[3] An attack from the north-west towards Bapaume seemed to offer the best chances of success if the allied forces were to maintain pressure on German High Command, but it must be attempted under great secrecy, and so the 63rd Division handed over its control of the Auchonvillers sector and travelled at night, to avoid detection by enemy spies or aircraft, to the small village of Souastre, ten miles north-west of Bapaume, arriving on 19 August. Here Lieutenant Colonel Fletcher learned of their task.

It was to be a surprise attack for the Royal Marines almost as much as the enemy as it was to commence the next day without any opportunity for the battalion to become familiar with the sector, but theirs was initially a supporting role, though a vital one. The plan was for the 37th Division of IV Corps, already in position on the front line, to push forwards, after which the 5th and 63rd would pass through them to the line of Irles – Bihucourt – Gomecourt, and then further up to the Achiet-le-Grand to Arras railway line. The first objective, the 'Brown Line' ran along the eastern edge of Logeast Wood by the village of Achiet-le-Petit and was to be taken by 188 and 189 Brigades (with the assistance of sixteen tanks), who were then to proceed to attack the 'Red Line' of the railway as it passed through Achiet-le-Grand. Finally, 190 Brigade, in support until then, would pass through them to capture the final objective line between the villages of Bihucourt and Irles with their own supporting tanks.

The approach to the jumping-off line was made on the night of the 20th, assisted by white tapes laid out by compass by the battalion intelligence officer at Fletcher's insistence, conscious of the uneven and unfamiliar nature of the ground. They arrived only ten minutes before the attack was due to begin and the morning was foggy, but in the early morning summer light the 37th Division set off on time behind their artillery barrage and quickly captured their objective. Now, at 4.55am, it was the 63rd's turn to advance, making excellent progress for the first forty-five minutes before the right flank was held up by sustained machine-gun fire from huts on the road at the corner of Logeast Wood. C Company and two platoons of D Company 1/RMLI wheeled on to the target and attacked in text-book manner, capturing a 5.9-inch gun, 250 men, 6 trench mortars and much more besides. So far both advancing brigades had captured their first objectives with few casualties and no loss of time.

Here there was a short pause for the tanks to catch up with the infantry, as the divisional artillery could provide no support beyond the Brown Line. The second objective for 188 Brigade lay ahead and they pushed on behind the support of the tanks, but in the confusion of the fog and the unfamiliar ground Hood Battalion advanced diagonally to the right, and the 2/RI too far to the left, leaving a weakened centre of the division as they approached the railway embankment. The 1/RMLI reached the objective, but at this point the division came under fire from the huts of a former British Army camp, whose sunken floors, designed to shelter the occupants from shrapnel, also turned them into excellent machine-gun posts in the hands of the enemy. Major Poland led C and D Companies of the 1/RMLI in a desperate attempt to capture the post, but they were driven back, their commander killed. As the fog lifted it became clear that the German defenders also had new anti-tank weapons, with the result that one by one they went up in flames: the weakened divisional centre began to waver and then fall back, forcing the flanks to do the same, back towards the Brown Line. The last marines pulled back at 3pm, receiving casualties from short-range artillery fire, and they consolidated their position about 500 yards in front of Logeast Wood, but in the absence of the tanks no further advance could be made until the divisional artillery was brought up. Three counter-attacks were successfully beaten off that afternoon, including one repelled by Captain Vance who continued to lead his men even after having an arm blown off.

The divisional artillery was brought up with great effort overnight, ready to repel the expected early-morning counter-attack of which Lieutenant Colonel

Fletcher had learned from a prisoner, but most of the night passed quietly apart from the work of the regular offensive patrols preventing a surprise attack by the enemy. At 4.45am the expected barrage began, and further attacks were successfully broken up at both 5am and 11am, but the third, at 1.30pm began to break through the exhausted British line. The division's left flank, comprising the 7/RF and Anson began to be pushed back, and while the marines held their ground a further wave at 3pm also forced the partial withdrawal of the battalion to their right. The 1/RMLI began to follow, falling back through the centre of Logeast Wood, but Fletcher would not allow such a thing: gathering his battalion HQ staff he rallied the withdrawing troops and led them himself back towards the enemy on the far side of the wood. Despite being severely injured in the leg he refused to be carried away from the action until he was certain that he could report to division that the line had been restored. For this he was awarded a bar to his DSO, and his acting adjutant, Lieutenant Spraggett, received an MC. Second Lieutenant Stone was also awarded an MC, for manning a Lewis gun himself once its crew had been killed or injured, driving off a large number of the enemy. Sergeant Trigg received a DCM for a similar action. In total one DSO, five MCs, four DCMs and seventeen MMs were awarded for the battalion's actions in that one 24-hour period.

That night 188 and 189 brigades were relieved by the 37th Division – the 1/RMLI at 5.30am on the 24th by a battalion of the Rifle Brigade. Major Sandilands took over command of the battalion in the absence of Lieutenant Colonel Fletcher and continued the CO's policy of immediate reorganisation and retraining, but their part in the assault had not yet come to an end. The 37th Division continued the attack on the following day and, alongside the 5th and New Zealand Divisions, succeeded in capturing Achiet-le-Grand, but the villages of Grevillers and Warlencourt remained in German hands and further action was required. The commander of IV Corps decided to follow up immediately on his successes and instructed that the attack take place at 7.30 that evening, with the 63rd advancing from Loupart Wood (between the two villages) east towards Bapaume to capture the small settlements of Le Barque, Ligny-Thilloy and Thilloy. With the NZ Division on their left and the 5th on their right, 188 and 189 brigades would advance with 190 Brigade in support and six tanks to assist.

Unfortunately, when the corps commander sent his instructions General Lawrie, commanding the division, was out inspecting the men of his brigades after their heavy fighting the day before, and he did not pass on the order to brigade commanders until 3pm. Brigadier General de Pree, commanding 189 Brigade, had misgivings beyond simply the short-notice of the order. He was unsure whether the enemy had yet been driven out of Loupart Wood, a critical piece of information about his intended assembly position.

He therefore took his mounted battalion commanders and inspected the wood himself, right through to the far side. Satisfied that the enemy had withdrawn, he returned to his brigade to find that in his absence two battalions, Hood and Howe, had been bombed and machine-gunned by low-flying enemy aircraft and were in no state to mount an attack. With dusk falling fast and only fifteen minutes left before the intended zero hour he made a fast but important decision. As senior officer present (the divisional commander being at his HQ several miles away), he would delay the attack, taking whatever consequences there may be from division or corps. It was a risky decision, but one made very much with both the likelihood of success and the welfare of his own men in mind and had to be immediately justified to the chain of command. Leaving Commander Egerton of Hood Battalion in temporary command of his brigade, de Pree set out to offer his explanation to General Lawrie. In the event both divisional and corps commanders entirely supported his decision and new orders were swiftly issued for the attack to happen as previously planned but early the next day, 25 August.

Major Sandilands led the 1/RMLI from their assembly positions to their station on the left of the line in the darkness of the early morning. Once more they set off in fog, and once more it concealed their advance to their first objective. Grevillers trench, between that village and the wood, was taken by 5.40am with almost no resistance once an enemy machine gun had been single-handedly captured by Private W. Brindley of Chatham. The second objective, a further trench 1,000 yards off, was similarly taken by 6.10am and the battalion had begun to take many prisoners from amongst the German troops retreating east towards Bapaume, hoping to pass unnoticed in the early-morning murk: by 7.45 they had taken 150 prisoners, two trench mortars and six machine guns. An hour later the fog began to lift as the day warmed, and the battalion could accurately assess its position: they had reached their final objective, passing the village of Le Barque and establishing themselves on its eastern side, facing towards Bapaume, but the rest of the division had failed to take Thilloy and Ligny-Thilloy.

It was at this moment in 189 Brigade that Commander Daniel Beak DSO MC*, who had joined the RND as an ordinary seaman and was now commanding Drake Battalion, staged an extraordinary attack on an exposed German machine-gun position with the assistance of just one volunteer, for which he was awarded the Victoria Cross. His men followed him with a loud cheer. The remaining villages were situated on higher ground and strongly defended, so the brigade took up defensive positions to the west and waited for the villages to be bombarded. At 1pm the first of several attempted counter-attacks was received and defeated, with the line still held at nightfall. Supply lines were becoming tenuous, so a novel method of delivery was used, by which boxes of rifle ammunition were dropped from aeroplanes onto the brigade below. Thilloy remained in the enemy's possession and a frontal assault was considered impracticable as the NZ Division were not able to advance any further, so 188 and 189 brigades attempted to take the village by 'infiltration' – house by house using heavily-armed patrols. Still the enemy held out, and on the 27th a further attempt was made by the fresher troops of 190 Brigade, but to no avail. That night the RND was relieved by the 42nd Division, the 1/RMLI by the 8/Manchesters whom they had known and fought alongside in Gallipoli. Casualties had again been high – the week's fighting had cost the lives of 5 officers and 46 men. Withdrawing to Miraumont to reorganise, there was to be little time to rest.

A period of comparative rest followed, during which Major General Blacklock, late of the King's Royal Rifle Corps, took command of the 63rd Division. However, it was not to last. The allied advance had pushed the enemy into a northern extension of the Hindenburg Line known as the Drocourt-Quéant Switch, south of the River Scarpe, and XVII Corps, to which the 63rd Division had recently been reallocated, were to push left with the Canadians in order to attack the line from the north while the VI Corps were to simultaneously push to the right of the line. In the early hours of 2 September 1918 the 88th Division, including the RMLI, assembled in the valley of the Sensée River between the villages of Croisilles and Fontaine, with 189 Brigade in support. The attack began at 5am, and the 1st Canadian Division, along with the British 57th Division made swift advances, with the trickle of German prisoners being escorted back a sure sign of their success. General Blacklock had been granted the discretionary power to advance if he was certain that the first wave had achieved their objective, and so he gave the order to advance at 7.20am. His belief was proved correct as the 1/RMLI and 2/Royal Irish advanced through the troops of the first wave towards the Green Line, the third objective of the morning. Reaching the trenches of the Drocourt system the RMLI wheeled to the right to attack the line from the north, exactly as detailed by the Corps' plans. The day was a great success for the 63rd, not least because of the extraordinary leadership of Commander Beak of Drake Battalion, and Quéant and Pronville had been taken by midnight.

The morning of 3 September dawned brightly and 9am brought a message of congratulations from Field Marshal Haig for the previous day's successes, but there remained much work to be done.

Enemy resistance became stronger as the day wore on and the 63rd fought through the village of Inchy to capture the first crossings over the strategically vital Canal du Nord. This continued throughout the afternoon, and at 9pm 189 Brigade, including the RMLI, were ordered to establish a strongpoint on the bank of the canal in order to allow a forced crossing by 190 Brigade at dawn. It was at this same moment that a message was received from the First Lord of the Admiralty which, though its arrival may have seemed a little incongruous, certainly served to remind the 63rd that their efforts were not going unnoticed:

> 'On behalf of my colleagues on the Board of Admiralty and myself, I congratulate you and the troops of the Royal Naval Division under your command most warmly, on your share in the brilliant success, which was achieved in storming the junction of the Drocourt-Quéant and Hindenburg lines yesterday. The praise bestowed on you by the F.M. Commander-in-Chief will be most gratifying to all ranks and ratings of the Royal Navy and Royal Marines.'

At 5am on the 4th D Company 1/RMLI, under Lieutenant Buckley MC moved forward to assist the Hawke Battalion in their attack on the crossing-point south of Inchy, at the same time that A Company, under Lieutenant Hardisty, assisted Hood Battalion in their attack to the north. These crossings were successful (and Lieutenant Buckley was awarded a second bar to his MC in the process) but were thereafter held up as the brigades on either side had not made as much progress. This allowed the 63rd a period of tense rest and consolidation. At 6.40 a heavy German bombardment to the northern crossing point gave warning of a possible counter-attack following quickly behind, but that was repulsed by A Company and the line re-established under Lieutenant Hardisty's inspiring leadership and example. Here the advance stumbled as both sides fought to regain control of the canal bank and crossing points on either side of Inchy, and showers of both rain and shells continued until the 1/RMLI were relieved at 11pm on 7 September.

The Canal du Nord

A well-deserved and needed period of rest followed the relief of the division at Inchy, including a divisional race meeting, but with the speed of the allied advance ever increasing it could not last forever. On 23 September the division received warning that they would soon participate in the capture of the Canal du Nord itself and three days later they moved up towards the village of Moeuvres ready for the attack. At 5.05am on the 27th the artillery barrage began and at 5.30 the 1/RMLI moved off from their position in 'Tadpole Copse' to cross the now dry canal and the Sains-Havrincourt road with ease to reach their jumping-off point west of Bourlon Wood. The advance of 188 Brigade, who had all crossed largely unhindered, began at 7.58am with the 1/RMLI advancing with a front three companies wide. Here the division's advance was slowed by enemy concentrations located in a factory by the main road. Three officers were killed and repeated attacks failed until the strongpoint was taken by two tanks after an artillery bombardment and the village of Anneux was taken by the Canadians, including a large number of enemy guns. By 4pm the village seemed secure, but the threat of counter-attack was ever present and indeed came on strongly at 6.45. The 1/RMLI briefly faltered but skilful work with the battalion's Lewis guns by Lieutenant Buckley drove off the attack and secured the village for the night.

The Canal du Nord had been taken, but the Canal de l'Escaut remained. The corps commander sent a message which read 'Well done. Reported that German Naval Division is waiting for you on Canal de l'Escaut. When Greek Meets Greek.'[4] It can hardly have made for a calm night's waiting. As dawn broke the division spent its time reorganising on the 'Brown Line' of the German trench system that they had reached the day before. They were to have a vital role in the capture of Cambrai, waiting for the 57th Division to secure the high ground east of the canal before passing through their lines and around the south of the town to prevent the enemy garrison from retreating further east.

The advanced guard, including 189 Brigade, moved off at 1.15 but the 57th had not yet secured the crossings and so the advance quickly halted. As the rest of the division moved up at 3pm only a few men had succeeded in crossing the canal, so it fell to the Divisional Engineers of the 63rd to construct two pontoon bridges under fire and the cover of darkness. The morning of the 28th saw three companies of Hawke Battalion RND across the canal and an artillery bombardment assisted the capture of Cantigneul mill. Now it was time for the 1/RMLI to come to the fore and at noon they passed 189 Brigade and passed through the woods and parkland of La Folie. Crossing the canal at 1.30pm, they advanced up the slopes towards the suburb village of Proville, immediately south-west of Cambrai. The town was still heavily defended, with machine guns placed on the roofs of houses, and at 3.30pm the advance of the 1/RMLI was halted by enfilade fire from Proville to the right, causing significant casualties, though Lieutenant Colonel Sandilands fought on with his battalion for which he was awarded the DSO.

A comparatively quiet night ensued, during which the final brigade of the division, 190, crossed the canal in support. The next day saw further efforts to break through the suburbs of Cambrai and in the middle of the morning 188 Brigade attacked a trench system extending south from Proville in front of the Faubourg de Paris, capturing their objective after a five and a half hour struggle. D Company 1/RMLI and a company of Anson Battalion attacked a strong-point at the Faubourg and successfully drove out the enemy, only to be themselves trapped by a counter-attack at 6.10 the following morning and they could not be rescued until a battalion of the Royal Scots Fusiliers pushed through the line at dusk that evening, 1 October. Making use of their relief in darkness, the 1/RMLI formed up on the road and retired to bivouacs near Anneux. It had been a remarkable day of fighting all along the line; only 200 of the 1/RMLI remained fit for action, including fewer than a third of the officers, but the French had taken St Quentin and in a few short days the Hindenburg Line would be in allied hands.

The Battle of Cambrai

After such an intensive few days of action the 63rd Division could justifiably have expected a period of rest, and that certainly was the intention; they were to travel by train to a rest area and leave had begun to be granted when, at 6.30pm on 4 October, XVII Corps HQ sent a signal cancelling the order and instead indicating that further operations were to be expected. The divisional commander was summoned and informed that the 63rd would be involved in the attack on the village of Niergnies, immediately to the south of Cambrai and the capture of the open ground between there and the village of Rumilly further to the south, the site today of Cambrai airport. Though the offensive was postponed by twenty-four hours, it was to go ahead on the 8th. A first wave, comprising the 2/Royal Irish, was to capture a trench on the road (now under the airport) leading south-east to Seranvillers, after which the 1/RMLI were to pass through their lines to capture the second objective, the Rue St Ladre to the east of Niergnies, allowing Anson Battalion to follow behind and encircle the village without fear of attack from the east, after which Anson and Hood battalions would together sweep north to capture the village itself. The 1/RMLI was to be protected on its left flank by three tanks in order to deter any harrying attacks from Niergnies while the battalion fought past the southern edge of the village.

At 7.30pm on the 7th the battalion fell in on the Cambrai-Rumilly road for a hot meal before moving off into the dark. Niergnies had been bombarded with incendiary shells during the preliminary barrage and so presented a clear target ahead as zero hour, 4.30am, approached. The Royal Irish achieved their objective with comparative ease and relatively few casualties by 6.10am and at 6.44 the 1/RMLI, in attack formation, took advantage of the lifted barrage to pass through the line and advanced eastwards until halted by machine-gun fire from defended German positions in the cemetery, located in fields just to the south of the village itself. After severe casualties had been sustained the enemy positions were destroyed by the accompanying tanks and the battalion advanced again towards the second objective, which was captured along with four machine guns and thirty enemy soldiers. Lance Corporal Child was awarded the DCM for his actions in which he fought off an enemy tank with his machine-gun section once the capture of the objective had been consolidated.

An extraordinary action ensued in which the German troops occupying the village counter-attacked using seven captured British tanks, while the 63rd Division fought them off using captured German anti-tank guns. Several more awards for gallantry were earned in the course of the morning. By 9.55am the village was in British hands, occupied by Anson Battalion, while the flanks were protected by Hood, Hawke and the 1/RMLI. A strong counter-attack emerged from the German line at 1pm, however, and both sides struggled to gain the upper hand throughout the afternoon until the 63rd Division was relieved by the 24th at 9.30pm.   It had been a long day; 2 officers and 9 NCOs and ORs had been killed, with a further 120 wounded and 14 missing, but the tenacity of the RMLI had made the capture of Cambrai by the Canadians on the following day a significantly easier task by removing the risk of assault from the south of the town. As the division left XVII Corps the corps commander made his gratitude apparent:

'I wish to express to all ranks of the Royal Naval Division my appreciation of and sincere thanks for the splendid work, which they have done since joining the Corps on 31st August. The Division has always been in the front of any fight and has never failed to get its objectives, however difficult the task; its final performance, the capture of Niergnies with 1,000 prisoners, could only have been effected by troops imbued with determination and soldierly spirit. I congratulate all ranks and wish them good luck and success in the future. It will always be a matter of pride to me to have been associated with the Royal Naval Division during this eventful period of the war.'[5]

At long last a period of rest had arrived.

Armistice

On 1 November 1918 the 1/RMLI travelled by a convoy of buses to an area near Douai where they spent three days training before joining XXII Corps at Aulnoy, south of Valenciennes, on the 5th. The roads of the area were in a terrible condition, made worse by recent heavy rain but after some contact with the enemy on the 7th, the division's advance towards Mons was largely without incident beyond sporadic machine-gun fire from remaining pockets of resistance. At 6am on 10 November the 1/RMLI left the village of Sars-la-Bruyère and found considerable German presence around the Chateau de Bourgnies and Harmignies. One officer was killed and the commanding officer, Lieutenant Colonel Sandilands, was injured, his place being taken by the adjutant, Captain R.H.P. West. A line was established east of Harmignies at 3.30am and an attack further east was ordered at 5am, but that was amended at 7am to the effect that the division should proceed if possible, but any casualties should be avoided. Something was clearly about to happen, and at 8.30am this communication was received from the divisional commander, Major General Blacklock:

> 'Hostilities will cease at 1100 hours, November 11th. All troops will stand fast on line reached at that hour, which will be reported to Divisional Headquarters. All defensive precautions will be maintained and an outpost line established. There will be no parleying with the enemy who if he attempts to come over, will be sent back over.'[6]

On 15 November 200 men of the 1/RMLI under Captain T.H. Burton MC marched into Mons as part of the official allied entry into the town. Less than a week earlier they had sustained their last casualties, but now they marched behind the band of the Hood Battalion as triumphal victors. Five days later they transferred to St Symphorien, coincidentally the site of the grave of both the first and last British casualties of the war, and then six days later to the adjacent villages of Eugies and La Bouverie, south of Mons, where they spent six months in billets. The 1/RMLI swelled to over 1,100 men as individuals and small groups rejoined from attachments and courses in skills which would no longer be required. The colours of the Chatham Division were sent out from England and the long months of peace negotiations were passed in peacetime military routine and in educational courses useful for the resettlement of the men. Finally, at the end of May 1919 they entrained for Antwerp and, now only at cadre strength, sailed for England, leaving France for the first time in three years.

Billeted in South Kensington, on 6 June they paraded with the other remnants of the division before the Prince of Wales on Horse Guards Parade. The Royal Naval Division may have been something of a military anomaly, but they had not been forgotten, as the prince made quite clear:

> 'It is a great pleasure to me to see you all here today, and it is a privilege to inspect you on parade. More than four years have

passed since the King at Blandford Camp inspected the Royal Naval Division, on the occasion of your departure for the Dardanelles. Since then the story of the war has unfolded itself, and after many vicissitudes and disappointments, strange turns and changes of fortune, the complete victory of our arms, and of our cause, has in every quarter of the world been attained. In this you have borne a part which bears comparison with the record of any division in the armies of the British Empire. In every theatre of war, your military conduct has been exemplary. Whether on the slopes of Achi Baba, or on the Somme, or in the valley of the Ancre, or down to the very end, at the storming of the Hindenburg Line, your achievements have been worthy of the best traditions both of the Royal Navy and the British Army.

There are few here today to whom the King bade farewell in February 1915. Some were lieutenants who have risen to be generals and have gained the highest honours for valour and skill. The memories of those who have fallen will be enduringly preserved by the record of the Royal Naval Division and of the Royal Marines. They did not die in vain. I am proud to have been deputed by the King to welcome you back, after so many perils and losses to your native land, for which you have fought so well.'[7]

With that, the Royal Naval Division marched off the parade and out of existence.

Chapter 5

The Royal Marine Artillery

The Royal Marine Artillery has been a much neglected element of British military history, particularly in studies of the Great War, and that is even more surprising when it is considered that, though small, they mounted the largest guns used ashore by the British armed forces of that conflict and they played a part in almost every major engagement on the Western Front.

Upon the withdrawal of the Royal Marine Brigade from Ostend in 1914 the Admiralty decided to remove the Royal Marine Artillery from the brigade altogether, but had not initially come to a conclusion about what to do with it instead. Some suggested that it should form four brigades – three of field artillery and one of howitzers – so as to provide artillery support to the Royal Naval Division in the same way as the army, but such an idea was rejected. Instead, the Director of Naval Ordnance provided three batteries of Mk VII 6-inch guns mounted on field carriages, while the War Office provided the tractors with which to draw them, and the new batteries were delivered to Eastney Barracks, the historic home of the RMA.

Training commenced in September 1914 under Major and Brevet Lieutenant Colonel G.R. Poole, who had gained considerable experience of heavy artillery during earlier service in Canada. However, though his programme of training was progressing well, within a few weeks these batteries were removed and transferred to the Royal Garrison Artillery instead, soon seeing service in the First Battle of Ypres. Though they were to prove invaluable in that capacity, the RMA was again left adrift and new tasks had to be found. In the short term, many members of the corps were sent to reinforce the RMLI in Antwerp and Dunkirk, but the decision was then swiftly made to establish two new brigades, both of which were to serve for the remainder of the war – one of howitzers and one of anti-aircraft guns.

The Howitzer Brigade

The early weeks of the war had provided something of a surprise on the artillery front. The cities of Liège, Namur and Antwerp were each ringed with the most modern of fortifications, some of which were only two years old, and which had been designed to withstand artillery fire comparable to their own armament. However, artillery development was outstripping that of fortification and at the outbreak of war the German army had at its disposal the first two operational examples of the Krupp-manufactured M-Gerät siege howitzer. These huge guns had a calibre of 42cm, which was exactly twice that of the guns designed to be withstood by the Brialmont forts of Liège and Namur. Swiftly named 'Big Bertha' by the German army and civilian press, the *Panzergranate* (armour-piercing) shells of these guns made light work of the Belgian defences. In addition to these, eight Austro-Hungarian Mörser M.11 guns, built by Škoda with a calibre of 30.5cm, were lent to assist the prosecution of the Schlieffen plan. These guns had in fact been commissioned in 1908 specifically to be capable of penetrating the defences being built in both Belgium and Italy at the time, and so could pierce up to two metres of concrete with a 384kg shell. The effectiveness of both of these guns, and the speed with which the Belgian forts fell, was of great concern to the allied governments and the underemployed RMA were an obvious choice to be equipped with something of similar power.

Such a gun had already been under development in Great Britain for quite some time. In 1900 the British government purchased a Škoda 9.45-inch Howitzer from Austria for use in the Second Boer War, but the Royal Garrison Artillery was dissatisfied with elements of its performance and so the Coventry Ordnance Works was commissioned to design an improved alternative, the prototype of which, with a calibre of 9.2 inches, was received in October 1914. It was an immediate success and the Coventry works was emboldened to develop a larger version in the hope that the design could be sold to the government. The War Office was immediately suspicious of the larger gun's utility, but the works had a close association with the Admiralty that it could, and did, exploit. The managing director was the 46-year-old Rear Admiral Sir Reginald Bacon, who had taken early retirement from his appointment as Director of Naval Ordnance in order to accept the position. Bacon's career had been impressive: his preceding two appointments had been as the first Inspecting Captain of Submarines and as the first commanding officer of the cutting-edge HMS *Dreadnought*. His naval experience, technical flair and eye for improvement made him a natural fit, but he was not beyond calling upon old acquaintances when required. Instead of the War Office, Bacon offered the 15-inch design to Winston Churchill as First Lord of the Admiralty.

Churchill, seemingly seeking ways for the navy to be involved in the war ashore, sponsored several such innovative ideas, and indeed the development of the first tanks benefitted from his patronage in a very similar way. It was thus that twelve of the new howitzers were ordered for use by the Royal Marine Artillery, without any recourse to the Army Ordnance Board who would normally be responsible for such orders of land artillery. Bacon couldn't resist the opportunity to see the new guns in action and insisted that he himself would take them to France, and so he stood down from his position at the Coventry works and was temporarily commissioned as Colonel Second Commandant, Royal Marine Artillery.

The building of the first gun was duly completed in Coventry and it was sent to the Shoeburyness ranges on the Thames Estuary for testing. After a satisfactory performance gun crews began to be trained at Eastney before moving to Essex to drill on the prototype gun itself. The 15-inch shells weighed 657kg and could be fired a maximum distance of 9.87km, with a muzzle velocity of 341m/sec. This was in fact rather less than had been anticipated, and the lack of protection for the gun crews when well within the range of enemy batteries was to remain a concern for the duration of the war. At Shoeburyness a great deal of experimentation was needed to calculate the range tables and the best methods of mounting and dismounting, particularly considering the soft ground of the coastal ranges, but it was the platforms which provided the greatest difficulties, which were to continue on active service in France.

An Admiralty committee was soon established to organise and equip the brigade, as well as to oversee the design and building of the remaining guns and their transport. When emplaced, each gun weighed an extraordinary 94 tons, and the gun and mounting was broken down into six constituent parts to be transported – the barrel, the jacket and breech fittings, the cradle (with recoil buffers), the carriage, the pivot and the racer. The gun and carriage sat on a platform of cross-hatched steel girders dug into the ground, which took a considerable time to construct whenever a gun had to be moved. Each whole single-gun battery was transported by five huge specially-built 105-horsepower motor tractors manufactured by Foster-Daimler of Lincoln. Each tractor pulled two eight-wheeled trucks (except for one which was required to pull three) and there was also a mobile workshop for each pair of guns. One spare tractor was also provided for each pair and was often needed. The scale of the equipment and of the operation was unlike anything that any British artillery unit had been required to undertake before: considerable technical expertise, as well as that in gunnery, was required by both officers and men, and the sheer number of personnel involved was quite astounding. Each howitzer required:

   1 commanding officer (a captain or major)
   1 gun officer
   2 observing officers
   1 motor transport officer

1 artificer
1 battery sergeant major
1 battery quartermaster sergeant
55 NCOs and men
25 drivers

In total the RMA Howitzer Brigade amounted to nearly 1,000 men, including armourers, staff surgeons and sick berth attendants attached from the Royal Navy. The first two batteries sailed from Southampton on 15 February 1915, with the newly-appointed Colonel Bacon in command. A total of fourteen officers accompanied the first two guns to the front in order to gain experience of their operation in the field, and No.1 Battery fired in action for the first time at Locre on 6 March, much to Bacon's delight. No.3 joined them in Belgium on the 26th under Captain Ledgard, but on 19 April was sent south by train to Marseille: it had been decided by the Admiralty that a heavy howitzer would be of excellent use at Gallipoli. No one appears to have considered that such a heavy weapon would be entirely unsuited to the sandy beaches and rocky hills of that theatre until it was too late, so upon arrival it wasn't even unloaded and was instead sent to Mudros, where the gun crew spent several months of happy inactivity, before being directed on again to Alexandria for an even longer period with very little worthwhile employment.

Finally, No.3 Battery returned to France in March 1916 and was sent north just in time to participate in the Battle of the Somme that summer. Bacon had handed over command of the brigade to Major Lumsden on 10 April 1915, after his appointment as Admiral of the Dover Patrol (his naval experience being much in demand), and his successor was to be awarded the VC, CB and DSO as the war continued, but he too handed over command of the brigade after a short period of time, this time to Lieutenant Colonel Poole, who continued in charge until the end of the war. From May 1916 that command was to be a more distant one as he had been appointed to lead the 26th Heavy Artillery Group, of which the RMA howitzers became a constituent part.

In total ten of the twelve constructed guns were to see action (No.7 was retained at Shoeburyness for testing and No.9 became the training gun for recruits at Eastney), and in general they were very well regarded by the officers of the RMA. Their accuracy was admirable, but the problems with the platforms mentioned above continued to plague operations. There was a tendency for the whole structure to slip backwards upon firing, or even to slew to one side, which sometimes necessitated the untimely and arduous re-siting of the gun pit after as few as fifty rounds. In addition to that, the huge force of the recoil from firing such a large shell could distort the steel girders used in the platform, meaning that it was impossible for the structure to be disassembled without the bolts being drilled out and replaced upon remounting. The ammunition itself was relatively new to the Admiralty, as 15-inch guns had only recently been introduced to warships, and at first supply wasn't exactly plentiful. The great weight of the shells also meant that they had to be transported by light railway wherever available, but that was often not the case and the ammunition column struggled with inadequate road transport.

As well as their comparatively short range, the sheer size of the shells and the explosions they caused meant that they had to be used very cautiously anywhere near allied infantry and, though very effective in destructive shoots against observation posts and buildings, the nature of the war meant that they were never used against their intended targets of heavy fortifications such as those in Belgium. Even so, when the Duke of Connaught visited No.5 Battery on the Somme in October 1916 they gave him a demonstration of their efficiency, firing three rounds in nine minutes (quite a feat with a gun of this size), destroying their windmill target with the second. In short, they were certainly adequate for the employment to which they were put, but debates continued throughout that time as to their relative merits compared to the army's 12-inch alternative. Indeed, when several guns were condemned for excessive scoring in the rifling in the autumn of 1918 it was the 12-inch howitzer which replaced them. The army had no intention of paying for any more of the navy's behemoths.

With the exception of No.3 (noted above) the RMA howitzers were employed exclusively on the Western Front and participated in almost every major offensive between the spring of 1915 and the end of the war. On the first day of the Somme they were mounted at Mailly-Maillet, Englebelmer, Sailly-au-Bois and Albert, firing at targets that included such well-known sites as Thiepval, Pozières and Delville Wood. In fact, a 15-inch shell from No.1 or No.2 Batteries was excavated in recent years when the new Thiepval Memorial visitor centre was constructed – both of these guns were firing at that site several times between July and September 1916. In the course of the war the casualty rate of their crews was comparatively low: Captain M. Williams and Lieutenants Warman and Hart were killed in action, while Lieutenant Boissier was accidentally drowned in a car accident and two others were gassed but survived. Of the other ranks, 35 were killed, 97 wounded and 69 gassed, though most of these were sustained in the Passchendaele offensive, when Nos.11 and 12 batteries were heavily involved and so suffered accordingly.

Only one gun was actually lost during the war: No.1, which had to be abandoned by its crew when its transport became bogged down in the mud during the retreat from Albert in March 1918, though the breach and barrel were successfully got away, rendering the gun inoperable. The brigade diary described the situation:

On 21st [of March] the German offensive was launched and No.1 came into action. Fired their last round at 11.55am on 22nd and prepared to move into Moislains. At 3pm the breech block was got away in a lorry; at 9.30pm the tube and jacket; the dismount, except the platform, was finished at 1am. On 23rd: they were told they could not go through Fins as it was occupied by the enemy; therefore moved by Metz-Equancourt road, which after the first mile was only a track; Enemy in Fins and Neuville; about half way the front tractor became hopelessly bogged, and the train had to be abandoned. Proceeded to Equancourt, here a party of infantry informed them that there was no one between them and the enemy and they marched to Moislains arriving 5.30am on 23rd. Leaving at 7am they went to Combles: eventually picked up tractor and lorry with breech block and jacket at Bray and marched to Corbie and so to Amiens. Lieutenant Foster awarded M.C. for his gallant attempts to save the gun.[1]

Several other guns were damaged at various times – No.8 was out of action for four months from 27 June 1916 when a shell from No.2 exploded prematurely during firing near Mailly-Maillet, killing two men and damaging No.8's recoiling gear. They had at the time been participating in the preliminary bombardment for the first day of the Somme and were perhaps the only guns engaged in that task capable of destroying the deep, reinforced German dug-outs along the front. In November 1917 No.2 itself received a hit on the carriage from a smaller enemy shell when operating near Dunkirk, putting it out of action until the middle of December. In April 1918 No.5 had to be blown up and temporarily abandoned (after the breech had been removed) to stop it falling into the hands of the enemy, and on 14 July of the same year a premature shell burst tore the rifling out of the barrel of No.4, after which it was replaced by No.9, sent out for active service from its training role at Eastney.

By the Armistice in 1918 the RMA's howitzers, now universally known as 'Grandmother', had fired a total of 25,332 rounds, often to devastating effect on the enemy. The slowness with which they could be moved, however, made it difficult for them to keep up with the infantry once the enemy began to retreat, and on 11 November the remaining guns were in the following locations:

No.1 Siege Battery (Nos. 5 & 6 guns) – Vaux Audigny.
No.2 Siege Battery (Nos. 11 and 12 guns) – Poperinghe, moved to Bisseghem that morning.
No.1 Gun – Lealvillers
No.2 Gun – Orchies

No.3 Gun – Acheux
No.4 Gun – Beira Farm, then moved to Menin during the morning.
No.8 Gun – Bourlon
No.10 Gun – Forceville

The War Office had had material responsibility for the guns since 1916 but had never been entirely complimentary about their design or performance, very possibly because Churchill had ordered them for the RMA without any recourse to the Ordnance Board. Indeed, it described them as 'a waste of money and material', and so there was never any real possibility of them being taken into permanent military service after the war. Consequently, they were moved north towards the coast and each battery reduced to cadre strength in June 1919. All guns and stores were handed in and the detachments sailed from Le Havre in the SS *Lydia* on the 14th. At 3pm the next day they arrived at Eastney Barracks, the home of the Royal Marine Artillery, where with little ceremony they were dispersed, and the RMA Howitzer Brigade was no more. The guns themselves were broken up shortly afterwards.

Regardless of the disdain of the War Office, the brigade's service had not gone unnoticed and a considerable number of honours and awards were made to members of the brigade, of which the most significant are listed here.

CMG – Lieutenant Colonel G.R. Poole.

DSO – Lieutenant Colonel G.R. Poole, Major C. Micklem, Major R.C. Morrison-Scott, Captain T.S. Dick, Captain W.R. Ledgard, Captain G.L. Wills (att. Tank Corps).

DSC – Major G.L. Raikes, Captain T.C. Cuming, Lieutenant F.L. Robinson.

MC – Captain C.C. Carus-Wilson, Captain L.L. Foster, Lieutenant M.H. Collet, Lieutenant H.N. Elphick, Lieutenant A.E. Holton, Lieutenant T.A. Ryder, Lieutenant S.H. Wood.

DCM – BSM C. Dadd, Staff Sergeant Mech. H. Williams, Sergeant E.C. Tye, Sergeant A.C. Woodhouse, Corporal F. Cross, Corporal T. Forsyth, Corporal R.E. Payne, Bombadier W. Pike.

MM – Sergeant A. Chatfield, Sergeant C. Inman, Sergeant J. Heaton, Sergeant T.J. Lee, Sergeant H. Tarbottom, Corporal S. Berry, Corporal H. Bland, Corporal N.F. Brown, Corporal T.C. Lockley, Corporal G.E. Wood, Bombardier F.J. Brighten, Bombardier S.M. Curtis, Gunner W.G. Blundell, Gunner W. Frew, Gunner R. Fulton, Bombardier E.J. Goff, Gunner J. Halden, Bombardier L. Hinchcliffe, Bombardier S. Hooper, Gunner J. Howarth,

Gunner A. Hutchinson, Bombardier W.S.C. Jeffery, Bombardier J. Morris, Gunner F.H. Parkes, Gunner S.E. Pearce, Bombardier E.J. Redman, Bombardier A. Shepherdson, Gunner E.A. Bevan, Gunner A.S. Butchers, Gunner H.H. Jarman, Gunner G.L. Willis, Gunner T.H. Woodrow, Gunner W. Wright.

The Anti-Aircraft Brigade

At the same time as the Howitzer Brigade was being formed during November and December 1914, across the barracks at Eastney Lieutenant Colonel C.A. Osmaston was busy creating the RMA's other new formation, the Anti-Aircraft Brigade. Anti-aircraft gunnery was an entirely new concept in 1914, since aircraft had not before been used in war, so Osmaston was instrumental not only in the development of the brigade, but of the skills required for this type of warfare in general. The brigade was to comprise four batteries, each with four guns, the specification of which varied over time, but the initial outfit was of Vickers 2-pounder pom-poms, capable of firing four rounds per second. Lieutenant Colonel Osmaston further adapted these for their special purpose by mounting them on special high-angle, all-round mountings, with adapted sights. They were mounted onto armoured lorries which also carried the crews and ammunition and each brigade also had other lorries for extra personnel and equipment with Wolseley Stellite cars or motorcycles for the officers. In this way each battery was entirely independent and mobile. This method, though efficient and effective, required an unusually high proportion of officers amongst the brigade personnel, particularly for technical and observing duties, as will be seen.

Three months of technical and gunnery training at Eastney ensued and the first battery, 'B', was ready for action at the end of March, but it wasn't until 23 April that they, with the brigade headquarters staff, ammunition column and elements of C Battery, sailed from Dover for Dunkirk. Their lorries and guns arrived in the port on the following day and so, while they remained billeted in a suburban factory at Coudekerque, Lieutenant Colonel Osmaston reported to Brigadier General the Earl of Athlone, head of the British Mission with the Belgian Army, that the Royal Marine Artillery Anti-Aircraft Brigade was ready for duty for the very first time. He received orders for B Battery to remain in the Dunkirk area to assist the French Army, and on the afternoon of the 28th they fired their first shells at an enemy aircraft, much to the surprise of the pilot. Later that day they moved along the coast to Nieuport, little knowing that elements of the brigade would spend the next three and a half years in or near that town. On the 26th the remainder of C Battery, under Captain Aman, arrived at Dunkirk with their guns, stores and most of their vehicles, and only three days later they moved to Malo where they too excitedly engaged the enemy for the first time on the 29th.

On the very next day Lieutenant Berrington arrived with all the personnel and equipment required to complete the first two batteries, and it was that same afternoon that B Battery shot down its first enemy aircraft, swiftly demonstrating the efficacy of Lieutenant Colonel Osmaston's theory and methods. As mentioned above, the unusually high proportion of officers required for observing meant that they accounted for 27 of the total 280 men between the two batteries, though that did include certain elements of A and D Batteries accompanying their counterparts for experience until their own guns were ready.

On 2 May 1915 Lieutenant Colonel Osmaston reported to the Commander Royal Artillery, V Corps, at Abeele, offering his guns to assist in the increasingly fragile defence of Ypres. As such, B Battery was sent into Poperinghe under Captain Aman, the column comprising four guns mounted on their lorries, with two further lorries for stores, two for ammunition (500 rounds per gun) and six armoured cars. Upon arrival they were attached to the 28th Division, under the orders of V Corps, who sent one section of two guns to the bank of the canal into Ypres and one to the north of the city. They were periodically moved over the succeeding weeks to keep their location from the enemy and to site them where they were most needed, including participating in the Battle of Frezenberg Ridge, but brigade headquarters remained in the former factory buildings at Coudekerque where they had been billeted on their first night at the front.

Anti-aircraft gunnery remained in its infancy but began to rapidly develop with such a high degree of practical experience. The RMA gunners quickly became adept at firing at fast-moving targets, but their range was limited to the fact that they only had standard, single-ring fuses. However, in June double-ring fuses began to be manufactured, extending the shell's range by 200 yards (once they reached the batteries in September), and new sights allowed vertical elevation to be added independent of elevation due to range, meaning that firing could be ever more accurate. Consequently, they would rapidly attract the attention of German shrapnel shells whenever they began firing, but the guns of B and C Batteries were constantly in use during the spring of 1915, to the regular acclamation of British and French commanders. It wasn't just in their commitment to their primary duties of gunnery that they stood out either: on 24 May Captain Richards, temporarily attached to C Battery, was travelling near Potijze with B4 gun and its detachment when they were overwhelmed by a sudden gas attack. The drivers of the two cars, Rudd and Kemp, though gassed themselves, struggled on to get the men clear to Vlamertinghe before seeking help for themselves, as did Gunner Everill, who brought in two men on his motorcycle. Once the rest of the battery heard of the attack Lieutenant March took car C7 to search for more survivors, bringing in many men of different units who had succumbed to the gas.

On 16 June Captain Forster and Corporal Stone both displayed great bravery and calmness in bringing in many wounded men of the King's Shropshire Light Infantry, all the while under heavy shell fire at Tuileries near Ypres during the Battle of Bellewarde. Captain Forster was subsequently awarded the DSO and Corporal Stone the DCM. Inevitably casualties were taken too, and on 16 July the first officer of the brigade was killed, as Lieutenant S.C. Knight was mortally wounded after refusing to leave his observation post when under heavy fire in order to allow his battery to continue firing. On 26 July one section of B Battery was moved to the busy St Pol aerodrome at Dunkirk and one section of the brigade was to be stationed there continually thereafter.

On 8 August A Battery came into being, with the delivery of a further two guns and vehicles from England, as well as the necessary crews. With numbers expanding, a brigade training school was established at St Pol, being now a permanent base of the batteries, and it was at this point that the composition of the RMA Anti-Aircraft Brigade was finally fixed, as follows:

Headquarters	4 officers, 1 warrant officer, 18 other ranks.
Four Batteries (in total)	28 officers, 8 warrant officers, 4 staff sergeants, 24 sergeants, 8 armourers, 8 mechanics, 180 other ranks, 120 drivers.
Ammunition Column And Workshop	3 officers, 1 staff sergeant, 1 sergeant, 20 mechanics and drivers, 5 other ranks.
Medical Details	2 officers, 2 drivers, 18 other ranks.
Base Details	1 lieutenant and quartermaster, 1 quartermaster sergeant, 3 other ranks.

Each battery consisted of:

    4 guns
    4 armoured five-ton lorries for guns and equipment
    2 armoured lorries for ammunition
    1 unarmoured lorry for ammunition
    2 unarmoured lorries for baggage and stores
    2 6cwt lorries for baggage and stores
    3 Wolseley Stellite motor cars
    5 motor cycles

The lorries chosen to carry the guns consisted of a 5-ton Pierce-Arrow chassis with a 14-foot wheelbase, with a body frame carrying 0.3-inch armour plating (0.2-inch on the earliest examples). The wheels were of the wooden-spoked artillery variety and were doubled on the rear axle in order to spread the weight of the gun. The whole vehicle was driven by a 30hp four-cylinder Wolseley engine, and as well as the crew's rifles, each lorry also carried a Maxim machine gun for defence which could be mounted on one of four positions in the gun bay or at the co-driver's position in the cab.

On 22 August A Battery went into action for the first time, at Nieuport, but only two days later one gun of C Battery was completely destroyed by a direct hit from a German 5.9-inch HE shell. Thankfully the crew had taken cover and were uninjured, but C Battery's firepower was reduced until a replacement could be provided and adapted to the brigade's needs. The extended range afforded by the double-ring fuses meant that enemy aircraft were rarely able to get close enough to accurately spot for their own artillery, but lucky hits still occurred. It was also C Battery who heard, on 21 October, that they were to join the Third Army and so headed south to the Somme: while the Admiralty retained authority over the brigade throughout the war their employment was directed by the War Office. Consequently, throughout the winter of 1915-16 the batteries were actively engaged right across the British-held sectors of the Western Front and were much in demand for their expertise. That expertise was exemplified by Lieutenant Colonel Osmaston, who continually experimented with the guns and ammunition, particularly the fuses, in order to use them to best effect against enemy aircraft, but it was also this which led to his appointment to the Ordnance Board on 7 February 1916, forcing him to relinquish command to Major Barr in order to return to London. Major Barr himself was invalided home only three weeks later, leaving Captain Forster in command of the brigade.

Over the first six months of that year A, C and D Batteries began to lose their Royal Marine identities too, as more and more personnel were replaced with members of the Royal Garrison Artillery instead, with the result that brigade headquarters returned to Eastney in June, but Captain Aman remained in charge for a further year under army orders.

As the aerial war had continued to develop, the operating ceiling of enemy aircraft had reached higher and higher and with the Battle of the Somme looming there was a possibility that they would soon be able to operate entirely out of the 6,000-ft reach of the RMA's 2-pounder pom poms. Replacement guns were required, it was clear, and so C Battery took delivery of Royal Field Artillery 13 and 18 pounders, mounted on cartwheels for a wide arc of fire, but these proved inadequate and were themselves replaced by 3-inch 20cwt guns as soon as possible, since the latter were specially mounted for anti-aircraft gunnery, though it took much strenuous effort from

Major Cartwright (a former England rugby captain) before the Admiralty approved their use.

B Battery continued very much as an RMA-badged operation and between September and October 1916 they were employed in protecting the 12-inch Mk X Naval Gun at Dominion Farm, Adinkerke, which had been landed by Admiral Bacon from a ship of his squadron and was operated by the RMA Heavy Siege Train. Not only were the Germans understandably keen to locate this gun, but their aircraft were also spotting for their own 11-inch guns of the T4 or Tirpitz Battery, and both tasks were made considerably harder by the efforts of B Battery. In March 1917 it was determined that the Nieuport guns, remaining at that post since their arrival in France, perhaps required a greater degree of protection than hitherto afforded. Consequently, two of the 3-inch guns were mounted in concrete gun-pits near to Nieuport-Bains, the construction of which took six weeks and was completed entirely by RMA labour, without any assistance from the Royal Engineers. That such 'amateur' built defences should then stand up to 11-inch shells was a source of huge pride for B Battery, and rightly so, as such specialist work had never been carried out by artillery units themselves before.

As well as the larger guns, the battery also received regular shelling from German 6-inch guns, and one of those barrages very nearly brought its existence to an end when, on 31 July 1917, it caused the detonation of an ammunition dump that left a crater an acre in size, the edge of which was only a few yards from the guns. Many were wounded, but Lieutenant Haszard and Gunners Walker and Bristow rescued a large number of injured men under continued enemy fire: consequently, Bristow was awarded the DSM and Haszard a bar to the DSC he had already received earlier in the war.

Shortly before the New Year of 1918 Major Cartwright returned to Eastney and was replaced by Major Briscoe: his task was not to be an easy one when, in March 1918, the final German offensive began and the battery was in action on every day that flying was allowed by the weather, including against the new larger bombers at night. Firing sometimes continued for sixteen hours a day. In June the brigade's numbers were augmented when Major Cartwright arrived at Dunkirk with a new battery that Major Briscoe had been training at Eastney before his arrival in France. But the night-bombers were not all intercepted and on the night of 16 September a bomb fell on the base depot at Coudekerque, by now the brigade's home for over three and a half years, destroying the majority of stores and spares for the guns and their transport.

The battery continued in its task, however, until it fired its last shot on 10 October 1918 – after that the speed of the enemy's retreat eastwards and problems of supply rendered any ideas of keeping up with the advancing infantry impossible. Even using vehicles, the choked roads proved too problematic. B Battery, the final remnant of the Royal Marine

Anti-Aircraft Brigade, had a quiet final month of the war, therefore, and in January 1919 sailed for England, and its own disbanding parade at Eastney. The head of the British Military Mission wrote:

> *It has been a great pleasure to me and to the officers of the mission, to have been associated with such an efficient battery. Having come across the RMA before, it was not a surprise to me to find that they were so good, but with these weary long years of stability and little to relieve the monotony, I must congratulate you on the manner in which you kept them in form, and very good form at that. This to my mind is the test of well-disciplined troops, and I therefore congratulate both officers and especially the NCOs at their success. Many regrets at not seeing you and thanking you personally.*[2]

The Anti-Aircraft Brigade had led the way in the development of a new form of warfare which would become more and more vital to success on the ground, and so inevitably it also received its fair share of honours and awards:

CB – Lieutenant Colonel C.A.F. Osmaston

OBE – Lieutenant G.F. Haszard

DSO – Major E.H. Barr, Major V.H. Cartwright, Captain & Brevet-Major A.L. Forster

DSC – Captain D.L. Aman, Captain G. Evans, Captain W.G.A. Shadwell, Lieutenant G.F. Haszard and bar, Lieutenant H.R. Lambert

MC – Lieutenant W. Russell, Lieutenant R.H. Sawyer

DCM – Corporal W.J. Stone

DSM – Battery Sergeant Major C. Bryan, Acting Sergeant Major W.T. Clarke, Acting Sergeant Major F. Merckel, Sergeant S. Bull, Sergeant F.S. Chapman, Sergeant E.S. Lewis, Sergeant W.H. Rogers, Sergeant A.J.E. Thorburn, Corporal H.C.B. Callaway, Corporal L.H. Tomlin, Gunner A.H. Bristow, Gunner E.G. Chamberlain, Gunner J.H. Messum, Gunner R.G. McCurrack, Driver F. Baker, Driver Glass, Driver J.E. Thompson.

Royal Marine Artillery Heavy Siege Train

When the war began the Royal Marine Artillery already had considerable experience, mostly gained at sea, of the successful operation of some of the biggest artillery pieces fielded by the United Kingdom. After the Germans occupied Ostend in 1914 they established several heavy batteries in order to guard against allied attack. One of these, known as T4 or 'Tirpitz' comprised four 28cm (11-inch) guns located in the south-western suburbs of the town. With a range of some 30,000 yards it was immediately apparent that this battery in particular could pose a significant problem to allied shipping and the warships of the Dover Patrol. Indeed, the September 1915 bombardment of Ostend by four Lord Clive Class monitors of the Royal Navy made it clear just how dangerous T4 had become. Admiral Bacon consequently landed four 9.2-inch and one 12-inch guns soon after the raid, and though the 9.2-inch guns were mostly manned by Royal Navy personnel, the 12-inch example was to be served by the RMA. They were moved by the same Daimler-Foster tractors and eight-wheeled trucks as the 15-inch guns of the Howitzer Brigade and the larger gun, on a girder mount also similar to that of the howitzers, was mounted at St Joseph's Farm near Adinkirke. This placed it some 27,000 yards from T4, therefore within the range of that battery's guns, but out of the reach of the others surrounding Ostend.

The gun itself was a BL 12-inch Mk VIII naval gun, originally mounted in one of the Majestic Class of pre-dreadnought battleships, and with a barrel of 35 feet 5 inches, the barrel and breech alone weighed 46 tons. Its original range of only 13,700 yards had been very much lengthened by increasing the maximum elevation from 13.5 degrees to 30, thereby allowing the constant artillery duels with T4 which subsequently lasted for several years. The work to mount the gun was undertaken by Canadian railway troops, and in honour the RMA named it 'Dominion'. Covered by a light skeleton barn designed to look like those of the area's farms, the emplacement began operation in April 1916 after Captain W.P. Dyer RMA and sixteen other ranks arrived at the farm from specialist training undertaken at the Coventry Ordnance Works during the preceding weeks. Only two months later Dyer was relieved by Captain H. Peck, and the battery remained under the command of Admiral Bacon in order to safeguard the operations of the Dover Patrol against the Ostend guns. Only one of the 9.2-inch guns was operated by RMA personnel, named 'Eastney' after their home establishment, under the command of Captain J.H. Hollingsworth in a concrete emplacement by Groenendijk, on the coast immediately west of Nieuport Bains.

In the first few weeks of 1917 it became apparent that the intended allied operations in Flanders would require a greater number of heavy guns than had hitherto been landed and so in February the Royal Marine Artillery Siege Train was formed under Major R.E. Kilvert, with Captain Peck brought in from Dominion Battery to serve as adjutant. The whole organisation was borne on the books of HMS *Attentive II*, depot of the Dover Patrol. As well as 'Dominion', two further 12-inch guns were landed from the monitors, followed closely by three more 9.2-inch Mk X guns and eight 7.5-inch Mk III guns removed from the secondary armament of the decommissioning HMS *Swiftsure* in April. These last guns formed part of the Royal Navy Siege Gun Unit, though they were in fact manned by soldiers of the Royal Garrison Artillery. Moved into position by the tractors and transport staff of 2 and 3 Batteries of the RMA Howitzer Brigade, one 12-inch gun, imaginatively named 'Nameless' was sited adjacent to 'Dominion' at St Joseph's Farm, as well as one of the additional 9.2-inch guns named 'Henri', and they too were camouflaged with false barn structures. The other 12-inch gun was named 'Jutland' and sited six miles to the rear of 'Dominion' at Leffrinckoucke, near the imposing but obsolete Fort des Dunes, under Captain Connew. The final two 9.2-inch guns were mounted in concrete emplacements immediately east of the straight road that links Coxyde with Coxyde Bains on the coast.

On 10 July 1917 the enemy began a heavy and sustained bombardment of Dunkirk as part of Operation Strandfest, their successful attempt to prevent a British landing between the German line and the outskirts of Ostend to the north (Operation Hush*)*. The RMA played their part in this action, with the guns of the siege train and the Howitzer Brigade sharing the same observation posts, though the enemy advances made the continued manning of some batteries a dangerous occupation in the face of machine-gun fire. Casualty rates were mercifully low, with two officers and two ORs killed during 1917. One of them was Lieutenant Thomas Hulme, the poet and critic who had written earlier of his experience of the artillery duels in which the RMA were now engaged:

> It's not the idea of being killed that's alarming, but the idea of being hit by a jagged piece of steel. You hear the whistle of the shell coming, you crouch down as low as you can and just wait. It doesn't burst merely with a bang, it has a kind of crash with a snap in it, like the crack of a very large whip. They seem to burst just over your head, you seem to anticipate it killing you in the back, it hits just near you and you get hit on the back with clods of earth and (in my case) spent bits of shell and shrapnel bullets fall all around you. I picked up one bullet almost sizzling in the mud just by my toe.[3]

On 28 September 1917, only four days after his thirty-fourth birthday, Hulme's own time had come. During a heavy bombardment of his battery at Oostduinkerke by the German guns the rest of his crew had taken cover from an incoming shell, but Hulme didn't appear to hear it. Apparently lost in thought, the shell hit him directly, leaving scant remains to be gathered and buried in the military cemetery at Koksijde.

The Heavy Siege Train of the RMA and the Royal Navy Siege Gun Unit were both regularly proving their value against the bigger guns of the German artillery, but the Admiralty was increasingly keen to withdraw naval personnel, and so at Christmas it was decided to combine the two units as the RMA Siege Guns. Major Kilvert was awarded the DSO for his efforts in command up to that point, but the increased size demanded a lieutenant colonel in command, and so Brevet Lieutenant Colonel R.T. Ford arrived shortly after the new year of 1918, to be himself relieved by Lieutenant Colonel P. Peacock in March. Upon his arrival the unit took its final form, and with the moving of some guns to new emplacements the establishment comprised:

RMA	31 officers, 2 warrant officers, 425 NCOs and ORs.
RN	3 medical officers, 23 armourers and carpenters.
RE/RGA	1 officer, 8 signallers.
Canadian	1 officer, 12 ORs.

The RMA Siege Guns were thereafter divided into three groups, each under the command of a major, in batteries named as follows:

A Group (Major A.W. Ridings, then Major Morrison-Scott)
    12-inch Guns 'Dominion', 'Nameless' and 'Jutland'
    9.2-inch 'Henri'
    2x 9.2-inch 'Stella'
B Group (Major J.B. Chancellor)
    2x 9.2-inch 'Carnac'
    2x 9.2-inch 'Terrible'
    9.2-inch on a railway mount.
C Group (Major H.E. Iremonger)
    2x 7.5-inch 'Saskatoon'
    2x 7.5-inch 'Diana'
    2x 7.5-inch 'Langley'

The siege train depot was established at Dunkirk, alongside that of the Anti-Aircraft Brigade, whose workshop and transport were made available for use under Lieutenant and Quartermaster W. Holloway.

The life of the gun crews was relatively comfortable, as the extended range of the guns meant that they were out of the range of all enemy weapons except the long-range guns that they were themselves targeting. This conveniently meant that they could be billeted in the buildings of the farms on which the batteries were constructed, as the ground beneath the inland guns was water-logged just below the surface, making dug-outs impossible. The cordite charges were stored in splinter-proof shelters for the safety of the crews, but the shells themselves were laid out in long rows on the grass of the fields. The garrisons of the guns located in the sand dunes along the coast instead lived in concrete bunkers covered with sand, and though the glacis required constant maintenance it provided adequate cover even against the largest German guns such as the 38cm 'Leugenboom'.

The spring of 1918 proved to be a busy time for the siege train. In March the Germans bombarded Dunkirk more heavily than ever before, and the 12-inch guns were called upon to fire at extreme range, which they did very accurately due to the extraordinarily meticulous and skilful work of Captain Hollingsworth, for which he was awarded the DSC. On one occasion, however, he made a mistake which caused something of a panic, as the range sheet had been made out so that the shell would fall 200 yards short of its 32,000-yard target. The siege train had always been extremely careful to only target the military and industrial establishments of the docks, but now the officer commanding the battery had terrible visions of burning houses and churches. Quickly checking the maps to hand, he was relieved to find that if the shot was on target then the shell should be just about to fall on the officers' mess of the German Marine Corps!

By October it became clear that the German retreat east would soon put the RMA's guns out of action as the enemy would no longer be within the range of their fixed emplacements. On the 15th and 16th the German guns 'Leugenboom', 'Tirpitz' and 'Jacobnissen' were extremely active, heavily shelling many areas behind the allied line, and rumours that they were expending their remaining ammunition were confirmed as the evening of the 16th arrived and many fires and explosions could be seen as the enemy gun crews destroyed their positions before evacuating. The RMA immediately began to dismount its guns in case they could be moved further forwards to be put into action again, but the opportunity did not arise, and after the armistice the guns, their crews and stores began to return to Eastney where the Siege Train finally disbanded in March 1919.

The locations of the RMA's siege batteries meant that they had always maintained close relationships with the Belgian forces, and that became even more apparent after the war ended: at the invitation of the Belgian general staff five officers and fifty ORs of the RMA were present at King Albert's ceremonial entry into Brussels on 21 November 1918. Though they had not strayed far from the sand dunes of northern France at any point during the war, their contribution was simultaneously significant ashore and at sea, in the finest tradition of the Royal Marines, and must be so recognised.

Weapons used by the Royal Marine Artillery during the Great War

RMA Howitzer Brigade
Mk I BL 15-inch Howitzer

Calibre	15 inches (381mm)
Overall weight	94 tons (incl. mounting)
Effective range	10,795 yds (9871m)
Muzzle velocity	1117 ft/s (341 m/s)
Ammunition	HE 14,500 lb (657.7kg)
Recoil	Hydro-spring 31 inches constant (790mm)
Breech	Wellin interrupted screw
Designed by	Coventry Ordnance Works
Constructed by	Coventry Ordnance Works
Number used by the RMA	12

Mk II BL 12-inch Howitzer

Calibre	12-inch (304.8mm)
Maximum range	11,340yd (10,370m)
Muzzle velocity	1175 ft/s (358 m/s)
Ammunition	HE 750lb (340kg)
Recoil	Variable hydropneumatic
Designed by	Vickers
Constructed by	Vickers
Number used by the RMA	As required to replace 15".

RMA Anti-Aircraft Brigade
Vickers QF 2 Pdr

Calibre	1.57-inch (40 mm)
Overall weight	527lb
Effective range	1200 yds (1000 m)
Muzzle velocity	1920 ft/s (585 m/s)
Ammunition	2lb
Rate of fire	200 rpm
Designed by	Vickers
Constructed by	Vickers
Number used by the RMA	16

QF 13 Pounder

Calibre	3-inch (76.2mm)
Effective range	5900 yd (5400 m)
Muzzle velocity	1675 ft/s (511 m/s)
Ammunition	HE 12.5lb (5.7 kg)
Recoil	Hydro-spring 41inch constant (100 cm)
Designed by	Vickers
Constructed by	Vickers
Number used by the RMA	Not known (experimental mount)

Mk III QF 18 Pounder

Calibre	3.3-inch (83.8 mm)
Effective range	9300 yd (8500 m)
Muzzle velocity	1615 ft/s (492 m/s)
Ammunition	HE 18.5lb (8.4 kg)
Recoil	Hydro-spring 26-inch constant (66 cm)
Designed by	Armstrong Whitworth, Vickers, Royal Ordnance Factory
Constructed by	Multiple
Number used by the RMA	Not known (experimental mount)

QF 3-inch 20 cwt

Calibre	3-inch (76.2 mm)
Effective range	5330 yd (4870 m)
Muzzle velocity	2000 ft/s (610 m/s)
Ammunition	HE 16lb
Rate of fire	16-18 rpm
Recoil	Hydro-spring 11-inch constant (66 cm)
Designed by	Vickers
Constructed by	Multiple
Number used by the RMA	16

RMA Heavy Siege Train
BL 12-inch Mk X Naval Gun

Calibre	12-inch
Effective range	25,000 yd (22,860 m), (further with high angle when mounted ashore)
Muzzle velocity	2700 ft/s (823 m/s)

Ammunition	HE or armour-piercing 850lb (385.6 kg)
Recoil	Hydro-spring 41-inch constant (100 cm)
Designed by	Vickers
Constructed by	Vickers
Number used by the RMA	3

BL 9.2-inch Mk X Naval Gun

Calibre	9.2-inch (304.8 mm)
Effective range	29,200 yd (26,700 m)
Muzzle velocity	2643 ft/s (806 m/s)
Ammunition	HE or armour-piercing 380 lb (170 kg)
Overall weight	28 tons (barrel and breech)
Designed by	Vickers
Constructed by	Vickers
Number used by the RMA	8

BL 7.5-inch Mk III Naval Gun

Calibre	7.5-inch (190.5 mm)
Effective range	14,200 yd (13,000 m)
Muzzle velocity	2765 ft/s (843 m/s)
Ammunition	HE or armour-piercing 200 lb (90.7 kg)
Overall weight	28 tons (barrel and breech)
Designed by	Vickers
Constructed by	Vickers
Number used by the RMA	6

Royal Marines Attached to the Royal Garrison Artillery

The German 'Spring Offensive' of March 1918 caused a great deal of consternation in the War Office as the Army struggled to replace the casualties and prisoners of war that had resulted from the German army's rapid advance. The Admiralty had fared comparatively well over the same period, with recruits continuing to enlist in strong numbers, and so four decisions were made by which the Royal Marines would assist with the rebuilding of the British Army in France. Firstly, all Royal Marine recruiting was to be halted immediately for a period of one month, thereby diverting all potential recruits to the army instead. Secondly, 400 men of both the RMA and RMLI were to be seconded to the Royal Garrison Artillery to provide crews for additional heavy batteries with which to halt the German advance and to replace those lost in the hasty retreat. Thirdly, the two RMLI battalions in France were to be augmented by extra drafts of men from the depot at Blandford and finally RMA recruits who had been trained in naval gunnery but who were too young to serve overseas were to be used to replace older medically fit men of the RGA in coastal batteries, thereby allowing the latter to replace casualties in France.

The RGA had already formed four new siege batteries at Lydd, in Kent, each armed with four Mk XIX 6-inch guns capable of firing 100lb shells over 18,000 yards, but though the artillery could provide officers and technicians, they could not provide enough men to form the gun crews themselves. Consequently, four RMA officers from Eastney accompanied 160 RMA NCOs and ORs, and 229 men of the RMLI barracks in Portsmouth, Plymouth and Chatham who arrived at Lydd on 3 April 1918. The officers were all recently commissioned long-serving men of the RMA. A month of training on the Lydd ranges ensued, after which the four new batteries, numbered 525 to 528 in the RGA, concentrated at Hilsea, by Portsmouth, as each was mobilised and despatched for France over the course of May. The first to be mobilised, on 3 May was 527 Battery under the command of Major Moore MC RGA, with the assistance of Lieutenant C.W. Stiles RMA, with eighty men of the RMA and twenty from the RMLI's Stonehouse Barracks in Plymouth.

With an ASC ammunition column comprising sixteen lorries, a car and four motorcycles, they arrived in France on 22 May 1918 and went into action for the first time on 6 June from positions established approximately 4,000 yards west of Lens, where they remained for six weeks until 15 August. During this time they suffered heavily from German mustard gas attacks, as they had done since their second week in France, but on 15 August they transferred towards Arras as part of Field Marshal Haig's push through the Somme valley and came into action again at Villers-Cagnicourt on 30 August. Three days later on 2 September 527 Siege Battery supported the Canadian and British assault on the Drocourt-Quéant line which forced General Ludendorff to withdraw behind the Canal du Nord. Five days later the battery had itself crossed the canal and came into action at the village of Marquion, north-west of Cambrai. It was here that on the 10th an 11-inch German shell hit one of the column's ammunition lorries, causing a huge explosion which could have been devastating, but which somehow didn't cause any fatalities, though one officer and fourteen men were wounded.

The 525 Siege Battery was the second to mobilise at Hilsea, under the command of Major Gaskill RGA, with the assistance of Lieutenant O.S. Smith RMA, plus eighty men of the RMLI from Chatham, twenty from Stonehouse and fifty from the RGA. Upon mobilisation they completed their training in the new weapons at Codford Camp, between Warminster and Salisbury in Wiltshire, and arrived at Le Havre on 1 June 1918. From there they entrained for Saulty, south-west of Arras, where they continued to train, though the guns fired in anger for the first time while deployed in pairs at the adjacent villages of Monchy and Berles-au-Bois. They subsequently played an important role in the allied halting of the German advance at Villers Bretonneux, and on 8 August 1918 their bombardment of enemy positions and communication lines was a vital part of the opening day of Haig's great offensive that ultimately led to allied victory.

The speed of the allied advance meant that the guns were usually fired with their wheels wedged rather than mounted upon the heavy platforms which accompanied the batteries. This at least allowed them to remain in action, an option not available to the howitzers of the Royal Marine Artillery, who were soon left behind. The 6-inch batteries were a regular target for German artillery and bombing raids, such was their ability to harass the enemy withdrawal, and this made them very unpopular with the lighter batteries of the Royal Field Artillery with whom they were increasingly deployed. When the Armistice arrived 525 Battery was located in the village of St Martin outside Valenciennes, right up by the Belgian border, and it was from here that they slowly returned west until they were demobilised a few weeks later.

The 526 Siege Battery mobilised on 9 May 1918 under the command of Major Oliver RGA, assisted by Lieutenant F.H. Durham RMA and manned by eighty men from the RMLI's Forton Barracks in Gosport, twenty from Stonehouse and fifty from the RGA. Landing at Le Havre at the very end of the month, they spent a week encamped before moving to the well-known town of Poperinghe and mounted their guns at Roam Farm, on the road north from Vlamertinghe. From here they could bombard enemy positions to the north of the Ypres Salient, and they moved closer in to the outskirts of the town on 23 September. At this moment however, they were detailed to support General Sir Herbert Plumer's advance across Flanders with the Second Army, and so by Armistice Day the battery found itself at Enghien, only 20 miles from Brussels. From here they were demobilised at Bierghes and returned to England on 19 April 1919.

As these batteries were not brigaded there are few war diaries or other records available to detail their movements, and very little is known of the service of 528 Battery beyond the fact that it was also located in the Ypres sector under the command of Major Ryan RGA, with Lieutenant W.J. Backhouse RMA under his command and Colour Sergeant Fell of the RMLI serving as Battery Sergeant Major.

Chapter 6

The Raid on Zeebrugge

It may seem a little odd to include an operation that arrived by sea in a record of actions on the Western Front, but it did indeed take place there and was conducted by the Royal Marines, so it very much deserves its place.

Ever since 1916 plans had been considered for the disabling of the North Sea ports from which the Kriegsmarine's U-boats were able to sail in order to interrupt allied shipping, both merchant and naval, thereby having an increasingly serious effect on Britain's food supply. Rationing had become more and more severe and action was required if it was not to begin to have serious consequences for the British population's continued support for the war. The army's attempts to push north-west towards the sea had stumbled and fallen at Passchendaele, as the deadly struggle through the winter mud had failed to reach its objective, so a radical alternative was required. One of the great centres of U-boat activity, perhaps unexpectedly, was the inland city of Bruges. Linked to both Ostend and Zeebrugge by broad sea canals, U-boat parts could be transported there by rail from their German factories for assembly and the finished vessels sailed downstream to their new home ports on the coast. The Royal Navy had attempted to shell the canal lock at Zeebrugge in order to prevent such movements, but that plan too had failed, and in any case a greater degree of destruction was required if the port was not to be quickly back in action.

A new, almost fantastical idea was suggested by Rear Admiral Roger Keyes, Admiralty Director of Plans, but little happened until he was appointed to the command of the Dover Patrol with promotion to the rank of vice admiral, allowing him to put his plan into action without the requirement for any higher authority. His plan was essentially that the two sea canals should be put out of action using obsolete British warships as blockships, sinking them in the channel and preventing the passage of the U-boats. They could, of course, be removed in time, but it would take a great deal longer than the repair of shelled lock gates. At Ostend the plan should have been simple enough, as the channel was well-known, well-marked and largely open to the sea, though still of course heavily defended.

The Royal Marine Barracks, Chatham.

The Royal Marine Barracks, Deal.

R.M.L.I., Forton Barracks.   The Main Gate

Forton Barracks, home of the RMLI's Portsmouth battalion.

The officers' mess, Forton Barracks.

Stonehouse Barracks, home of the RMLI's Plymouth Division.

Men of the Royal Marine Artillery Battalion filling their water bottles outside Ostend, August 1914.

RMLI signalmen at Ostend.

Lt Col F. W. Luard, commanding officer of the Portsmouth Battalion who were devastated in their withdrawal from Antwerp.

Royal Marine prisoners of war in German custody after the defence of Antwerp in 1914.

New recruits at the Deal depot, early in the war.

Above: Temporary officers under training at Forton Barracks, early 1916.

Left: Maj Gen Sir Archibald Paris KCB.

Maj E. F. P. Sketchley, the long-serving staff officer killed by the shell which injured Gen Paris and led to his withdrawal from command of the 63rd (Royal Naval) Division.

The memorial at Beaucourt for the men of the RND who fell at the Ancre in November 1916.

The officers of 1/RMLI at the time of the Battle of Passchendaele.

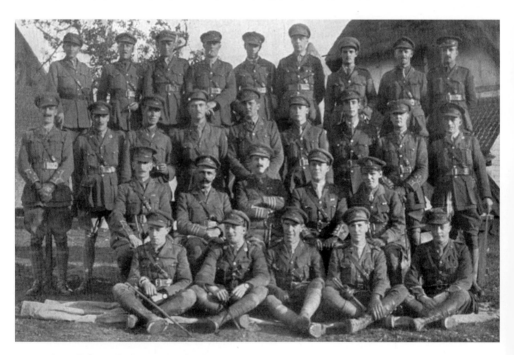

The officers of 2/RMLI in 1917.

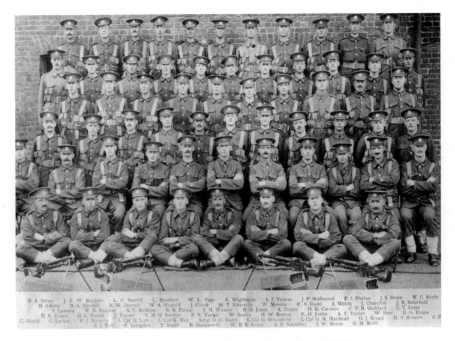

H. A. Sabey   J. R. W. Burgess   L. C. Harfill   L. Stoddart   W. L. Page   E. Wightman   A. J. Veness   J. F. Stallwood   P. J. Phelan   J. S. Straw   W. C. Boyle
  H. Adams   B. A. Randall   S. W. Dorrell   W. S. Niepold   J. Crook   H. T. Edwards   W. Mennie   P. A. Dadd   S. Mitton   J. Churchill   J. R. Seterfield
    S. Lawson   W. B. Bamber   A. C. Erskine   R. K. Parker   J. H. Weaver   R. O. Jones   A. Coutts   H. K. Carman   C. P. R. Goddard   C. V. Lines
      D. E. Evans   G. L. Parish   J. Turner   V. H. G. Sexton   P. E. Taylor   W. Speirs   H. W. Barton   E. H. Joslin   A. T. Davies   W. Barr   D. G. Evans
  G. Gould   C. Larkin   F. J. Roberts   L. Cpl G. Lott   L. Col G. May   Sergt O. C. Budd   L. Cpl G. Greenfield   L. Cpl G. H. Hardstaff   G. J. Broad   H. V. Roberts   A. E
        R. J. Tew   E. Longden   T. Smith   B. Duckworth   W. B. B. Avery   A. E. Saunders   J. W. Morse   G. M. Knill

The Machine Gun Company at the Deal Depot, September 1917.

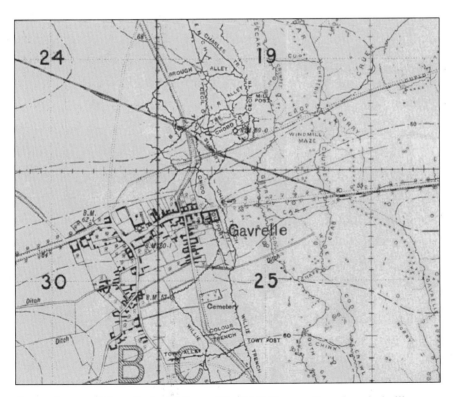

A trench map of Gavrelle at the time of the RMLI's assault on the windmill.

Fort Cumberland, training location for the RMA's new howitzer and anti-aircraft brigades.

Loading a 15″ howitzer.

One of the RMA's 15″ howitzer's in action at the Battle of the Somme.

An RMA tractor and mobile workshop at the Somme in 1916.

Gun No.1 of C Battery, RMA Anti-Aircraft Brigade.

Hon 2Lt Anthony Wilding, the five times Wimbledon champion who volunteered himself and his car for service in the Royal Marine Motor Transport Company.

One of the 7.5″ howitzers fitted to HMS Vindictive for the raid on Zeebrugge.

The remains of HMS Vindictive after being sunk as a blockship in a later attack on Ostend.

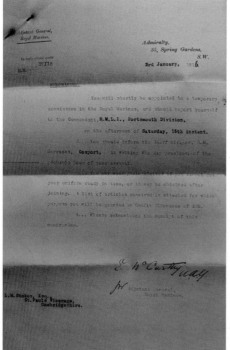

Above: The England rugby team of 1905; Vincent Cartwright (later Maj V. H. Cartwright DSO RMLI) is second from right in the middle row.

Left: The letter offering a temporary commission in the RMLI to Louis Stokes.

2Lt L. M. Stokes RMLI, killed in action 13th November 1916.

Maj Edward Bamford VC DSO RMLI.

Sgt Norman Finch VC.

Lt R. D. Sandford VC RN.

Zeebrugge, however, was an entirely different matter. The canal there emptied into a harbour protected by a mole of a mile's length, extending far into the sea before curving to the north-east at its far end. At the landward end an iron viaduct connected the mole to the port and carried a railway line which could be used to swiftly visit any part of its length, including first a seaplane base, then a bombproof submarine shelter, two storage sheds, an anti-aircraft battery and finally, at the end of the line, a concrete blockhouse containing three German 5.9-inch guns. From the end of the line the mole continued out to a lighthouse at its extremity, as well as a further six guns of 4.1-inch calibre. To attempt any hostile approach, therefore, was an extremely hazardous business, particularly considering the batteries ashore that were also capable of disabling any would-be attacker.

The mole itself was also a considerable construction: from the seaward side it comprised 29 feet of smooth granite and concrete from sea level at high tide, increasing to 44 feet at low tide. If anyone did manage to scale such heights they would arrive on top of a parapet 4 feet above an 8-foot wide walk-way with a railing stretching the length of the mole, and from there it was a 16 feet further drop down onto the roadway and railway line of the mole itself. This alone presented many problems, but combined with an estimated garrison of 1,000 men, any success of an attempted attack seemed almost impossible.

Keyes' plan, however, was so bold as to convince others of its likely success. He planned to send not one but three blockships to close the canal, while at the same time a fourth ship landed a diversionary force to engage the defences of the mole. Bombs dropped from British aircraft would aid the assault, while two submarines wedged under the viaduct and blown up would prevent reinforcements from arriving on foot or by vehicle. Subsidiary actions would do as much damage to the harbour and shipping as possible, but the primary task was the blocking of the canal. The plan required an eye-opening 162 vessels of various kinds for its completion: the blockships themselves, HMS *Vindictive* which would carry the landing force, fast motor launches, destroyers, monitors with which to bombard the port and a steam pinnace with which to pick up the submarines' crews.

Much has been written in the past about the raid on Zeebrugge, but it is the scope of this book to concentrate on the role of the Royal Marines. In November 1917 a 4th Battalion had been raised for possible service in Ireland, comprising three companies of RMLI and one of RMA. That service did not materialise and the men of the RMA company were required to man the batteries in France, but the other three companies were not to be left unemployed. In January 1918 a meeting took place at the Admiralty between the First Sea Lord, the First Lord of the Admiralty and the Adjutant General Royal Marines, Sir David Mercer, to discuss their use in Vice Admiral Keyes' planned raid.

Orders were therefore issued to stop all drafts from the battalion and Lieutenant Colonel F.E. Chichester was placed in command to draw up a programme of training for what was necessarily, from its inception, a highly secret operation.

On 6 February the orders for the official formation of 4/RMLI were issued, with Major Bertram Elliot DSO as second in command, but only four days later a medical examination found Lieutenant Colonel Chichester unfit to continue and so, to his huge disappointment, he was replaced by Elliot, promoted to lieutenant colonel for the appointment. On the 13th Elliot led his new battalion to Chatham, but a week later they moved to Deal where they were to train for their unusual and particular task. Meanwhile, a signal had been sent to the fleet asking for Royal Marines willing to volunteer for a 'hazardous' task, but no further details were given. Even when two officers and fifty men of the RMA and two officers and eighty men of the RMLI who subsequently volunteered had arrived in Deal they had no idea of the plan. The RMLI men formed platoons and the RMA men a trench mortar section, and the composition of the battalion was fixed as:

- Bn HQ – 4 officers, 46 ORs
- Machine Gun Section – 2 officers, 56 RMLI ORs
- Trench Mortar Section – 2 officers, 51 RMA ORs (later augmented by 1 officer and 30 ORs from the RMLI)
- Chatham Company A – 6 officers, 165 RMLI ORs
- Portsmouth Company B – 6 officers, 165 RMLI ORs
- Plymouth Company C – 6 officers, 165 RMLI ORs
- Medical staff – 2 officers, 6 RN ratings

Secrecy was of the utmost importance above all other matters. It was suggested, and allowed to be thought, that the battalion was being prepared to be attached to the Royal Naval Division in France for a special raid that required a good deal of demolition and the 'mopping up' of a large enemy ammunition dump and store. This would apparently take place on the bed of a drained 15-foot deep canal, the practice of entering which therefore exactly mimicked the drop from the parapet onto the mole at Zeebrugge. The ground was taped out on the grass at Freedown, Deal, to allow the battalion to understand the locality, but without any mention at this stage of water or ships. Instructors, sent from Chatham, were also kept in the dark, being informed by a 'Confidential Circular' that:

> 'The object of the training is to get the men physically fit, full of dash and accustomed to short sharp raids at night, equipped in the lightest order.

The company must therefore be worked up in Bayonet, Bombing, Rapid Shooting at short range, Snap Shooting (especially standing), and Trench fighting.

Heavy marching is not required. Marches should be from 5 to 10 miles without packs, to get men in condition only. Wrestling, football, running, boxing (when gloves are available) and such games as prisoners base, can easily be carried out during instruction hours (these sort of games now form a great feature of Army instruction).

Practice in Trench fighting is essential. Lewis gunners and Bombers must be thoroughly trained. They must be exercised respectively with Ball Ammunition and live Bombs at night.

Lewis gunners are not required to be mechanical experts, but men who can get in to action quickly, keep their guns going and instinctively remedy stoppages. Similarly, the Bombers are not required to be skilful throwers of the Mills Grenades, and not to know the construction of a variety of grenades.

All the company should be put through a Musketry Course with Mk VII Ammunition, the practices being framed to develop rapid shooting at short ranges and snap shooting.

Practice in night fighting is essential.

It is suggested that in the daily programme should be included:

1 hour Bayonet and Trench fighting (not necessarily continuous)
½ hour Swedish.
½ hour Games at odd times, and running.
½ hour Section, Platoon and Company Training.
½ hour Musketry Instruction, chiefly rapid snapping, with
   marches of 5 to 10 miles without packs.

Practice in night work, even if this can only be carried out in a very elementary way, is essential.

Digging is not required, but men should be practised in quickly passing up filled sandbags.

Open warfare tactics are not required and should only be occasionally carried out as a change.

Officers should practise with the revolver.'

Even the king himself was not informed of the true nature of the preparations when he inspected the battalion at Deal on 7 March. To him they were simply a new battalion being trained for service in France and Belgium.

The trench mortar battery was to be required to use a variety of heavier weapons, including new 11-inch and 7.5-inch howitzers, and so its two officers and the crews for those guns (one for the former and two for the latter) were sent to Shoeburyness on 23 February for instruction from the Royal Artillery, and on the 27th the machine-gun section arrived at Deal from its short period of training at Browndown, after formation at Forton Barracks in Gosport.

Though the Royal Marines were still unaware, the plans for the raid had now been finalised by the Admiralty. The action was to open with the shelling of Zeebrugge by the monitors HMS *Terror* and *Erebus* (whose guns were also manned by the Royal Marines), while the RMA siege batteries near Dunkirk engaged the defences of Ostend. Following that aircraft of the 65th Wing RAF would bomb the port from their base at Dunkirk. Storming parties of Royal Marines and Royal Navy seamen would be embarked in HMS *Vindictive*, a 21-year-old second-class cruiser selected by Vice Admiral Keyes, and would disembark onto the mole to engage and destroy its defences.

She had been prepared for the task by the planking-over of her boat deck to bring the storming parties closer to the height of the top of the mole, and fourteen hinged brows had been added to her port side to enable them to disembark. Her foretop had been strengthened too and heavily armed to allow guns to be brought to bear inside the mole from that greater height. The mainmast had been removed, with a portion of it projecting from the port quarter to prevent the propeller on that side from striking the mole underwater, and large fenders had been placed on the port bow to cushion the blow of the ship against the granite structure. On the upper deck three howitzers had been placed, one on the bow, one amidships and one on the stern, and as much protection as possible had been given to all crews working these weapons using extra armour and sandbags. Two Mersey ferries, the *Daffodil* and the *Iris*, had been temporarily taken into Admiralty service: not only would they carry additional storming parties, but once towed across the channel by *Vindictive*, the *Daffodil* would be used as a tug to hold the larger ship against the mole until she had been secured by seamen with parapet anchors, while the *Iris* landed her party ahead of them both. The approach of all three ships would be hidden from view by a smoke-screen laid by fast motor launches using a system designed by Wing Commander Frank Brock, pilot and inventor, who himself accompanied the raid as an officer of HMS *Vindictive*. As well as the smoke screen, his design for flame-throwers was also to be used, two of which were housed in armoured compartments on the upper deck of the ship. At the same time two C Class submarines, *C1* and *C3* with minimal crews, would be aimed towards the viaduct and, after setting their auto-gyro steering, the crews would escape in attached skiffs to be picked up by a steam launch.

During the distracting and demolition work on the mole three blockships, the elderly cruisers HMS *Thetis, Intrepid* and *Iphigenia* would be steered into the harbour and towards the entrance of the canal by skeleton crews of seaman officers and stokers, guided by red flares from seamen on the mole itself. Once in position the crews would be evacuated by the minesweeper HMS *Lingfield*, and at Ostend a similar plan would utilise HMS *Brilliant* and HMS *Sirius*, though without the need for the complex plans dealing with the mole. Vice Admiral Keyes would direct the operation from his flagship, HMS *Warwick*, offshore under the command of Commander Victor Campbell, while to the north the Harwich Force would deter any enemy ships from interfering by sea.

At 7.45am on 6 April the 28 officers and 704 other ranks of the battalion entrained at Deal station for an unknown destination. In fact they were only going to Dover, a short distance down the coast, where they embarked in the transport ship *Royal Edward*, transferring to the *Daffodil* at sea off the Mouse Lightship. The former Mersey ferry took them to the Swin, a passage in the Thames Estuary, where the force was assembling and where they transferred to HMS *Hindustan*, depot ship for the operation, except for C Company who transferred direct to HMS *Vindictive*. It was only now, already at sea and a few hours from their objective, that the plan was finally revealed in the battalion orders issued by the adjutant, Captain Chaters. Battalion HQ was to be embarked in HMS *Vindictive* with B and C Companies, plus the Lewis guns of the machine-gun section under Captain Conybeare and the majority of the trench mortar section under Captain Dallas-Brooks. A Company was to be embarked in the *Iris* with the Vickers Guns under Second Lieutenant Sillitoe and two Stokes mortars and their crews under Lieutenant Broadwood. Each company received its orders, having drawn lots to decide who would land first:

'2 – The position to be attacked and held by the Battalion in this operation is the Zeebrugge Mole. The object of the attack is the destruction of the guns on the seaward end of the Mole, and the causing of as much damage to the materiel on the Mole as practicable. A seamen demolition party under the command of Lieutenant Dickenson and Sub-Lieutenant Chevallier R.N. has been organised for this purpose.

3 – The operation will be carried out as follows:

'C' Company (Major Weller D.S.C.) less two platoons, will carry out phase 1, and will disembark first and establish a point-d'appui by occupying and consolidating the Mole to the West (shore) end up to and including the No.3 shed and the A.A. battery, clearing up all points of resistance, as far as point 600. Nos. 11 and 12 Platoons under Captain Palmer will turn to the left and advance towards the battery and capture the guns.

'B' Company (Captain Bamford) will then disembark and forming up under the cover of 'C' Company attack along the Mole, securing the bomb ammunition dumps, shed and shelters as far as point 1200; the end of this sector is to be secured and held at all costs. The advance is to be covered by overhead fire from the 2 Vickers guns of the Machine gun section operating along the raised pathway.

'A' Company (Major Eagles) when disembarked from Iris is to follow 'B' Company and carry out the fourth phase, that is the occupation of the remainder of the Mole including the aeroplane base, and the attached quarters for aircraft personnel, actual length of sector is 650 yards. The advance is to be covered by the 4 Lewis guns of the Machine gun section operating from the raised pathway which are also to co-operate in the defence of the position; the two Stokes guns from the Iris are to be landed and act under orders of O.C. 'A' Company.'

Interestingly, nowhere do the Royal Marines' orders mention the blockships which were, after all, the primary reason for the raid. They simply had to follow their own orders and, if they did so that would allow the rest of the raid to progress as planned. Each man carried sixty rounds of ammunition, two Mills bombs, a swimming belt and his respirator in the alert position. All men landing ashore wore rubber-soled plimsoles instead of boots to prevent them from slipping on the smooth stone of the mole. Every platoon had a Lewis gun and a flame thrower, plus two ladders and four scaling ropes to descend from the parapet onto the mole itself. They were equipped, they were briefed and they were ready to attack. A final message arrived from Vice Admiral Keyes, making it quite clear just how important their objective was:

'The object of the enterprise that we are about to undertake is the blocking of the entrances to Zeebrugge and Ostend. These ports are the bases of a number of torpedo boats and submarines, which are a constant and ever-increasing menace to the communications of our Army and to the trade and food supply of our country. The complete achievement of our aims would have the most favourable and far-reaching effect on the Naval situation.

I am very proud to command the force which has the great privilege of carrying out this enterprise. Drawn as this force is from the Grand Fleet, the Harwich Force, the Dover Patrol, the three depots, and the Royal Marine Artillery and Light Infantry, it is thoroughly representative of our service.

I am very confident that the great traditions of our forefathers will be worthily maintained, and that all ranks will strive to emulate the heroic deeds of our brothers of the Sister Service in France and Flanders.

(Signed) ROGER KEYES, Vice-Admiral, Dover Patrol.'[1]

No further communication with the shore was allowed in order to ensure absolute secrecy. The following day, Sunday 7th, was a day of rest and church parade onboard HMS *Hindustan*. On Monday they prepared for the attack and were visited onboard by both the First Sea Lord and the First Lord of the Admiralty. Finally ready, two days passed before suitable weather arrived, and at 1.30pm on the 11th they embarked in the *Iris* and *Vindictive*, but less than 24 hours later they had returned. Only 16 miles from their objective, at 12.45am, the wind had changed, making the smoke screen impossible, and Vice Admiral Keyes had to make the decision to turn back, though astonishingly the large flotilla had not been spotted, so the element of surprise remained. For a further four days they planned to sail but were hampered by the weather, and the changing of the tides meant that there would be a further delay of at least a week so as to ensure that the men could get ashore using the temporary brows. The longer they waited, the more anxious the Admiralty became, and though games and competitions were organised for the men onboard, a week at anchor is a testing time when faced with the knowledge of impending extreme danger. The Royal Marine buglers, usually unarmed, requested to be armed for the event, but their young age meant that the usual rifle and bayonet would be too heavy, while revolvers were considered too dangerous, and so eventually they were issued with cutlasses, as much to satisfy their demand as to provide any offensive power.

At last the time had come. The 22nd was the first day on which the tides were again suitable, and with favourable weather they left the depot ship for the last time at 11.40am, sailing at 1.10pm for the long journey to Zeebrugge. The battalion diary for the day is unhelpfully sparse:

'23rd April, St. George's Day; operation carried out; Vindictive reached Mole 12.05am; left Mole about 1.00am; arrived Dover 8.15am. Battalion arrived Deal 10.30am.'

After several hours of slow steaming in silence, at 11pm the battalion proceeded quietly to its action stations. In *Vindictive* B Company 4/RMLI was in the

Port Battery, with C Company in that to starboard. The Royal Navy storming party, landing first, were on the upper deck. Elsewhere in the ship the two companies' Lewis guns were in sand-bagged positions along the upper deck, and of the RMA two crews manned Stokes mortars on the forecastle, while others manned the 11-inch howitzer on the stern, one 7.5-inch howitzer amidships on the port side and another also on the forecastle. The two pom-poms and several Lewis guns were in the foretop under the command of Lieutenant Rigby. Battalion HQ occupied the port side of the signal bridge from where they would be able to monitor operations on the mole. In the *Iris* A Company were split between the main and upper decks, with a sand-bagged Vickers gun on the port bridge wing and a Stokes mortar forward.

As they approached their objective the weather worsened and the wind picked up. At 11.20pm the monitors opened their bombardment, but that in itself was no indication to the port's defenders of anything out of the ordinary. Heavy rain held off the bombing raid, so the sign that something was underway was the roaring engines of over thirty motor launches laying the smoke-screen. Searchlights flashed on and swung across the scene. It was clear that an attack of some kind had begun, but shortly they had their answer: just before midnight, potentially disastrously for Keyes, the wind suddenly changed and swept the smoke-screen from in front of the flotilla. HMS *Vindictive*, *Iris* and *Daffodil* were in clear view of the enemy, illuminated by countless searchlights and flares; 250 yards from the mole Lieutenant Rigby opened fire, the signal for all guns to engage, and the air filled with noise and steel. As the ship closed on its objective the fire intensified, and this was when the majority of casualties were sustained. Twelve of the brows were shot to pieces and in the confusion *Vindictive* secured alongside several hundred yards closer to shore than intended, meaning that the storming parties intending to capture the batteries by the lighthouse had much further to go under extremely heavy fire. The two remaining brows rose and fell alarmingly as the ship rolled, but Lieutenant Campbell in command of the *Daffodil*, despite being shot in the face, used his vessel to force the cruiser up against the wall, allowing the storming parties to stream ashore.

The intended RAF bombing raid had been expected to scatter any ships alongside, but its absence meant that a German destroyer was moored on the inside of the mole and the exposed foretop took the full power of its guns. Lieutenant Rigby and his crew were all killed with the exception of Sergeant Norman Finch, who kept firing a Lewis gun until he too received a further wound, though he survived. Now alongside, the RMA howitzers came into action, but the crew of that on the forecastle had been killed on the approach and their gun remained silent. The midships howitzer had been hit by splinters, but its crew worked feverishly to repair the damage and it was later brought to bear as the ship left the mole.

Heavy casualties amongst C Company meant that a rapid change of plan was required, and so No.5 Platoon of B Company were soon led ashore first, by Lieutenant Cooke and Captain Bamford, quickly killing a party of enemy snipers who were firing into the disembarking troops. Lieutenant Cooke was quickly injured, but Captain Bamford ensured that the remaining party could withstand the enemy. Nos.9 and 10 Platoons of C Company landed next, though only ten of the forty-five members of the latter remained, and with their scaling ladders descended onto the mole and raced to secure the landward end of Shed 3. On their way they bombed and shot at the destroyer that had shelled the *Vindictive's* foretop, before establishing a strong position from which to prevent the enemy moving up the mole from the shore. They also blew up the shed before re-embarking, completing their task entirely.

Shells, bullets and bombs raced through the air in every direction and as the platoons descended the ladders, the bodies of the defenders began to mount. The seamen of the storming party sent to the seaward battery began to falter so Major Weller of C Company sent his No.12 Platoon to reinforce them under Lieutenant Underhill, as well as the few remaining men of No.11 who had not yet been killed or injured. Meanwhile, submarine C3, commanded by Lieutenant Sandford, had been picked out by enemy searchlights as it approached the viaduct. Ignoring his orders, Sandford steered the boat directly for its target and the crew of six stayed onboard until the charges had been set. Escaping in the skiff, they found that its propeller had been damaged by machine-gun fire on the approach and, rowing furiously away from the mole, three of them were hit, Sandford twice. The charge blew, leaving a gap of 30 yards between the mole and the shore, and the crew of C3 were picked up as intended by the picket boat commanded by Sandford's brother, who immediately turned towards Dover.

Captain Bamford strode forward again; having collected Nos. 5, 6 and 8 Platoons of B Company he led them down the mole towards the 4.1-inch battery near the lighthouse, an outstandingly inspiring leader throughout. Still under intense fire they were readying their attack on wire-filled trenches when the signal for the general recall came from the *Daffodil* – it was to have been given by *Vindictive* but her forward funnel was in tatters and barely recognisable, with both sirens shot away. However, it was shortly ascertained that the battery had been put out of action and the withdrawal began. The enemy were firing at the mole with every weapon available, and the dead and dying of friend and foe lay on all sides. The numbers of all platoons of the 4/RMLI had been seriously depleted, some now being commanded by their sergeants, but those left retired in good order up the ladders and across the swaying brows, taking as many of the wounded with them as possible.

With some ladders shot to pieces by the intensity of the machine-gun fire, Captain Tuckey remained on the mole encouraging his men up a ladder as quickly as possible until he was shot and killed. He had served with the corps since Antwerp and throughout Gallipoli, yet he was only 23. No.9 Platoon was the last to re-embark and a rearguard was provided by Captain Palmer of C Company with two sergeants, a corporal and ten privates. In protecting the re-embarking platoons, they themselves were left behind and captured by the enemy after *Vindictive's* departure at 1am, though the senior naval and marine officers assured her commanding officer, Captain Carpenter, that all survivors were onboard.

Throughout the operation the *Iris*, carrying A Company, had been struggling to secure alongside. She came under intense fire, with most of the bridge being destroyed and her commanding officer, Commander Gibbs, losing both legs, but after the decision had been taken to secure alongside *Vindictive* rather than attempt another landing on the mole, A Company had not yet landed when the general recall was sounded, so she was compelled to let go again to allow the withdrawal to begin. She now came under extremely heavy shelling from the shore batteries – a fire broke out on the upper deck and Lance Corporal Bugler Heffernan was killed attempting to remove ammunition from the flames – and then a shell fell amongst the company's officers, killing or wounding all but one, including the company commander, Major Eagles, who was killed by the blast. Still manoeuvrable, the *Iris* turned for home.

After leaving the mole no more casualties were sustained in the *Vindictive* and the *Daffodil*: it is quite extraordinary that none of the shells, some of quite considerable size, damaged any of the ship's machinery or the hull below the waterline, but the superstructure was a tangled wreck. Still, she made a good 17 knots back towards Dover, and at 5am Vice Admiral Keyes signalled from his flagship, 'Operation successful, Well done *Vindictive*'. Somehow against massive enemy firepower the three blockships had entered the harbour and been sunk in the canal entrance. The defences and military facilities of the mole had been destroyed and, while many casualties had been sustained, the operation had indeed been a complete success militarily. No more U-boats would be leaving Zeebrugge for quite some time, though the parallel attempt on Ostend had failed.

At 8.15am the upper decks of the ships in Dover harbour were lined with men, and the promenade full of early-morning workers were amazed at the scene unfolding. The torn, twisted funnels of HMS *Vindictive* proclaimed her battle honour as she entered the harbour accompanied by dozens of smaller craft. None had known of the operation before it began, so the sight could have been the herald of a disaster, but soon cheers began to spread through the crowds as the message of a great victory became apparent. Some, however, looked nervously for the *Iris*, which limped in appreciated and cheered by the ship's company of *Vindictive* a few hours later.

At 9.30am the remains of the 4/RMLI marched down the gangway and formed up to march to the station. Tired, bloodied troops were not an unusual sight in Dover, but none could claim to have returned from an action as daring as this, and in an hour they had returned from the scene of the fighting to their home depot. They had completed their allotted task and returned home to a grateful country, as their action was one of few seen in the war which directly affected the home front as much as those in uniform.

It had come at a great price, however, and the officers suffered particularly, leading from the front. Of the battalion's 28 officers who sailed on the 22nd, 10 were killed, including Lieutenant Colonel Elliot, 6 wounded and 1 taken prisoner. In total 101 men of the battalion had given their lives to achieve their aim. Lieutenant Colonel Elliot had been killed when a shell hit the signal bridge, along with many of his battalion HQ, and he was buried at Chatham, his home base. Of those killed 66 were buried together in a communal grave in the cemetery overlooking the harbour at Dover on 27 April, with naval chaplains of each denomination presiding together.

There was much to reward too, as well as much to lament, and the king gave the honour of two Victoria Crosses, to be awarded under provision of the decoration's ninth statute, whereby they may be awarded by secret ballot when a large group of individuals have all acted with great gallantry. The ballot was taken and two names clearly emerged – Captain Bamford and Sergeant Finch, who received their medals from King George and the fact of the ballot was entered upon the records of all those whose names were entered. Their citations from the *London Gazette* clearly show why they were the popular choices and illustrate different elements of the action:

> *Captain E Bamford, R.M.L.I. for most conspicuous gallantry. This officer landed on the Mole from HMS* Vindictive *with numbers 5,7 and 8 platoons of the Marine storming force in the face of great difficulties. When on the Mole and under heavy fire he displayed the greatest initiative in the command of his company and by his total disregard of danger showed a magnificent example to his men. He first established a strong point on the right of the disembarkation, and when satisfied that that was safe, led an assault on a battery to the left with the utmost coolness and valour.*
>
> *Sergeant N.A. Finch, Royal Marine Artillery, was second in command of the pom-poms and Lewis guns in the foretop of the* Vindictive *under Lieutenant C.N. Rigby. At one period HMS* Vindictive *was being hit every few seconds, chiefly in the upper works, from which splinters caused many casualties.*

It was difficult to locate the guns which were doing the most damage, but Lieutenant Rigby, Sergeant Finch and the Marines in the foretop kept up a continuous fire, changing rapidly from one target to another and thus keeping the enemy's fire down to some considerable extent. Unfortunately, two heavy shells made direct hits on the foretop which was completely exposed to enemy concentration of fire. All in the top were killed or disabled except Sergeant Finch, who was however severely wounded, nevertheless he showed consummate bravery remaining in his battered and exposed position. He once more got a Lewis gun into action and kept up a continuous fire harassing the enemy on the Mole until the foretop received another direct hit; the remainder of the armament being then completely out of action. Before the top was destroyed Sergeant Finch had done invaluable work and by his bravery undoubtedly saved many lives.[2]

In addition to these many more decorations were awarded to members of the battalion for their actions on that St George's Day: one Companion of the Bath, three Distinguished Service Orders, five Distinguished Service Crosses, three Conspicuous Gallantry Medals and twenty Distinguished Service Medals. In total the combined force received eight Victoria Crosses, and Keyes himself was knighted on the very day he returned from Zeebrugge. Indeed, though he had not known of its inception, the king himself was astounded by the raid's audacity and success, and his secretary wrote to the Adjutant General Royal Marines to express…

…His Majesty's high appreciation of their gallant conduct during the recent operations undertaken at Zeebrugge and Ostend. It is a matter of special interest to the King to remember that the 4th Battalion, which took part in the fighting, was at Deal on the occasion of His Majesty's inspection on March 7th.[3]

No more valiant action than this stands in the collective British memory of the Royal Marines' contribution to the Great War, and indeed the corps declared that no other Royal Marine unit would ever be known as the 4th Battalion. And so, with a characteristic humility, the 4th Battalion Royal Marine Light Infantry ceased to exist on 27 April, its former members returning to their own headquarters carrying the memory of a heroism few, if any, could ever exceed.

Chapter 7

A Subaltern on the Somme

Of the thousands of Royal Marine casualties on the Western Front, most remain no more than a name to the modern reader. Though all were someone's son, and often a husband and father too, unless they commanded a battalion or were rewarded for gallantry the sheer number of those killed and wounded means that their lives and deaths can easily sink into obscurity. Every so often, however, collections come to light which give us a narrow window into the lived experience of the Great War. One such collection is that of Second Lieutenant Louis Stokes of the 2/RMLI. Found in a suitcase on a top shelf in the Rugby School archives, it is an extraordinarily comprehensive collection of letters, photographs, school reports, bills and receipts detailing the school and military life of a young man killed at the Ancre in November 1916.

Louis was born on 19 July 1897 in Cambridge, where his father was Vicar of St Paul's Church. The Reverend Dr Henry Stokes was an amateur antiquarian of some note, and of the type sadly no longer to be found amongst the clergy in the face of modern administrative requirements. Louis' mother Sophia was a daughter of the highly successful Mander family, paint and ink manufacturers from Wolverhampton whose firm continued until taken over in the late 1990s. Louis and his three sisters, Margaret, Mary and Amy, spent a happy childhood in St Paul's vicarage with their parents, a cook, a nurse, two maids, a dog and two cats. They played under the chestnut trees in the garden, rowed to picnics on the Granta and Louis kept a detailed diary of his birdwatching trips around the Cambridgeshire countryside. The girls were to be educated at home, but Louis was sent at a young age to St Faith's Preparatory School amongst the water meadows that line the river between Cambridge and Grantchester.

As the end of Louis' prep school days approached his parents decided upon Rugby for his senior education. Several of his Mander uncles had attended the Warwickshire school, famous for its version of football which spread rapidly around the world, and it was perhaps a point of honour to Dr Stokes that his own children should receive the same level of education as those of his wife's family. A vicar's stipend, generous though it was, was barely enough to pay for the fees of a major public school as well as running a not insignificant household, and so Louis was entered for a scholarship. He sat papers in English, Maths, French and Latin (all of which survive) and while he was not successful in his application, his papers caught the attention of the headmaster, Dr Albert David (later Bishop of Liverpool). Until the pressures of modern headmastering prevented it in the 1960s, the headmaster of Rugby was also the house master of School House, the oldest and largest house in the school, its imposing gate tower looming at the top of the town's high street. On the strength of his scholarship papers Dr David decided that he would have Louis in his own house and so, after a short spell in a 'small house' (a temporary solution until a bed was found) he moved into School House at Christmas 1911. Rugby had led the way in the establishing of the structures and practices of the British public school under the renowned leadership of Thomas Arnold seventy years earlier, but subsequent headmasters had continued the tradition of reform and Dr David was no exception. In his first couple of years most of the houses changed hands and many new younger masters were brought in. Dr David very much had the welfare of the school at heart, even to the point of buying the vacant Springhill estate for the school with his own money in order to safeguard the school's green link to the countryside.

The school of Louis' experience was very much the stereotypical example of fagging, games and corporal punishment, but he nonetheless hugely enjoyed his education. He idolised the best rugby football players such as his Head of House, William Clarke (killed near Kemmel with the 3rd Battalion Worcestershire Regiment in March 1915) and even more so the Old Rugbeians who had gone on to play for their country. Ronald Poulton Palmer, for example, was very much the ideal rugbeian hero when he returned to the school to play against the XV for the University of Oxford. Louis' letter home when he heard of Clarke's death is an extraordinary example of the Edwardian schoolboy's stiff upper lip:

> *By the way, will Dad please just mention that he gives me leave to go in for the Crick run? I have already been round the course. I went on Thursday with two masters, Odgers and Raven, and two boys. We got caught in a snowstorm six miles from home along a straight road with the snow blowing straight in our faces. Horribly cold. Dreadful it was.*
>
> *The boy who was Head of House for my first year, W.H. Clarke, was killed at St Eloi last week. His brother had already been killed at the Aisne. His father is in command of a Division. Horrible I think the war is.*

The beginning of the war had hardly gone unnoticed in Rugby, as the town billeted a battalion of the King's Own Scottish Borderers and the school sanatorium was filled with Belgian refugees. Louis recounted a tale to his parents in which a Belgian man called at School House to ask for directions to the convent on Hillmorton Road. The headmaster invited him back for lunch on the following Sunday and the only boy in the house who could speak French was called upon to translate. When he returned to the dormitories that afternoon he regaled the other boys with the story of how Dr David, carving lamb, tried to make his Belgian guest feel at home by enquiring *'Voulez vous le mouton?'*, to which the man replied in broken English that it was a very kind offer, but because of the war he had nowhere to keep sheep.

The declaration of war had also prompted a large number of boys to clamour to join the Officer Training Corps. Dr Stokes was largely pacifist in his approach to conflict and so became increasingly alarmed at his son's determination to serve at the earliest opportunity, particularly as he had long intended Louis to sit for a scholarship at his former college, Corpus Christi, Cambridge. Mrs Stokes had her own concerns, and had long considered Louis to be physically frail, preventing him from boxing at school. Louis protested in his letters home:

> *Well, the thing is I have a reputation for being strong. A master Mr Raven, said to another boy here who told it me 'Stokes is very strong' – I am back for my house, and though I have not played for the school at Rugger, I have played among the 1st 30 players last season. I have run for the school. I have been 3 years in the House Relay Team (I am the only member left who ran 3 years ago). I am in my house XI – Mr H.C. Bradby wanted me to play at Lords against Marlborough. Boxing – when I hoped to attempt some skill at it, you stopped me. There is only one fellow in the school now besides me who was in each Cock House team last year. This eulogy is all entirely with the view of showing you that here I am looked upon as strong.*

Before long an ever-increasing number of boys Louis had known at school were listed as casualties, as if to reinforce Dr Stokes' fears. The names came to be reported so regularly that the headmaster stopped announcing them in chapel, and instead termly memorial services were held, to which the men's families were invited. Others returned to Rugby uninjured and their stories of death and horror did little to dampen the enthusiasm of the younger boys for king and country:

> *There was a boy down here to see us last week who was here in the house this time last year. Since then he has been to Flanders and wounded and is back. He had some disgusting tales to tell,*

and exciting ones. Some of our trenches – being old German ones – have communication trenches that lead forward into the present German trenches. One day this boy turned down one of these trenches and saw two rifles at the far end trained on him. He went down like a shot in the mud – the next second two bullets passed over his head. He lay not daring to move for about half an hour. They pulled the trigger of these rifles with string from round the corner. When he did at last venture to get up he found he was stuck in the mud – and it was with great difficulty that he got out. He says many soldiers are drowned in mud in this way as they drop down in the mud, wounded, and sink in and their wound is too painful for them to struggle out. Various other stories he had – not very suitable for writing down.

In spite of such accounts Louis still determined to leave school at the end of 1915 in order to join up. Dr David sensed the familial tension and intervened as a mediator. In May 1915 he wrote to Dr Stokes, setting out their agreed course of action:

Dear Dr Stokes,
Thank you for your letter. I do not think it is at all impossible that your son should be successful in the Scholarship Examination next December, provided that he does not aim too high. I had a long talk with him last night and suggested a Scholarship to him as quite a practical ambition. I ventured to go a little further and to say that if at half term he had shown us that he had adopted it as a serious ambition for himself and was working accordingly, I would do my best to assist him, if you consent, to get a temporary Commission in January, 1916. I told him that his chance of going to the front in the present War is very small, for they are very unwilling to send any boy under 19, but there is also, as you know, the greatest possible need of boys between 18 and 19 who can be trained at home and, after three months, can take the place of an older Officer who is needed for service abroad.

I hope very much that you will agree with me in this programme for him. I have suggested a similar programme to other boys who are equally restless, and I find that they all accept it as reasonable that the Scholarship should be disposed of first. This gives them a good working aim which they can combine with such special preparation as we can provide in the Class of Instruction for Officers. Would you therefore be willing (1) That he

should join the special Military Class this term with the others,
(2) That he should take all opportunities that we can provide in
the way of special preparation for the Scholarship Examination
in December, 1915, and (3) That he should be available for
a temporary Commission, if they are still being offered, in
January 1916?

Believe me,
Yours sincerely
a a David

Perhaps unsurprisingly, given his mediocre academic career at Rugby, Louis' scholarship application was not successful, but his mind was firmly set upon the war, and it was Dr David's suggestion of the Royal Marine Light Infantry which immediately caught his imagination. He quickly applied and was accepted for a temporary commission, and his brief career thereafter gives an example of the many dozens of young men who followed the same path into the RMLI during the war.

Louis left Rugby for the last time at the end of the Advent Term, 1915. A letter arrived at St Paul's Vicarage on 3 January from the Assistant Adjutant General Royal Marines, stating that 'You will shortly be appointed to a temporary commission in the Royal Marines, and should report yourself to the Commandant, RMLI, Portsmouth Division, on the afternoon of Saturday, 15 instant.' It also indicated that he was to receive a uniform allowance of £30, and a uniform was quickly procured in Cambridge over Christmas in time for the new temporary Second Lieutenant Stokes RMLI to travel to Portsmouth by train twelve days later. The attached kit list was rather sparse and lacking in detail, instead relying upon the experience and expertise of naval and military tailors:

1 x khaki jacket
Badges (Globe and Laurel)
1 x pair khaki knee breeches
1 x pair khaki trousers
1 x khaki cap
Cap badge (globe, laurel and bugle)
1 x khaki greatcoat
1 x khaki waterproof coat
1 x pair khaki puttees
2 x pairs brown lace boots, with plain toe caps
4 x khaki flannel shirts
6 x khaki collars

1 x khaki tie
1 x set Sam Browne belt and slings.
1 x pair brown regulation gloves
1 x whistle and khaki lanyard
1 x haversack
1 x waterbottle (with slings. Can be obtained at headquarters on arrival)
1 x Wolseley valise
It will not be necessary to provide yourself with a sword or revolver.

Louis left home in Cambridge on the morning of the 15th and upon alighting from the train in Portsmouth he was somewhat startled to be saluted and had little idea of how to respond. Guided to the Gosport ferry and thereby to Forton Barracks, the whole experience of his first day in the Royal Marines was novel and not altogether unintimidating:

Forton Barracks
Gosport
Hants

Dear all,
As I have told you, I got here all right. When I got out at Portsmouth Harbour I was saluted by a huge Marine who inquired if I was coming to the Forton Barracks, and then showed me the way up. Portsmouth harbour is amazing to me, big ships lying about and Nelson's 'Victory' a few hundred yards out from the quay, seagulls flying about. Hundreds of sailors, marines and soldiers who salute you from many yards away. You get into a steamboat which takes you across the harbour past big buoys... I went down into Gosport and got my hat badge put right, feeling very small when great sergeants saluted me and sentries came smartly to the 'shun', and passed various barracks. Then I came back and went into the officers' mess and sat down and read papers. There were only three officers there as nearly everyone else was on leave. One officer (a lieutenant risen from the ranks) had the decency to say good afternoon. I felt a bit out of place, but after a bit another temporary arrived called Clanchy, a very decent chap. After some tea we reported ourselves to the adjutant whom we found in his shirtsleeves pasting pictures, picture-postcards, etc on a screen for his small daughter. He was very decent to us and we helped him do his screen... This adj told us that we should stay here probably for three to four months, after which

we might be drafted to the front, possibly Servia [sic], but since the Dardanelles business had stopped we might stay here longer.

Tomorrow we start work, he told us, which will be drill at 8.15 for an hour. A bit later physical drill for which we shall need white flannel trousers which you might send at the earliest opportunity and send the bill to me. Then a lecture till lunch and 2-4 in the afternoon something else.

After mess dinner (7.45) at which there were only two or three officers, I and Clanchy went down to Portsmouth and to the shore and saw the Isle of Wight in the distance and all sorts of red and white lights between Hayling Island and the Isle of Wight where there is a great harbour barrier. Then we went back to barracks and to bed (11 o'clock).

This morning, breakfast (8), church parade, to which the temporaries marched off independently after falling in. Here we met some more temporaries, eight or ten, very decent men, rotten service and hopeless chaplain, whose name I don't know or want to.

Thus ended Louis Stokes' first 24 hours in the Royal Marine Light Infantry. His cabin in the officers' mess was furnished, but he was required to hire bedding and any additional items from a firm in Gosport High Street. He opened his first bank account with army agent Cox's & Co, received his first cheque book and had calling cards printed. Less than a month after leaving School House Second Lieutenant Stokes suddenly appeared to be an officer. His early letters during this period give a fascinating insight into the daily lives of temporary officers under training at the mid-point of the war. The routine was very regular, as he described to his father in a further letter dated 31 January:

My routine is not very exciting, being drill 8.15 to 10.30 with a ¼ hr's break, and 11-12.30, lecture on field work. Then in the afternoon 2-3 and 3-4 either drill or lecture or drill and signalling or drill and drill. This is the routine regularly for every day. The exceptions are that on Wednesdays there is a route march parading at 8am and finishing at about 2.30 at the earliest, and on Fridays a 3/6d expedition into the country for fieldwork parading at 9.30 at the station and home about 3.00. On Saturdays there is nothing after 12.30 and Church Parade on Sunday at 9.00. Every evening there is mess dinner for all who are not billeted out; this you must attend unless you ask the Mess President for leave off... Breakfast in the morning at 7.30. I get my servant to call me at 6.30.

Even after a year and a half of war the routines of mess dinners and church parades remained, though temporary officers were not expected to purchase mess dress for the duration of their service. At the end of January 1916 Louis received his first pay – £16.13.0, of which £13.10.0 was his pay and £3.3.0 his 'war allowance'. £3.8.9 was deducted to cover his mess bill. Contrary to his expectation, life became rather mundane at Forton Barracks and distractions were welcome, such as when, reading the newspaper in the mess one evening, Louis heard a bugle call that he knew to be the fire alarm, and so he and the other young temporary officers trooped down the road to watch the local cinema burn to the ground.

Perhaps unconsciously Louis and his fellow temporaries had begun to absorb the practices and expectations of the corps. The huge sergeants became less intimidating, drill more natural, and he met some of the great characters of the corps, such as Colonel G.E. Matthews CB who had led the Plymouth Battalion at Ostend in 1914 before also serving at Gallipoli with Portsmouth:

> There is a colonel here called Col. Matthews, who has a great string of ribbons across his chest and is a great friend of Kitchener, who thinks a lot of him. He went with the Portsmouth Battalion to the Dardanelles. I have heard two accounts of his behaviour there which are interesting as coming from two very different points of view. The first was from our drill instructor, a quartermaster sergt, a splendid man (he was a sergt major in Gallipoli but they always take away those temporary ranks when they come back – he had a platoon there). This man went to Anzac, the worst place of the lot in Gallipoli and saw some awful things. He was wounded. He said 'a man told me that Colonel Matthews walked about on the beach at Anzac just as if he was on parade with shells and bullets flying all round him, taking no notice.' The other account was from Colonel Evans... He said 'I believe Colonel Matthews ought to be a dead man several times over through exposing himself unnecessarily.' Several people have told me that.

As winter wore into spring Louis' training became less theoretical and more practical; he wrote home in May that 'I, with my platoon, have been digging trenches, marching and shooting this week; also some bombing.' The dozen or so temporary officers at Forton Barracks received letters from the Admiralty asking if they wished to serve at sea but, though that had been Louis' original intention before he left school. '...I have since changed my mind. If I went to sea, I should not get on a ship till the beginning of next year, whilst the

Naval Division may be in France in a few months' I think it would be rather last to go to sea as matters stand. I don't know what you think...' As the summer solstice approached news came to the temporaries that their time at Forton Barracks, somewhat longer than had been anticipated, had come to an end, and on 20 June Louis rather incautiously wrote to his father:

> *On the 28th June, we are to go to a place called Blandford in Dorsetshire, to join the Royal Naval Division. We are to form a Reserve Battalion to the Royal Marine Battalion now serving as part of the RND with the French at or near Verdun. From Blandford we shall be drafted to the front as they require us. This will be a change of air and scenery, but not routine. But I like Portsmouth very much, especially the harbour, and shall be sorry to leave it. My routine now is digging, marching, trench fighting (bombing particularly).*

Louis' impression of Blandford seems to have been altogether more positive than almost every other opinion recorded at the time, but that is probably due to the fact that he arrived in the warm late June of 1916 and spent only a few days there before sailing for France. What for those in the winter of 1914/15 had been a frozen, windswept quagmire now appeared as a rural idyll, as Louis described to his father on 2 July in a letter which also gives an interesting insight into the daily routine of troops preparing to deploy for the first time:

> *Well we arrived at Blandford after a good send-off at Gosport by the population, and here we are. We are 3½ miles from Blandford up on the downs in the direction of Salisbury. Where we are is an absolutely ripping place. I do not remember anywhere like it except perhaps the hills behind the vicarage at Childerditch or the downs at Hunstanton where we once went in a donkey cart. From west to east there is about ¾ mile on each side of us open down, rolling up and down with nothing in the way of it. On the eastern horizon, certain clumps of trees and a lot of black huts, where the Naval Division are. On the western horizon are more trees and more huts; these last huts are the hospital. In the middle we are; about a hundred tents, besides about fifty RND tents. North of us, the downs go up to the skyline, and about a mile away... they roll down into a cultivated land of hill and lake looking very pretty, though the corn is still green. There are miles of huge cornfields and turnip fields and ploughed fields, and here a wood and there a little village*

> *among trees. It is absolutely topping and nothing shuts out the*
> *sky all round. The air is searching usually, hot sometimes when*
> *the sun has been shining for long... and really cold at night.*
> *Already I have been for three long walks among the fields by*
> *myself. I very much enjoy it, sleep beautifully, and though I do*
> *not wake up any earlier, am not sleepy when I wake. Our routine*
> *is parade at 6.15, physical training for all till 7 o'clock, breakfast*
> *7.30, then from 8.45 till 4.30 in the afternoon – with a ½ hour*
> *break for dinner (12.30-1) – we do all sorts of field training,*
> *(that's training for service in the field and includes everything*
> *that you want to know about active service except the real thing).*

Louis' stay at Blandford was always to be of an indeterminate time, for as he had written the young temporaries were to be drafted to the front as they were required. As soon became apparent, he had arrived at Blandford on the same day as the first day of the Battle of the Somme, and though the RMLI had not been in action that day, the terrible casualties inflicted had prompted a reinforcing of the battalions. Consequently, Louis sent a telegram to his parents at 6.35am on 5 July 1916 which simply said *'Going to France Friday coming home today please have some breakfast for me between 9.30 and 10. Stokes.'*

This was to be his last 24 hours at home in the vicarage with his parents Henry and Sophia, his three sisters and Pickles the dog. On the morning of Thursday 7th he sailed for France to join the 2/RMLI, his first front-line battalion. The battalion had been in billets at Frévillers, south of Béthune, for a week and a half completing training by companies in wiring, Lewis Guns, PT, bayonet fighting, sniping and scouting, but Louis's journey, though smooth, was not simple, and he described his first impressions of France to his parents in a letter dated 8 July:

> *I am at this moment in my tent on some hills at a place in cis-*
> *alpine Gaul of which, for military reasons, it is inexpedient to*
> *say anything further; (ahem), beyond that we heard the guns*
> *roaring in the distance this morning, so I suppose we are less*
> *than 100 miles from the battle line.*
>
> *My train got into London in fairly good time but the train at*
> *Charing Cross was packed, and several of us had to go down in*
> *a 3rd class carriage, with some Derby recruits. We had a smooth*
> *crossing. We passed three lightships, with no names on that*
> *I could see. One of them, near France, was painted up all red*
> *and white stripes like a circus girl.*

A SUBALTERN ON THE SOMME

When we landed at – we had about six hours to wait before our train started. Reporting ourselves and seeing to our gear took a long time. Then we (I and Dewar) had supper at a place for British officers. The French servants and ways were very amusing; the food was good. Then we took a walk round, through dark cobbled streets with old high houses on either side looking strange and romantic in the clear evening dusk; past little leaping and screaming French girls and boys and dark handsome mothers and French policemen and soldiers in their unfamiliar uniform. After a bit we passed under a dark gloomy archway and turned into a sort of avenue or grove of mighty trees leading up to a stone, ancient-looking building on one side, and to a great stone wall on the other, in places wide enough to drive a horse and cart along, with semi-circular embrasures which we leant over and saw through the branches of high dark trees, a road 100ft below glowing white. It was now quite dusk, and this strange old grove seemed to us very romantic and typical of old France that you read of. And as we lay in the grass watching a blood-orange sunset over the fortified wall, a lovely light shone on a river far in the distance. Then, like Little Shenford bells, from the ancient stone building the bells rang for mass... I slept well in the train, and we arrived here at about 4.30. I slept till 8.30 about, then went into the village or town and had omelettes, bread and café au lait at the hotel. Today, we have slept mostly, feeding from time to time. This afternoon we have got into tents and got our gear straight...

I do not know how long we are to stay here or anything about it. Please note address. Copy it exactly without additions. Love to you all, from Louis.

Second Lieutenant Stokes had not yet seen action and his months of training on Portsdown Hill had yet to be tested, but his time had now come as he and the eleven other young temporary officers travelling with him received orders to join the 2/RMLI at the village of Hersin, south of Béthune. On 12 July they drew iron rations, ate a hurried breakfast at 3am and then entrained for the front. The train was typically slow and by lunchtime had been replaced by motor lorries which took them on to Hersin itself where they had approximately thirty-six hours of final training and preparations before marching to the line. The experience remained novel and exciting for Louis, who was delighted to see one of the London buses of the Royal Marine

101

Motor Transport Company which he had read so much about in the British newspapers. He wrote:

We did gassing, practising with helmets on, and going through a gas trench with them on, and bayonet fighting. You would be surprised at how difficult it is to breath with the gas helmets on, especially if you exert yourself.

Finally, the time had come for Louis to experience the front line for himself, spending eleven days there in total, first in the firing line and then in reserve. The 2/RMLI war diary of the time gives the official detail of their subsequent actions:

'14th. 9.15pm Proceeded in accordance with Operation Order No.3 of 1st Bde. RND to BULLY GRENAY, B & C Coys billeted R.11.a. A Coy Corons D'AIX Trench, D Coy MECHANICS TRENCH.

15th. A & D Coys 4½ hours work improving BAJOLLE LINES during night of 14th-15th.

16th. Pm 141st Infantry Bde. carried out a small raid on the apex of enemy salient at M.32d.0.3. Smoke demonstration opposite salient M26c by 1st Bde. RND proved a successful 'blind', the enemy evidently expecting attack to come from there. This was proved by enemy clearing his front line & opening 'barrage' on it, then increasing his range to 'No Man's Land' & finally on to our front.

17th. Am line and support line. Raiding party found trench empty and no dug-outs but brought back some rifles. Zero altered to 1.00am. Battn. 'stood to arms' during the raid preparatory to moving upto 'Alarm Posts' viz BAJOLLE LINES. 2/Lt. Curtis & 4 ORs appointed Bde. Scouts & left the Bn.

18th. RN Divl. School opened at PERNES – 2 ORs to same. 119th Inf. Bde. on our LEFT carried out raid on enemy trenches at M15.D.3.5 at 12.15am 19th.

19th. Orders issued for the relief of 1st Royal Marines in ANGRES SECTION II. B & C Coys baths.
ANGRES II Sub-Section

20th. Took over ANGRES II sub-section from 1st RM. 19th RWF on our LEFT, ANSON Bn. on our RIGHT. Very quiet.

Relief completed at 4.50pm. Mine exploded on our left at 9.5pm. Enemy fired 2 green followed by 2 red lights at 10.30pm. Artillery active on both sides 10.30pm to 11.30pm. Our front and support lines shelled during these hours Sgt DORAN shot through knee and killed about 12.45am (21st) whilst out wiring. Wind N to NNW fine.

21st. 3 enemy aeroplanes crossed our line about 7.30am but returned quickly, another attempt to cross at 11am was driven off by our machines. Enemy shelled our front and support lines from 8.30am to 9.15am. We retaliated with 18lbrs & LTMs. Work done, recovering trench bounds & cleaning up trenches. We blew a camouflet 30x from long arm of BULLY CRATER, R.26a.1.9. The crater was reported by the Mining Officer to be negligible but on examination in daylight was found to be about 20x with lips 4' high. No enemy barrage. Wind N to NNE fine.

22nd. Day quiet. We tried to level out crater of mine R.26.a.1.9. with medium TMs but without success. Very heavy artillery bombardment heard continuously from the SOUTH also at times from the NORTH. Enemy shelled junction of BULLY ALLEY & front line to PYRENEES about 9.20pm. Casualties ORs 4 killed, 3 wounded, 1 of our Lewis Guns knocked out. 'Crater jumping' party connected long arm of BULLY CRATER to new crater & partially consolidated near lip of same. Wind N to NNW fine, colder at night. RWF relieved by 13th E, SURREYS on our left.

23rd. Intermittent bombardment during the afternoon in which our guns easily had the upper hand. Continued consolidating new crater & also both arms of BULLY CRATER at night. Wiring parties on rest of front. Wind N to NNW fine, wounded OR one.

24th. Trench Mortars & some artillery activity between 10.15am & 11am. Minenwerfers fired between 5pm & 6pm we replied with 4.5" Howitzers & 18lbrs, also with medium TMs during afternoon between 6pm & 7pm. Repaired damage done to new crater, Wind North fine.

25th. Orders issued for relief by 1st RMs & orders for defence on arrival in NULLY. 1st RMs relieved. C Coy moved to MECHANICS, B Coy to CORONS D'AIX & CAP LE PONT, A& D Coys billeted in BULLY.'

Thus ended Louis' first experience of trench warfare and he had returned safely to billets. The battalion had suffered some casualties, though not an unusual number, and in his usual way Louis found the positives in his situation, perhaps in order to try to reassure his parents that he fully intended to return home when the war ended. These excerpts from a long letter dated 26 July 1916 illustrate his attempts, with just a brief reference to 'sad things' hinting at the horrors he had already seen:

The day after I wrote to you we started off all loaded up like Santa Claus and with our steel shrapnel helmets on. We went about five miles and then put up for the night at a village. It had a few ruins in it, but was not shelled at all then. The men were billeted in an empty convent, and I with Dewar and another chap, over an estaminet, which is the same thing as a public house in England. Very interesting it was.

Next day we marched another five miles and after a bit turned off the road into a cornfield, up a trench. After going along this trench for a long way we came into the line we had to hold. We then stowed the men away in dug-outs and looked at ours. It was a very elaborate one; it is sometimes used as a Brigade HQuarters and we were using it as a Company H.Q., only five of us. There were steps leading into it; what I mean is that the ordinary dug-out for men goes straight down into the earth, but ours had steps leading down to the floor of the dug-out, then you go below the earth. On the right hand side of the steps was a raised sort of terrace with a seat. In the dug-out was a sort of room to the right with two beds with wire springs on each side, a room with one bed to the left, and a parlour in the middle with a mantelpiece and mirror over it. In the wall by the fireplace a deep dug-out went down twenty ft, and there another bed at the bottom of this. There we spent quite a happy time, eating and sleeping by day, and working at improving trenches further towards the firing line (which was about ½ mile off) by night, or keeping two-hour watches alternately through the night...

...In the line it was much harder work, very exciting at times and most of the time very tiring, but always fun, except when sad things happen...

...One thing here (besides the people) is simply lovely, that is the flowers in the trenches. As you go up along the communication trench it is like nothing I have ever seen anywhere. I could really go into raptures over them. They grow on top of the trenches and form a sort of arch bending over and meeting in the middle.

These are what I have seen: cornflowers, poppies, daisies, wild mustard, buttercups, purple vetch, white and pink vetch, rest harrow, fumitory, clover, a sort of white or cream flower, half wallflower half stock, I don't know the name, and many others some of which I forget, and others which I don't know. In places you look along, and in front of you are banks of the bluest cornflowers in the world, and the reddest poppies in other places...

...You have heard of the rats in the trenches, well unless you see them you can hardly imagine how many there are, nor how large. Walking along the trench on a watch of two hours, you can see a hundred easily if you hadn't anything else to look out for, and as it is, scores force themselves on your sight and, in the dug-outs, on your person.

Nor had he forgotten Rugby. It was still only seven months since Louis had left school, but in that time he had gone from being a smartly-dressed 'Sixth' (house prefect), sitting by the fire in School House's Old Hall to being a mud-spattered platoon commander sheltering in a dug-out from German trench mortars. In the first week of August Rugby played Marlborough College in their annual cricket match at Lords. News of a Rugby victory filtered through to its old boys at the front, and at the end of a long night watch on the 8th Louis scribbled a quick two-line postcard to his father in pencil, inscribed:

Just a line at 5am to let you know we are up again. I am doing nicely. Heard Rugby beat Marlborough. Floreat Rugbeia! Now goodbye, love to all.

Trench warfare required continuous training, not least for someone so new to its strenuous demands. Consequently, Louis was sent a week later to a bombing course for five days, and though it was only a mile or so away he couldn't stand being away from his platoon. The bombing course was immediately followed by one in the use of gas for two and a half days, billeted in a former hotel. Whether sincerely or not, he was happiest with the battalion in the line, so it was with frustration that he departed once more three weeks later to the IVth Army Corps Headquarter School of Signalling. This course was expected to last a month, though thankfully was foreshortened, as Louis wrote to his family that:

I am absolutely fed up with this signalling; it doesn't interest me one bit. In fact, it bores me to the verge of tears, all about cables and electricity and so on, that I don't understand and don't want to...

Back with the battalion by means of a former London bus which retained its advertisements for Pear's Soap, the experience of the trenches began to sour as the autumn set in and the notorious Somme rain began in earnest. Still, in the comparative quietness of the reserve line Louis found time to appreciate the colours of autumn, remembering such views in the Cambridgeshire of his childhood and finding beauty in the most unlikely of contexts:

> *Yesterday after tea I walked out of the village along the straight road lined with trees that always grow so here and turned off the road on to a great grass field on a rise, where the country stretched away, plough and pasture turning without hedge or ditch for miles to the wood in the far distance. I sat down by a haystack, a grey and dirty but dry-smelling haystack. Two kestrels rushed up and with loud screams fluttered wildly in the air nearby and departed ranging over the fields. As it got dark the flashes of the guns began to show in the distance; continual coming and going like summer lightning, and the bright Very lights ('star shells' the papers call them) rose slowly and hung like stars along the line; and from time to time a flash in the air like those in old picture books of the Matabele campaign or something showed where a shell was bursting; occasionally a string of green lights or green and red mixed floated into the distance, signals to artillery...*
>
> *...I look back on the last page I have just written, and estimate its worth at about a farthing a line. However, I think you may have it for nothing.*

Each letter home carefully avoided any mention of death or injury, or indeed to anything more than 'sad times'. Instead he wrote of what amused him, such as when the adjutant complained to his company commander that he *'...twiddled [his stick] like Charlie Chaplin'* on parade, or his excitement at watching dog-fights over the trenches or his first view of tanks in action. In mid-October the 2/RMLI were bivouacked near Englebelmer, close to the line near Beaumont Hamel but largely sheltered from German artillery by the rolling Picardy downs. The weather remained wet and with kit wearing out without being replaced the men of Louis' platoon grumbled somewhat. A letter home on 30 October described their difficulties, as well as a somewhat unexpected visit:

> *For the last ten days we have been living on a great plateau in tents and bivouacs; the men live in these last. I suppose there*

are not enough tents. Bivouacs are waterproof (?) sheets made into little sort of tents by being raised on sticks a few feet from the ground. Seven men get into one and as there is a good squash they are fairly warm I think, but I am afraid they are not very comfortable as they can't help dragging a lot of mud in with them. Washing and shaving is difficult especially as it had rained more or less continuously for a week... The mud round here is just wonderful, and nearly up to the knees in the trenches. It is a hard time for the men now starting, as they get wet through without anything to change into, day after day, while we have our valises just now and so can change.

We are doing plenty of work, which is just as well; it has been cold here lately. On Saturday (28th) Sir Douglas Haig came and inspected the battalion late in the afternoon. He stopped and had a short jaw with me. He asked me if the bivouacs were waterproof. I was sorry to have to say, 'No' (sir). He said 'H'm. H'm. Well good luck' and shook hands with me. He looked different from his pictures, much smaller, older and greyer, and tired. He had a great train of generals behind him, they all jingled by with pennants streaming. Quite an honourable sight.

My servant said he didn't want to see Sir Douglas Haig. He went and picked apples instead. I told him he should honour the Commander-in-Chief, and we held a long discussion upon military things, during which the Battalion Sergeant Major entered my tent on business, and affirmed that he honoured Sir Douglas Haig, and declared he was the finest soldier in the army.

October became November, and the plans for the last great offensive of the Somme solidified. If Haig was to have a strong hand to play at the forthcoming Chantilly Conference it was important to nip out the remaining German stronghold around the village of Beaumont Hamel, immediately north of the River Ancre. The 63rd Royal Naval Division was to have a vital role to play, as described elsewhere in this book, and the easing of the autumn's thunderstorms into a bright early winter made a surprise attack a more viable contemplation. The 2/RMLI continued to cycle in and out of the line and Louis was ever more grateful for the parcels that arrived regularly from Cambridge. His last letter home, dated 11 November 1916, described just such a night:

Dear all,
The night before last I came in at 12.30 having been on a long and muddy task since 3.00pm. I found a big parcel waiting for

me with a cake, fruitcake, apples, sweets, nuts, lozenges and socks within. Thereupon I took off my puttees and boots, put on my greatcoat, all ready to go to bed, and sat down together with the other officer who had been with me. Nor did I rise from the festive board (there were the remains of supper on the table of honey, butter, cake, jam, bread) till 1.30am when 'replete with every modern convenience', I retired to my valise and woke up at 8.30 and devoured a hearty breakfast. What ho!

I write this so because I am getting tired of saying 'thank you' for the parcels and letters I receive. I am quite sure you cannot imagine the joy your letters and parcels give, so I just briefly draw the brutal picture and leave you to believe or not as you please, that I am most grateful...

I wish I could tell you what we are doing, but I can't. However, I am having great fun, as I hope you are. Rotten letter this is. More follows.

Love from Louis.

At 2pm on 12 November 1916 the 2/RMLI moved forward into the line from where they were to attack in the second wave of the offensive, up the Ancre valley towards the small village of Beaucourt. Louis' great friend in the battalion, Second Lieutenant Lancelot 'Jack' Dewar wrote a last entry in his diary: 'We are waiting... pray for us all at this time. We need your prayers. God help us.' At 3am Louis shook hands with his company commander, Captain Albert Staughton, and together they climbed out of their trench and, with their troops, lay in the mud and wire of no man's land waiting for zero hour. That moment came at 5.45am and Louis, leading the left-most platoon of the battalion rushed forwards, revolver in hand. Captain Staughton, who later died of wounds sustained in the attack, wrote to Louis' parents that 'Stokes was last seen amongst a crowd of Scotch soldiers, the 7th Gordons, rushing forward to attack.'

At St Paul's vicarage on the morning of 13 November Mrs Stokes sat down to porridge for breakfast with her daughter Margaret. Dr Stokes was away in London, having been preaching at a friend's church and so there was surprise when the bell rang and a telegram boy stood at the door. Mrs Stokes opened the envelope in the hall and read the words she had hoped would never arrive: 'Deeply regret to inform you 2Lt L.M. Stokes RM killed in action 13th November. Admiralty.' She sat down at the breakfast table and Margaret told later in life of how her tears dripped into the porridge.

Louis' body was found by the 7th Gordon Highlanders with whom he had found himself mingled in the attack. His personal effects, little more than his uniform, notebook, binoculars and valise, were collected up and his muddy corpse buried in Mailly Wood Cemetery, where he lies today. Jack Dewar, too, was killed, and buried in the Ancre British Cemetery, located at the site of the right hand end of the Royal Naval Division's starting positions on the morning of the attack. His grave is regularly visited by members of his old school Oakham, in Rutland. The *Daily Mirror* of the following morning, 14 November, may have heralded a 'Magnificent victory – 2000 prisoners taken', but of course such news comes at great human cost, and that cost was borne by the families of those killed.

Dr Stokes could hardly contemplate the death of his only son. Having been Vicar of St Paul's for twenty years, he had moved to a new parish at Wilbraham within six months, unable to bear the memories of Louis which remained in every corner of the vicarage. He gathered up every record of Louis' life – his letters, photographs, even an invoice from Gosport, asking for payment for a pillow missing from Louis' cabin at Forton Barracks, and a small hand-written receipt for laundry done in a French village. Many items paint a picture of Louis' daily life – a telegram from the headmaster saying that he has been concussed in a rugby match sits alongside Louis' own letter apologising for not writing home for several days because of the same injury. The receipt from Salter's Outfitters for the top hat that he was required to wear in chapel may be seen along with Louis' letter to his parents describing how the hat was too large and had to be stuffed with newspaper to balance on his head on Sundays. When Dr Stokes died in 1931 that collection passed to Margaret, who placed it all in the suitcase in which it was discovered uncatalogued in the Rugby School archives, where it had been deposited after Margaret's own death in the 1980s.

Louis committed no famous feats of gallantry, nor was he awarded medals for bravery. His life and death were sadly typical of so many young officers in the Royal Marine Light Infantry on the Western Front, yet his letters serve to illustrate a life well-lived, if cut short, and to remind us that however large the number of casualties, each one was a real man who lived and indeed, died.

Chapter 8

Miscellaneous Units

Royal Marine Motor Transport Company

One of the stranger sights at the withdrawal from Antwerp in 1914 was that of dozens of London buses ferrying the Royal Naval Division to and from the front, many still retaining their hoardings advertising Heinz Sauces, Wright's soap and the latest plays at the Royalty Theatre. These formed the Royal Marine Motor Transport Company and its story is one of adaptability and ingenuity in time of need.[1]

As soon as the Royal Naval Division sailed for France it was apparent that a system of transport would be required. Through the ministrations of the First Lord of the Admiralty ninety 'B' Type buses were quickly procured from the London General Omnibus Company (LGOC),[2] complete with their drivers, who were attested into the Royal Marines at a London recruiting office before driving to Dover or Southampton, via Chatham or Eastney, in order to be issued uniform before sailing. The buses had been introduced into service in 1910, built in Walthamstow by the LGOC with a top speed of 16mph. Each could carry up to twenty-four soldiers and their equipment, though before long the windows were boarded up in order to prevent further breakages by slung rifles.

Upon arrival at Dunkirk the vehicles came under the command of Captain Dumble, a reserve officer of the Royal Engineers who had been temporarily commissioned as a lieutenant colonel in the Royal Marines, and who acquired the use of a large garage in the town for the maintenance of the vehicles and the services of Captain the Hon. G. Howard, Captain H.M. Leaf, Lieutenant Churchyard and Second Lieutenant F. Summers.

As well as the buses the Admiralty had also arranged with the Royal Automobile Club that the owners of private cars could serve as honorary second lieutenants, driving their own vehicles in the service of the division and provided with free petrol and tyres. They were somewhat overwhelmed by volunteers and though those chosen rendered valuable service, the compensation later paid to the owners of the large and expensive vehicles used was considerable. One of these volunteers was the New Zealand tennis player and five times Wimbledon champion Anthony Wilding,[3] who later transferred to the Royal Naval Armoured Car Division and was killed by shellfire at the Battle of Aubers Ridge in May 1915. To this day he holds the record for the highest number of consecutive victories in clay court matches – not losing a single one of his 120 matches between 1910 and 1914.

Upon arrival in France there was still no real operational command over the vehicles of the RM MTC and so on 1 October Captain Leaf and Lieutenant Churchyard took thirty-five of the buses to the Royal Marine Brigade HQ at Cassels in order to conduct trials on how best to operate under the orders of the divisional staff. Still with minimal experience and even less administration, seventy-five of the buses formed a convoy two days later which transported Commander Samson's RNAS units from Dunkirk to Bruges and on to Antwerp, though at no point in the journey did anyone in command have any record of which vehicles or personnel were involved. Indeed, at this point no arrangements had been made to ensure the pay and administration of the newly-recruited drivers, and it was only several weeks later that they were finally listed on the Eastney books and issued RMA service numbers.

By 6 October the German army was closing in on Antwerp and under cover of darkness the Royal Marine drivers moved their vehicles to the linoleum factory that lay within the inner ring of forts surrounding the town. The men were billeted in a girls' school and so found themselves in surprisingly comfortable accommodation, but less than forty-eight hours later it became clear that Antwerp was about to fall. Driving slowly through the crowds of refugees in the dark and carrying as many wounded men as possible, the convoy left the town across the River Scheldt and headed west towards safety, skirting south of the Dutch border via Tete de Flandre and St Nicholas. Early on the morning of the 9th six buses had to be abandoned at Selzaete as the promised fuel had not arrived in the confusion; others had broken down during the withdrawal, but the majority reached Bruges at approximately 8.30pm and were able to refuel before heading on further to Ostend.

For such a newly-recruited and loosely-organised unit they operated extraordinarily efficiently, and after a night's rest in Ostend the convoy arrived largely undamaged in Dunkirk. At this point the Royal Naval Division was evacuated to England, leaving the RM MTC unemployed until the Admiralty agreed that they could be employed under the command of General Gilpin, Director of Transport for the Army Service Corps at the new GHQ in St Omer. They arrived at their new home on 15 October with forty-six buses and twenty-three lorries, but only ten days later Lieutenant Colonel Dumble was recalled to Eastney in order to organise the transport of the RMA Howitzer Battalion and so Captain the Hon. G. Howard took command.

For a further ten months the Motor Transport Company provided vital support to the British Army, participating in the First and Second Battles of Ypres, as well as Aubers Ridge and Festubert. They often operated under fire, usually at night, and the drivers gave the most extraordinary service, never sleeping for more than two hours at a time in order to keep the engines warm, and with a rifle always in the footwell of the driver's seat. Finally, in August 1915 it was agreed between the Admiralty and the War Office that the latter would assume responsibility for all buses being used on the continent under the auspices of the Army Service Corps, who had already organised their own companies in addition to those of the Royal Marines. The RM drivers were offered the opportunity to transfer to the ASC with their vehicles, but few chose to do so as such a move entailed a drop in pay from ten shillings per day to six. Instead the majority returned to Eastney where they were mostly employed in the transport of the Howitzer and Anti-Aircraft Brigades of the RMA. So the heroic little London buses of the Royal Marine Motor Transport Company continued to trundle the roads of the Western Front; indeed a small number even returned to service in London after the war, and one remains, B2737, on public display at the London Transport Museum.

Medical Unit Royal Marines

Until the Great War there had never been a requirement for the Royal Marines to form their own medical units, supported as they were by the surgeons and sick berth attendants of the Royal Navy. However, the formation of the Royal Marine Brigade and their operations at Antwerp and Ostend made it clear that if the corps was to serve ashore in any numbers during the ensuing conflict then a more structured system would be required. The task was entrusted to Fleet Surgeon A. Gaskell RN as Assistant Director of Medical Services to the Royal Naval Division, with the assistance of Captain F. Casement RAMC, and the new unit was modelled upon army lines, with three field ambulances each comprising nine medical officers, one lieutenant and quartermaster, one sergeant-major and 171 NCOs and other ranks. Transport for casualties was provided by three horse-drawn and seven motorised ambulances per field ambulance. Each was commanded by a regular naval officer, with the remaining twenty-four originally comprising temporary Royal Navy surgeons, but it was soon decided by the Admiralty that they should instead be borne on the books of the Royal Marines instead, paid at the rates set down by the Royal Army Medical Corps.

The other ranks were principally recruited from the units of the St John's Ambulance in northern English towns, who brought with them a great deal of experience compared to the usual recruits of the RAMC. A significant number were also miners, whose peacetime employment also often required first aid training, and their physical strength proved invaluable in bringing in the wounded through the mud of the Ancre. They were trained at the unit depot alongside the RND at Blandford, where they also manned the camp hospital in order to gain further experience alongside their formal training. Each field ambulance was split into three sections, A, B and C, comprising twenty-four stretcher parties of ninety-six men, and by February 1915 the unit was fully formed and ready for deployment to Gallipoli.

The restructuring of the Royal Naval Division upon its transferral from Gallipoli to France also affected the RM Medical Unit. Though efforts to amalgamate them with the RAMC were resisted, the three field ambulances were renumbered 148, 149 and 150, under the army's numbering system, and the unit arrived on the Western Front under the command of Surgeon Commander E.J. Finch CMG RN. However, further RAMC officers arrived early in 1917, replacing many of the naval surgeons, and Colonel Clements RAMC took over as the Assistant Director of Medical Services in command. Surgeon Commander Finch was appointed instead to the staff of the Deputy Adjutant General Royal Marines with particular responsibility for ensuring that Admiralty regulations were adhered to in light of the War Office's influence over the unit. Further diversity was added by the arrival of American medical officers amongst the unit staff after the USA entered the war in April 1917.

The Royal Marine Medical Unit was perhaps something of an anomaly but is a further example of the Royal Naval Division's determination to maintain its independence even when administered by the War Office. It served with great distinction in every action in which the division was involved, which is clearly indicated as the other ranks alone of this small but vital unit received no fewer than 139 Military Medals between 1916 and 1918.

Divisional Engineers, Royal Naval Division

The divisional engineers were the very first new sub-unit of the Royal Naval Division to be formed after the establishment of the camp at Blandford upon their return from Ostend in 1914. To form an entire division with all of its necessary auxiliary units was an immense task for an organisation that had hitherto been required to provide little more than light infantry and naval gunnery. Many tasks therefore fell to experienced officers from elsewhere who were appointed to temporary commissions in the Royal Marines for the duration of the war. One such man was Major A.B. Carey of the Royal Engineers who was promoted to temporary lieutenant colonel and detailed to raise the RND's divisional engineers. With his adjutant, Lieutenant G.H. Harrison, he intended to recruit two field companies and one of signalmen and he approached his task by enlisting the help of the Institute of Civil Engineers in London, a shrewd decision which provided him with many highly experienced and excellently qualified men. The status of Lieutenant Colonel Carey's men was still somewhat uncertain, and so he rather unusually had them attested as both RNVR seamen and as marines, dressed in the Royal Navy's blue 'square rig'. However, at the beginning of October 1914 the Adjutant General Royal Marines assumed responsibility for the administration of the division, and after a short discussion it was decided that the divisional engineers would fall under the authority of the Royal Marines rather than the Royal Navy. Consequently, they were swiftly fitted out accordingly, allotted Deal service numbers and were paid and administered through that barracks, though extra clerks were added to the depot admin office to bear the weight of the new unit. Though attested, uniformed and administered as Royal Marines (with plain globe and laurel cap badges), an Order in Council was obtained which allowed the men of the RND's divisional engineers to be paid the same rates as the Royal Engineers.

The three companies were swiftly established and accommodated under canvas at Freedown, a 14-acre area of grassland outside Walmer, a short march from the depot at Deal (and later an aerodrome, established in 1917). The autumn of 1914 was terribly wet, but a miniature rifle range was constructed and training began. Many of the recruits had joined from the railway industry and it was immediately apparent that their technical expertise would allow swift progress. Thus the divisional engineers, who had not joined the expedition to Antwerp, transferred to the RND camp at Blandford and joined the rest of the division. No.1 Field Company was commanded by Major A.T. Chivers RM, No.2 Field Company by Major S.R. Adams RM, and the Divisional Signal Company by Major G.H. Spittle RM.

A good number of the corps served in the Gallipoli campaign, during the course of which a third field company was established by order of the War Office, under Major Aveling, but the entire unit arrived together in Marseilles in May 1916 and entrained for the Western Front. At this moment Lieutenant Colonel Carey returned to the Royal Engineers and his place in command was taken by Major G.H. Harrison RM. As the division fell under army command and the RMLI port battalions were reorganised into 1/RMLI and 2/RMLI, the divisional engineers too received new designations. The signal company's change was a simple one, adopting the division's new army number allocation as the 63rd Divisional Signal Company, but the field companies were numbered amongst those of the wider army and became in turn 247, 248 and 249. Across the division the War Office attempted relentlessly to absorb as many elements as possible, reducing the naval influence wherever it could, and the marine identity of the divisional engineers was one such casualty. The Admiralty found it harder to object to this change than to others as the engineers were already employed entirely on army terms and pay, and so on 1 February 1917 the signal and field companies, were transferred wholesale into the Royal Engineers, complete with their own officers and men, and they ceased to be Royal Marines. Throughout their service they had been an extraordinarily important part of the 63rd Division's work on the Western Front.

The Divisional Train, Royal Marines

The establishing of the Royal Naval Division upon an army model presented many challenges, not least that described above of forming the auxiliary units that would usually be provided by the corps of the army. One such requirement was a divisional train with which to transport and administer the huge amount of matériel required to keep a division operating in the field, a task which usually fell to the Army Service Corps. Major F.D. Bridges RMLI took up the task and arrived at the Crystal Palace, depot of the Royal Naval Volunteer Reserve, to recruit the necessary numbers of men. A good number of experienced hands volunteered, many of whom had previous service in the Royal Navy or Royal Marines, and though the service as a whole was rather unused to the routines required (and the management of such a large number of horses and mules), training began at once under the command of Major E.C. Chaytor RMLI, with the temporary rank of lieutenant colonel.

Rates of pay were set at the same levels as those of the ASC, though allowances remained on the naval scale (usually slightly lower than that of the army). Ranks and specialisations too were those of the ASC and the hitherto unseen specialisation badges of farrier, driver and wheelwright appeared on Royal Marine uniforms for the first time. Members of the divisional train were borne on the books of HMS *Victory* (then the name of the Portsmouth naval barracks as well as of Nelson's former flagship), but for RM administrative purposes they were affiliated to the RM depot at Deal. The unit's own depot was established alongside the camp at Blandford, with officers and NCOs trained at the Army Service Corps' school of instruction at Stanhope Lines, South Camp, Aldershot.

A total of 30 officers and 673 NCOs and men were recruited and trained, with an additional officer and 175 men under Major Chaytor's command specifically allocated to provide transport for the Royal Marine Medical Unit. By the end of 1914 the train was ready for deployment and at the end of January 1915 received 378 horses and mules from the War Office, along with 142 carts and wagons for the purpose of supply and transport. An additional 16 mules, 23 wagons and 21 motor ambulances were provided for the use of the medical unit. The Divisional Train gave outstanding service to the division both at Gallipoli and on the Western Front, working in the most terrible and dangerous conditions, often at night to avoid detection. Their service, therefore, is intimately bound up with that of the battalions and batteries as described throughout this book.

Royal Marine Labour Corps

By the end of 1916 there was something of a manpower crisis: all manual labour requirements in the ports and depots of the British military infrastructure took trained men away from front-line units. The supply of local French labour became more and more unreliable as those men joined their own armed forces. In particular, the huge amount of stores being unloaded at French ports to supply the needs of the British Expeditionary Force occupied an extraordinary number of man-hours, and the threat from submarines and long-range guns meant that any delay could be fatal. Consequently, on 2 February 1917 two companies of the Army Service Corps were transferred to form the core of a new unit, the Royal Marine Labour Corps. Recruiting was soon opened in all depot ports, open to men over the age of 41, the maximum age for active service in fighting units. Indeed, it was confirmed in Parliament in July 1918 that there was no upper limit for service and members of the RMLC could be retained for the duration of hostilities as long as they were physically capable of the work required. Consequently, many men joined in their late forties and into their fifties as they saw it as a way to serve the country overseas, an opportunity hitherto unavailable. Of course, that also meant that, though the men of the RMLC received little military training before deployment (since they were recruited to serve as uniformed dock workers), many of them had indeed seen active service in previous conflicts. Upon volunteering they were sent to the divisional headquarters at the RM Depot at Deal, from where their pay was also administered, and there they were issued uniforms and given a minimal degree of military training before they sailed for France.

The uniform issued was essentially identical to the blue serge tunic and trousers of the RMLI, with the exception of the red trouser stripe and the bugle surmounting the cap badge.[4] This latter point was to become a cause for concern for the RMLI, who resented the similarity to their appearance of the comparatively unmilitary-like members of the RMLC, not least after the appearance of articles praising their work in the RM journal *Globe and Laurel*. In consequence of these complaints, in early 1918 the PNTO issued an instruction that members of the RMLC were to wear their corps' initials in brass letters underneath the globe and laurel badge on the front of the Brodrick Cap. This addition, which resembled a large shoulder title, was immediately unpopular with the RMLC as the only other individuals required to wear any letters or numbers on their cap in addition to a badge were conscientious objectors with whom they were understandably keen not to be confused.

The consequent unhappiness inevitably began to impact upon the effectiveness of the men, and on 17 April 1918 the OC of the RMLC camp at Rouen, Captain J. Paterson, wrote to Lieutenant Colonel Cator to explain the situation:

> Sir,
>
> I have the honour to report that deputations of men from both the Rouen and Quevilly camps have interviewed me on wearing the letters RMLC in their caps. The latter has only now cropped up since the arrivals of the numerals and the issue of the same.
>
> There is a very strong feeling amongst the men about the wearing of this distinctive emblem. On enquiry from the representatives of the men, I find they are of the opinion they are being stigmatised in some special way on account of them belonging to a Labour Company, and they feel hurt that they, as a body of volunteers who are doing effective work in France, should be so distinguished.
>
> The feeling is that the order has been given to distinguish them from the RMLI, and they point out that they consider this unnecessary, as there is already distinction shown between the two regiments, by the fact that the letters RMLC are worn on the shoulders, no red stripes worn on the trousers, and no bugle on the cap ornament...
>
> ...I gathered the impression that the feeling was not that their services were not appreciated, but that they, personally as a body, were looked down upon as a Labour unit, also as many remarked, that their age prohibited them from joining a fighting unit, and they volunteered for this work instead...
>
> ...I have interviewed all my officers here regarding this matter and they consider with me, that it would be inadvisable to enforce this order against such active opposition.

As the situation concerned the RMLI as well as the RMLC, Lieutenant Colonel Cater felt unable to resolve it himself and so discussed the matter further with the Adjutant General Royal Marines, General David Mercer. He, in early May of 1918, sent a letter to every camp of the RMLC to explain that the letters were a simple means of differentiation and were in no sense intended as a slight to the honour or reputation of the corps, but that did little to quell the dissatisfaction and representations and letters continued to arrive. The PNTO, Commodore Macgregor heard more and more of the discontent present across the detachments, and wrote to express his concern to the Admiralty on 1 June 1918:

> *The order is causing the greatest discontent and will continue to do so. So much so that very few of the men will go outside their camps on ordinary leave. Seeing that the only other body of men which has to wear the initials of their Corps in their caps are the Conscientious Objectors, this is not surprising.*

Such unnecessary unhappiness could not be easily ignored, and so one week later General Mercer issued an order to remove the initials. He went further, in fact, and recommended that a distinctive cap badge be designed which would placate both the RMLC's desire for recognition and the RMLI's need for differentiation, with the consequence that on 26 August he proposed a design to the Admiralty. This comprised the globe and laurel surmounted by a sailing ship, under way, seen bows-on, and it was approved for wear on 17 September.[5] This satisfied all parties, though considering the large number now seemingly available to collectors compared to the very short period of issue it must be assumed that many which appear for sale are later copies.

When originally formed, the ASC troops were accompanied by their Company Commander, Major J.F. Cable, whose expertise in dock management was invaluable: he was therefore commissioned into the Royal Marines, attached to the Principal Naval Transport Officer (PNTO) and gave excellent service to the RMLC as its technical officer. The first commanding officer of the new corps was Major J.G. Horne RMLI, but very soon after his appointment he was replaced by Major R. Cator RMLI, who was later to be awarded the OBE for his excellent and most tactful handling of this unusual unit. His headquarters was established at GHQ, alongside the PNTO, from where he would regularly visit the detachments at their various ports, assisted by his adjutant Lieutenant J. Carroll RMLI. The numbers at each port varied, with the Dunkirk detachment being the largest at 1,132 and St Valery the smallest at 57, and each was commanded by a temporary captain with his own adjutant who, as time went on, was often promoted from the ranks of the RMLI as the men's previous experience and expertise became apparent. The larger detachments also had a sergeant major and quartermaster sergeant seconded from the RMLI, with smaller detachments receiving commensurate levels of supervision, though each port detachment also included an RMLI sergeant and one or two lance corporals for policing duties.

Though they were far removed from the trenches of the front line, the men of the RMLC did not survive the war unscathed. Air raids on the British-controlled ports were a regular occurrence, and the men's age did not help them to maintain their fitness in the face of continued hard physical labour. However, their work was extremely appreciated by those in command, even if the front-line troops who received the benefit of the smooth supply chain were more often than not unaware of the RMLC's role. Indeed, medical unfitness was not always a complete bar to service. In late 1917 it was decided to increase the Royal Navy's mine-laying capability in the North Sea and the subsequent labour requirements could not be filled by the extant fleet working parties, so a new unit was raised, entitled the No.1 (Home Service) Labour Company. They were billeted at the mining depot at HMS *Gunner*, Granton, on the southern shore of the Firth of Forth, under Major F. Athow RMLI. They received ASC rates of pay and were administered through the Chatham Division of the RMLI, until being disbanded in 1919.

In total 7,995 men volunteered for the RMLC, with 4,908 serving in France. Considering the manual nature of their work a surprising number received honours and awards for their service, with three OBEs, a DSC, seven DSMs and eleven MSMs (including attached RMLI). Their work was vital to the smooth operation of the British Expeditionary Force, which could not have functioned without the efficient and swift administration of the French ports through which all manner of men and matériel arrived. Though they may have been neglected in almost every history of the war, and though they were not perhaps as 'glamorous' to the British public at home, they certainly deserve to be known.

In total there were eight principal detachments, with small groups being allocated to smaller ports when required. The RMLC personnel were distributed as follows:

Port	Total RMLC	Total RMLI	OC
Dunkirk	1132	4	Major G. Havelock
Le Havre	977	4	Major W. Cross
Boulogne	726	4	Major E.H. Gill
Calais	725	4	Major J. Mackay
Rouen	559	4	Major J.A. Paterson
Dieppe	309	2	Captain J. Tait
Cherbourg	152	0	Lieutenant J.M. Walker
Truville	106	1	Second Lieutenant J.B. Bradley
St Valery	57	1	Lieutenant T.W. Howell
Other ports	165	0	GHQ, Administered by Sergeant Major W. Gregory

Royal Marine Cyclist Company

In November 1914 the Royal Marine Light Infantry battalions had returned from Antwerp and were regrouping and retraining at their battalion home barracks. At Forton Barracks in Gosport Major A.H. French, who was shortly to be awarded the DSO for his part in the earlier engagement and the safe withdrawal of the Portsmouth Battalion, was invited to form a Royal Marine Cyclist Company, principally to be used for scouting and messenger duties. The majority of the existence of this small and obscure unit took place in Gallipoli and so is not a subject for this book, but should certainly be mentioned since it was both formed and disbanded in Europe. They were originally established at 8 officers and 210 other ranks, under Major French's command, and they had three months to train on the spacious playing fields of Forton Barracks and in the surrounding countryside of Hampshire before they sailed for the Dardanelles in February 1915 onboard HMT *Somali*, along with the majority of the Royal Naval Division. During that campaign they distinguished themselves for their loyalty, ingenuity and, above all, their bombing capability, so much so that on 12 July Major French established the first allied bombing school on the peninsula, training troops not only in the use of the early designs of hand grenade officially available, but also in the construction and deployment of improvised devices such as the so called 'Tickler Bombs', made from jam jars.

Converted for a short while to a 12pdr gun battery, the Cyclist Company returned to France with the rest of the Royal Naval Division from the island of Mudros on 18 May 1916, landing at Marseilles soon after. Five weeks later, on 24 June, the RM Cyclist Company was disbanded at the large depot camp at Étaples, with its members being allocated to divisional HQ and 1 or 2/RMLI, making use of their trench mortar and bombing experience where possible. Only one of its eight officers did not survive the war – Brevet Lieutenant Colonel N. O. Burge RMLI, killed leading the Nelson Battalion into battle at Beaumont Hamel on 13 November 1916.

Chapter 9

Notable Personalities

Major General Sir Archibald Paris KCB RMA

Archibald Paris was born at Lansdown, Bath, on 9 November 1861. His father, the Reverend Archibald Paris, was Rector of Ludgvan in Cornwall, and his mother Elizabeth the daughter of the Reverend Sir Henry Broughton Bt. He was commissioned as a lieutenant in the Royal Marine Artillery on 1 September 1879, after training at the Royal Naval College, Greenwich, and was promoted to captain on 7 May 1890 and to major on 18 August 1898. From 1899 to 1900 he served with naval intelligence in South Africa and commanded a column of troops, being Mentioned in Despatches three times and consequently receiving a brevet promotion to lieutenant colonel in the South Africa honours list of June 1902. He remained in Africa for several months after the war ended with the Rhodesian Field Force, returning to Southampton onboard SS *Syria* in September. Upon his return he was appointed Chief Instructor at Woolwich, an indication of the esteem in which he was held by the Admiralty, a position he held for three years. In 1907 he was appointed a Companion of the Order of the Bath by HM King Edward VII.

In 1913 Paris was appointed Inspector of Marine Recruiting with the rank of colonel commandant, but on 25 September 1914 he relieved Major General Sir George Aston in command of the Royal Naval Division in the midst of the defence of Antwerp, as described elsewhere in this book. He was appointed personally by Winston Churchill as First Lord of the Admiralty and led the division with great skill and affection throughout the Gallipoli campaign and beyond. It was through his devotion and determination that the naval traditions of the division were able to be maintained, but upon their return to France he was severely wounded in the leg and arm by an enemy shell when inspecting the trenches of the Redan Sector near the Ancre on 12 October 1916. Though he survived he could not continue in command of the Royal Naval Division, which passed to the notorious Cameron Shute. Paris survived but his left leg was amputated and he remained in England for the duration of the war.

He was transferred to the Retired List in 1917, being appointed KCB shortly before. In addition to that award he also received the Belgian Order of Leopold (with swords) and both the Belgian and French Croix de Guerre. Archibald Paris died on 30 October 1937, in Switzerland. His son, also Archibald, reached the rank of brigadier in the Second World War, commanding 12 Brigade at the defence of Singapore before dying in the terrible circumstances of the sinking of the SS *Rooseboom*.[1]

Major General Sir George Aston KCB RMA

George Grey Aston was born in the Cape Colony on 2 December 1861, the son of Lieutenant Colonel Henry Aston of the Indian Army. After training at the Royal Naval College, Greenwich, he was commissioned into the Royal Marine Artillery on 1 September 1879, the same day as Archibald Paris. Between 1893 and 1895 he served as intelligence officer to the Royal Navy's Mediterranean Fleet. In 1896 his expertise was such that he was sent to the Royal Naval College at Greenwich as Professor of Fortification where he first met Maurice Hankey, a young RMA second lieutenant under training at the college who would go on to establish the role of Cabinet Secretary in 1916, a role he would fill until 1935.

In 1899 Aston's practical abilities were required for the war in the country of his birth and he was despatched to join the forces there as staff officer to the Assistant Inspector General, Lines of Communication and then Deputy Assistant Adjutant General for Intelligence. For his efforts in this role he was appointed CB in July 1902, and upon promotion to brigadier general a few years later he returned to South Africa, this time as a member of the General Staff, before further service at the Admiralty in London (being appointed KCB in 1913) where Aston found himself as war approached.

If there was to be a conflict then he was eager to see active service, and his record certainly supported his intentions, so with promotion to colonel second commandant he was appointed to his old haunt, the RMA barracks at Eastney, assisting with the training of the rapidly-expanding corps, but that post was a short-lived one as the opening skirmishes of the war saw him promoted to colonel commandant, in command of the Royal Naval Division's 1914 expedition to Ostend. After handing over command to Archibald Paris the 53-year-old Aston served out the last few years of his service at Eastney before retiring with the rank of major general in 1917. The last twenty-one years of his life were spent lecturing at University College London and the Royal Naval College Greenwich and writing books on naval warfare, military intelligence and fly fishing. He died at home in 1938.

General Sir Alexander Hutchison KCB CMG DSO

Born in Colombo, Sri Lanka, on 2 August 1871, Alexander Richard Hamilton Hutchison was commissioned into the Royal Marine Light Infantry on 28 March 1890. Promoted to captain on 6 December 1897, he served with the army in the Second Boer War and by the early stages of the Great War was serving as Deputy Assistant Adjutant General, Royal Marines. He relinquished this position in July 1915 and as lieutenant colonel he accompanied the RMLI battalions to Gallipoli. Upon their return to Europe and reorganisation he took command of the 2/RMLI, seeing them through the hard days of the Battle of the Ancre. In July 1918 he left the battalion upon his appointment as Assistant Adjutant General, Royal Marines and continued in administrative positions until his appointment as Adjutant General Royal Marines in March 1924, a post which he held until retirement in 1927. Alexander Hamilton died at home three years later in 1930.

Colonel Harold Ozanne DSO RMLI

Harold Ozanne was born in British Guiana on 10 May 1879 to a family of plantation managers and after education at Queen Elizabeth College, Guernsey, he arrived for training at the Royal Naval College, Greenwich aged 18 in 1897. He was commissioned into the Royal Marine Light Infantry on 1 June 1898 and thereafter spent the majority of the next fifteen years at sea. By the outbreak of war in 1914 he was back in England and accompanied the RMLI at the defence of Ostend, but upon his return volunteered to go back to sea. As OC of the marine detachment in HMS *Cressy* he was onboard when that ship was sunk by the German submarine U9 on 22 September in a swift action that cost the Royal Navy three ships and 1,459 men; 560 were lost from HMS *Cressy* but Ozanne survived, picked up by Dutch fishermen.

One year and one day later he was promoted to major and appointed to the battleship HMS *Warspite*, where he saw further action at the Battle of Jutland on 31 May 1916 in which the ship was severely damaged. For his service in the battle Ozanne received the Order of St Stanislaus from the Russian government. He then volunteered to serve ashore with the Royal Naval Division and arrived in France as second in command of the 1st Battalion RMLI in the midst of the Battle of the Somme on 2 October. Less than two weeks later he commanded a guard of 200 marines at the funeral of Major Sketchley, killed accompanying General Paris on his rounds by the same shell which cost the general his leg. At the Battle of the Ancre he was one of only two of the battalion's officers to survive unharmed, and on 11 February 1917 he was awarded the DSO for distinguished service at Miraumont.

At the Battle of Gavrelle in April 1917 the 1/RMLI received extremely heavy casualties, including three of its four company commanders and the commanding officer Lieutenant Colonel Cartwright. Ozanne took command and his position was confirmed with a mention in despatches and promotion to lieutenant colonel. He continued to command the battalion through the Battle of Passchendaele where he was wounded and mentioned in despatches again, before being brought back to England on 26 January 1918. After the war he continued to serve until retirement as colonel second commandant in 1927, taking up the position of commanding officer of Harrow School OTC. When the Second World War was declared Ozanne was recalled to command a Royal Marines depot, but finally retired in 1944 and died peacefully at home in Sawbridgeworth, Hertfordshire.

Lieutenant General Edward Stroud CMG RMLI

Edward James Stroud was born on 22 April 1867 and commissioned into the Royal Marine Light Infantry on 1 September 1886. On 28 July 1915 he was appointed as the first commanding officer of the 1st Battalion Royal Marine Light Infantry after the four port battalions had been amalgamated in Gallipoli and he was mentioned in despatches for his subsequent service. Upon their return to France he continued to command the battalion, with occasional periods as acting brigade commander.

Lieutenant Colonel Francis Cartwright DSO RMLI

Francis John Winsor Cartwright was born at The Wilderness, Richmond in 1875, the son of Thomas and Marion. After joining the Royal Marine Light Infantry he took temporary command of the 1st Battalion RMLI in Gallipoli and was later appointed to command the battalion permanently in France on 11 August 1916, being promoted to lieutenant colonel on 10 September. In February 1917 he was awarded the DSO for his conduct during the actions at Miraumont, with the citation reading:

> *For conspicuous gallantry in action. When the attack was temporarily held up by heavy machine gun and rifle fire he went forward to the front line, where he reorganised and supervised mixed parties of men of different units and pushed forwards to the objective.*[2]

On 28 April 1917 Cartwright was shot in the stomach during the battalion's hard-fought attack on Gavrelle and died of his wounds two days later.

Major General Gunning Campbell – RMA

Gunning Morehead Campbell was born in India on 6 January 1863 and educated at Wellington College only a few years after the school opened. Upon completion of his education, he began training at the Royal Naval College, Greenwich before commissioning into the Royal Marine Artillery on 1 September 1880. As a lieutenant he served in the Suakin expeditions of 1884-5 and was promoted to captain in 1891 and major in 1898, serving as adjutant of the Forfar and Kincardine Artillery. Further promotions followed to lieutenant colonel in 1905 and colonel second commandant in 1914, in which rank he commanded the RMA Battalion at Ostend and Dunkirk. With a long and varied career, he had a great deal of experience of what was required to serve in the RMA, and so in May 1916 he was promoted to temporary brigadier general as Inspector of Marine Recruiting. That promotion was confirmed on 24 September 1917 when he was appointed commandant of Eastney Barracks, a post he held for nearly three years, and it was he who greeted Sergeant Finch as he was pulled by his comrades in a car onto the Eastney parade ground after receiving his VC from the king at Buckingham Palace. Also, in September 1917 he was appointed Marine ADC to HM King George V and a Companion of the Order of the Bath in 1919.

In July 1920 Campbell was appointed Adjutant General Royal Marines in succession to Sir David Mercer but he died of a heart attack at the Caledonian Club in London on 29 November of that year and is buried in Highland Road Cemetery, Portsmouth. His son Keith had been lost in the sinking of the submarine C31 in 1915.

Colonel Frank Luard RMLI

Frank Luard was the son of the Reverend Bixby Luard, Rector of Birch in Essex and his uncle was Admiral Sir William Luard KCB. He was educated for a short period of time at Tonbridge School, but spent the majority of his education at Forest School in Walthamstow before joining the RMLI in 1884. In 1896 he both married and was appointed adjutant of the Portsmouth Division, a position in which he served for five years. Promoted to lieutenant colonel in 1910, he was appointed to the command of the Portsmouth Battalion of the RMLI shortly after the outbreak of war in August 1914. He was best known for his leadership of the battalion in its extraordinary retreat from Antwerp, examined elsewhere in this book, but continued in command after their return to England.

In Gallipoli he was shot through the knee at Gaba Tepe on 3 May 1915 and was consequently evacuated to Alexandria to recuperate. After recovering he returned to the battalion on the peninsula but was shot through the chest on 13 July after leading his battalion in a 400-yard charge on enemy trenches. He refused all attempts to remove him to medical care in case those carrying him should themselves be killed and died several hours after being shot. The battalion's chaplain wrote:

> *The Colonel knew no fear. He loved his officers and men, and they loved and respected him. Keenly they feel his loss... We have lost a gallant officer who was also a Christian gentleman, whose example will never fade from the memories of all who knew him.*

Lieutenant General Cunliffe Parsons CB RMLI

Cunliffe McNeile Parsons was born in India on 15 February 1865 and was commissioned into the Royal Marine Light Infantry on 1 February 1883 and promoted to major on 1 January 1901. Parsons commanded the Chatham Battalion RMLI throughout the Ostend and Antwerp actions of late 1914, and indeed they were the first battalion to land, at 3.30am on the morning of 27 August 1914, and as they were also the first to lead the withdrawal from Ostend they also managed to do so without incurring many casualties. Parsons was promoted to colonel second commandant on 11 April 1915, being appointed Companion of the Order of the Bath later that year. On 13 April 1917 he was promoted to brigadier general and served as commandant of the Royal Naval Division Depot at Blandford in Dorset, before being appointed aide-de-camp to the king in 1919. In January 1921 he was promoted to major general, and to lieutenant general in December 1922, but retired for medical reasons only a month later and died only six days after that.

Major Ernest Sketchley DSO RMLI

Though he never rose to general rank, Ernest Frederick Powys Sketchley gave many years of dedicated service to the RMLI, from being appointed brigade major at Ostend in the first month of the war to dying alongside General Paris in a Somme trench in 1916. A rugby player and son of a clergyman from Bromley, Sketchley was born on 6 August 1881 and educated at Dulwich College. He was initially awarded a place at the Royal Military Academy, Sandhurst, when he left school in 1899, but instead decided to apply for a commission in the Royal Marine Light Infantry. After training at the Royal Naval College, Greenwich, he was commissioned in 1902 and spent the next three years of his career serving in the new Cressy Class cruiser HMS *Aboukir* in the Mediterranean Fleet (she was later sunk by the German submarine *U9* in September 1914). In May 1905 Sketchley was appointed aide-de-camp, then personal secretary, to Admiral Sir Frederick Bedford, the Governor of Western Australia, during which time he met and married his wife Phyllis, with whom he had a son.

After three years in Australia he returned to the UK as adjutant to the Plymouth Division of the RMLI and was promoted to captain in 1911. Upon the declaration of war he accompanied the division to Ostend and Antwerp, where he was appointed brigade major, a role he was to fulfil with great devotion for the remaining two years of his life. Throughout the Gallipoli campaign he supported General Paris and was awarded the DSO for his service at Achi Baba on 13 July 1915. Upon their return to France in September the division was sent to the Somme, and it was there a month later that Sketchley was killed by the same shell that severely wounded General Paris, while accompanying the divisional commander on his rounds of the sector. He is buried in Forceville Communal Cemetery and Extension, north-west of Albert.

Victoria Cross Winners

These records are not of all the Victoria Crosses awarded to the Royal Marines during the Great War, but only those awarded for actions related to the Western Front.

Sergeant Norman A. Finch VC MSM

Norman Augustus Finch was born on Boxing Day 1890 at 42 Nineveh Road, Handsworth, Birmingham. His father John was a postman, married to Norman's mother, Emma. He was educated locally, first of all at the Benson Road Board School and afterwards at the Norton Road Council School, before being employed as a tool machinist for the nearby firm H.W. Ward & Co. He joined the Royal Marine Artillery on 15 January 1908 at the age of 17 – too young, in fact, for the service, and when that fact was discovered he forfeited 346 days' pensionable service. After basic training at Eastney Barracks he joined his first ship, HMS *Diadem*, in the Home Fleet on 17 June 1909, but only the following year joined HMS *Minotaur* on the China Station, where he remained for two years. After short spells at Eastney and onboard the cruiser HMS *Spartiate*, Finch joined HMS *Antrim*, based in Chatham, though serving as the flagship of Admiral Pakenham of the 3rd Cruiser Squadron at Rosyth on the Forth.

After three years in HMS *Antrim* Finch had some kind of nervous breakdown, never fully diagnosed, and was sent ashore, but it was here that he discovered his talent as a gunnery instructor. Promoted to sergeant on 15 March 1917, he qualified as an instructor at sea that November, but had only just joined HMS *Inflexible* in the Grand Fleet when he was recalled to assist the growing preparations for the Zeebrugge raid. On the day of the raid Finch was second in command of the pom poms and Lewis gun in the foretop of HMS *Vindictive*, which was to be vital in suppressing enemy fire over the top of the harbour mole. In the event, German ships and shore batteries poured fire into *Vindictive*, killing many of the Royal Marine and Royal Naval parties before they had even landed. After many hits two shells struck the foretop in quick succession, killing or disabling everyone except Finch, who nonetheless kept up effective fire until all weapons were out of action.

Subsequent to the action HM King George V directed that two members of the 4th Battalion RMLI would receive the Victoria Cross, to be chosen by ballot of the battalion members themselves. The ballot took place on the drill field at Deal Barracks and Finch was one of those chosen, alongside Captain Edward Bamford. He received the medal from the king at Buckingham Palace on 31 July 1918, and upon returning to Eastney was received by cheering crowds and pulled in a car by members of the battalion onto the parade ground where he was met by the commandant.

After the war he served until retirement in 1929, at which point he was also awarded the Meritorious Service Medal. He served again with the Portsmouth Division during the Second World War, after which he returned to his employment as a bank messenger and served as a divisional sergeant major with the Yeomen of the Guard. Norman Finch died on 15 March 1966 and his ashes were scattered at Porchester Crematorium. His medals were bequeathed to the Royal Marines Museum and as such have passed into the possession of the National Museum of the Royal Navy.

Brigadier General Frederick Lumsden VC CB DSO***

Frederick William Lumsden was born at Fyzabad, India on 14 December 1872. He was one of six siblings born to John, a member of the Indian Civil Service, and Margaret, but was educated in England at The Gym, Old Aberdeen and Bristol Grammar School. After school he was commissioned into the Royal Marine Artillery on 1 September 1890 and was promoted to lieutenant exactly a year later, but continued to accumulate qualifications in musketry, equitation, signalling, gunnery, torpedo and law before embarking for his first seagoing appointment, joining the battleship HMS *Nile* in the Mediterranean Fleet in December 1894, shortly after his marriage. Over the following ten years he served in the garrison of Ascension Island and in HMS *Penelope*, HMS *Resolution* and HMS *Formidable*, including promotion to captain in 1897. He attended the Staff College, Camberley in 1908 prior to spending several months in Germany to qualify as an interpreter, a skill which was to be of great value in subsequent years. Between 1910 and 1914 he served as GSO2 in the Straits Settlement Command, based in Singapore, but the outbreak of war required his service in Europe and a return to the gunnery skills of his early career.

After a short period in HMS *Illustrious* he joined the RMA Howitzer Brigade at Eastney to take command of No.1 Battery, sailing with them to France on 15 February 1915. No.1 was in action for the first time at the Battle of Aubers Ridge on 9 May, but by that time Lumsden was in command of four of the guns. He commanded his guns in support of the Battle of Festubert before he left the brigade in July 1915 for a series of promotions in quick succession: first of all as GSO3 to the First Army, then as a brigade major on 21 November and staff officer to the Canadian Corps only six days later. It seems that, though a graduate of the Staff College, Lumsden's abilities as a staff officer were not quite as impressive as his service in the field. Earl Stanhope worked with him in II Corps in 1916 and later wrote:

> *For many months Lumsden was most trying as he knew very little about staff work although a staff college graduate, was extremely slow and didn't like it if I drafted things out for him so that he could sign them and send them out without delay. A bad staff officer, he had no sense of fear and was a wonderful leader of men...*

His subsequent zeal and service were exemplary, and a further year with the Canadians brought him a DSO for his devotion to his duty in the New Year Honours List of 1917, but within five months he had been awarded an extraordinary two bars to the award, which were gazetted together in May, shortly after the action which had earned him his greatest accolade. On 3/4th April 1917 at Francilly in France several German artillery positions had been overrun, but it had not been possible to retrieve the guns from their positions in advance of the British line. Lumsden acted decisively and without hesitation, as his citation in the *London Gazette* recorded, dated 8 June 1917:

> *For most conspicuous bravery, determination and devotion to duty.*
> *Six enemy field guns having been captured, it was necessary to leave them in dug-in positions, 300 yards in advance of the position held by our troops. The enemy kept the captured guns under heavy fire.*
> *Maj. Lumsden undertook the duty of bringing the guns into our lines.*

In order to effect this, he personally led four artillery teams and a party of infantry through the hostile barrage. As one of these teams sustained casualties, he left the remaining teams in a covered position, and, through very heavy rifle, machine gun and shrapnel fire, led the infantry to the guns. By force of example and inspiring energy he succeeded in sending back two teams with guns, going through the barrage with the teams of the third gun. He then returned to the guns to await further teams, and these he succeeded in attaching to two of the three remaining guns, despite rifle fire, which had become intense at short range, and removed the guns to safety.

By this time the enemy, in considerable strength, had driven through the infantry covering points, and blown up the breach of the remaining gun.

Maj. Lumsden then returned, drove off the enemy, attached the gun to a team and got it away.

For this action HM King George V presented him with the Victoria Cross, as well as a DSO with two bars, at Buckingham Palace on 21 June 1917. He had won all three within one week. Returning to France he was wounded on 2 and 30 August, and on 27 November was promoted to lieutenant colonel in command of the 17th Battalion, Highland Light Infantry in order to qualify for a brigade command.

Never a man for a quiet life, on 2 December he earned a third bar to his DSO as a result of a large raid by his brigade on Volt Farm, Mallet Copse and Double Copse in the Ypres Salient. His accolades continued to mount: on 6 May 1918 he was appointed temporary divisional commander of the 32nd Division, and on 3 June HM the King appointed him a Companion of the Order of the Bath. On the very next day he was in his brigade's trenches at Blairville, near Arras, when intelligence indicated that an enemy attack was imminent. Lumsden moved into an exposed position in order to assess the situation and was shot through the head by a sniper, dying instantly. Brigadier General Frederick Lumsden was buried in Berles New Military Cemetery, Berles-au-Bois, south-west of Arras. He was posthumously awarded the Belgian Croix de Guerre, and his medals are in the possession of the National Museum of the Royal Navy.

Major Edward Bamford VC DSO

Edward Bamford was born on 28 May 1887 at 34 Langdon Park Road, Highgate, London. His father, the Reverend Robert Bamford, was chaplain to the Yeatman Hospital in Sherborne, Dorset, and so that is where Edward grew up with his two brothers Robert (one of the founders of Aston Martin) and Arthur (killed serving with the Grenadier Guards at Loos in 1915). After education as a day boy at Sherborne School, Bamford joined the Royal Marine Light Infantry on 1 September 1905. He excelled in training at the Royal Naval College, Greenwich, being the joint recipient of the King George King George V Prize Scholarship prior to promotion to lieutenant on 1 July 1906. Exactly a year later he joined the Portsmouth Division of the RMLI at Forton Barracks to await his first seagoing appointment. Indeed, he was to spend the majority of the next ten years serving at sea. On 5 December 1908 he joined HMS *Bulwark* shortly before she arrived in Devonport for repairs to her armament which lasted for more than a year. After a further year and a half's service in HMS *Magnificent* he joined *HMS Britannia* on 5 September 1911. He was onboard when she ran aground in the Firth of Forth on her way to join the Battle of Dogger Bank, but after the new year of 1916 Bamford had his first experience of the war ashore when he served with the Guards Division in the Ypres Salient for five months in what must have been a great shock to a seagoing officer.

On 2 May 1916 he was promoted to temporary captain and joined the newly-built light cruiser HMS *Chester* of the 3rd Battle Cruiser Squadron, in command of the ship's RMLI contingent. Only three weeks later the ship took part in the Battle of Jutland, the greatest naval battle of the war. HMS *Chester* was severely damaged, receiving seventeen hits by 150mm shells from the enemy. In the course of the battle Boy Seaman John 'Jack' Cornwell famously kept his gun firing after being severely wounded, for which he was awarded the Victoria Cross. Bamford himself was wounded and his face burned when a shell destroyed the aft gunnery control station he was commanding. He struggled on regardless of his injuries and assisted in extinguishing a dangerous cordite fire. For these two actions he was awarded the DSO and the Order of St Anne, Third Class (with swords) by the Russian government.

After a swift recovery he was confirmed in the rank of captain and returned to HMS *Chester*, and it was from here that he was appointed company commander in the newly-raised 4th Battalion RMLI in February 1918. He joined the battalion at Deal and spent three months training his company, amongst whom he swiftly developed a reputation for a humanity rarely seen in such appointments. On the day of the raid on Zeebrugge Bamford's company were embarked in HMS *Vindictive*. When alongside the harbour mole and under extremely heavy fire Bamford led three platoons of marines ashore across the few undestroyed brows and headed towards the right, ensuring that enemy reinforcements could not break through to repel the British landing, before rushing to the end of the mole to attack the battery that was bombarding the ships waiting offshore for the returning troops and the crews of the blockships. Miraculously unharmed himself, Bamford led his company in an ordered retreat once their task was complete.

Once back in Deal, Bamford was the second recipient of the VC to be chosen by ballot, in addition to Sergeant Finch. His citation in the *London Gazette* read:

> *For conspicuous gallantry at Zeebrugge. April 1918. This officer landed on the Mole from 'Vindictive' with Nos. 5, 7 & 8 platoons of the Marine Storming Force in the face of great difficulties. When on the Mole under heavy fire, he displayed the greatest initiative in the command of his company, and by his total disregard of danger, showed a magnificent example to his men. He first established a strong point on the right of the disembarkation, and when that was safe, led an assault on a battery to the left with the utmost coolness and valour. Captain Bamford was selected by the officers of the R.M.A & R.M.L.I detachments to receive the Victoria Cross under Rule 13 of the Royal Warrant, dated 26 January 1856.*

As well as the Victoria Cross Bamford also received the French Legion of Honour and promotion to brevet major. He continued to serve, largely at sea, for a further ten years, but in September 1928 he was visiting Wei Hai Wei in China during an appointment as small arms instructor in Hong Kong when he contracted an unknown but serious illness. HMS *Cumberland* sailed to take him to hospital but he died onboard on 30 September. He was buried in Bubbling Well Road English Cemetery, which was sadly later flattened for building development, so Major Edward Bamford, hero of Zeebrugge, is presently buried under a Shanghai shopping centre. His medals are in the custody of the National Museum of the Royal Navy.

Appendix

Honours and Awards Received by the Royal Marines on the Western Front

The honours and awards listed below are strictly those received while the RMLI and RMA were deployed on the Western front, and so do not include those received for service at Gallipoli or elsewhere. All individuals are listed as the rank that they held when that particular award was made. Those marked with an asterisk received the same award more than once.

Victoria Cross
Major E. Bamford DSO RMLI (Zeebrugge, 1918)
Sergeant N.A. Finch (Zeebrugge, 1918)
Major F. Lumsden DSO** RMA (Francilly, 1917)

CB
Brigadier General A.R.H. Hutchison CMG DSO RMLI
(Spring Offensive, 1918)
Lieutenant Colonel C.A.F. Osmaston RMA (AA Brigade)
Major C. Weller RMLI (Zeebrugge, 1918)

CMG
Lieutenant Colonel A.B. Carey RM (Divisional Engineers)
Major C.F. Jerram DSO RMLI (Crossing of St Quentin Canal, 1918)
Brevet Lieutenant Colonel R.C. Foster RMLI (Staff)
Lieutenant Colonel G.R. Poole RMA (Howitzer Brigade)

CBE
Lieutenant Colonel R. Ford (RMA Heavy Siege Train)

OBE

Captain P. Allard RM (Divisional Train)

Lieutenant Colonel J.F. Cable RMLC

Major & Brevet Lieutenant Colonel R. Cator RMLI (RMLC)

Major C.L. Chapman RM (Divisional Train)

Major W.E. Cooke RM (Divisional Train)

Lieutenant A.L. Dugon RM (Divisional Train)

Major A.K. Evans (Staff)

Lieutenant G.F. Haszard DSC RMA (AA Brigade)

Major R.H.D. Lough DSO RMLI (Staff)

Major W.K. McKay RMLC

Captain & Adjutant C.G. Murray RM (Divisional Train)

Major F.H. Smith RM (Divisional Train)

Conspicuous Gallantry Medal

Private W. Hopewell (Zeebrugge, 1918)

Sergeant F.J. Knill (Zeebrugge, 1918)

Private J.D.L. Press (Zeebrugge, 1918)

Distinguished Service Order

Major E.H. Barr RMA (AA Brigade)

Lieutenant Colonel F.J.W. Cartwright RMLI (Beaumont Hamel, 1916)

Major V.H. Cartwright RMA (AA Brigade)

Captain A.R. Chater RMLI (Zeebrugge, 1918)

Major N.S. Clutterbuck RMLI (Aveluy Wood, 1918)

Lieutenant T.F. Cooke RMLI (Zeebrugge, 1918)

Captain R.A. Dallas-Brooks RMLI (Zeebrugge, 1918)

Captain T.S. Dick RMA (Howitzer Brigade)

Major C.E. Eagles RMLI

Major M.C. Festing RMLI (Staff)

Major E.K. Fletcher RMLI* (Aveluy Wood, bar Logeast Wood, 1918)

Captain & Brevet Major A.L. Forster (AA Brigade)

Brevet Lieutenant Colonel R.F. Foster RMA (Staff)

Major A.H. French RMLI (Antwerp, 1914)

Lieutenant D.J. Gowney RMLI (Antwerp, 1914)

Lieutenant Colonel G.H. Harrison CMG RM (Divisional Engineers)

Lieutenant Colonel A.R.H. Hutchison CMG RMLI (Beaumont Hamel, 1916)

Major Iremonger RMA (Heavy Siege Train)

Major C.F. Jerram RMLI (Staff)

Captain W.R. Ledgard RMA (Howitzer Brigade)

Lieutenant Colonel T.R. McCready MC RMLI (Canal de l'Escaut, 1918)

Major C. Micklem RMA (Howitzer Brigade)

APPENDIX

Major R.C. Morrison-Scott RMA
  (Howitzer Brigade)
Major H. Ozanne RMLI (Miraumont,
  1917)
Lieutenant Colonel G.R. Poole RMA
  (Howitzer Brigade)

Major P. Sandilands RMLI
  (Anneaux & Cambrai, 1918)
Captain E.J.B. Tagg RMLI (Staff)
Captain G.L. Wills RMA (Howitzer
  Brigade, att. Tank Corps)

Distinguished Service Cross

Captain D.L. Aman RMA
  (AA Brigade)
Captain T.C. Cuming RMA
  (Howitzer Brigade)
Captain G. Evans RMA (AA Brigade)
Lieutenant G.F. Haszard RMA*
  (AA Brigade)
Acting Company Sergeant Major
  E.E. Kelly (Zeebrugge, 1918)
Lieutenant F.H. Lamb RM
  (Divisional Engineers)
Lieutenant H.R. Lambert RMA
  (AA Brigade)
Lieutenant Colonel R.W. Lamplough
  RMLI (Zeebrugge, 1918)

Captain J.M. Palmer RMLI
  (Zeebrugge, 1918)
Major G.L. Raikes RMA (Howitzer
  Brigade)
Lieutenant T.N. Riley RM (Divisional
  Engineers)
Lieutenant F.L. Robinson RMA
  (Howitzer Brigade)
Lieutenant R.H. Roe RM (Divisional
  Engineers)
Captain W.G.A. Shadwell RMA
  (AA Brigade)
Sergeant Major C.J. Thatcher
  (Zeebrugge, 1918)
Lieutenant G. Underhill RMLI
  (Zeebrugge, 1918)

Military Cross

Second Lieutenant C.H. Bailey
  RMLI (Aveluy Wood, 1918)
Lieutenant A.G. Bareham RMLI
  (Niergnies, 1918)
Lieutenant T. Buckley RMLI**
  (Aveluy Wood, Le Barque,
  Inchy & Canal crossings, 1918)
Captain T.H. Burton RMLI
Captain R.H. Campbell RMLI
  (Aveluy Wood, 1918)
Captain C.C. Carus-Wilson RMA
  (Howitzer Brigade)
Lieutenant M.H. Collet RMA
  (Howitzer Brigade)

Second Lieutenant E.W. Collier
  RMLI (Flesquières Ridge, 1918)
Lieutenant J.C.P. Curran RMLI
  (Logeast Wood, 1918)
Captain F.G. Eliot RMLI (Spring
  Offensive, 1918)
Lieutenant H.N. Elphick RMA
  (Howitzer Brigade)
Captain A.K. Evans RMLI (Staff)
Major C.G. Farquharson RMLI
Captain L.L. Foster RMA (Howitzer
  Brigade)
Lieutenant J. Franklyn RMA
  (Howitzer Brigade)

Captain H.V. Fuller RMLC

Second Lieutenant E.A. Godfrey
RMLI (Gavrelle, 1917)

Lieutenant G.R. Goldringham
RMLI* (Passchendaele, 1917)

Lieutenant H.L. Hardisty RMLI
(Le Barque, 1918)

Lieutenant A.E. Holton RMA
(Howitzer Brigade)

Captain E.J. Huskisson RMLI
(Arleux & Oppy, 1917)

Captain H.B. Inman RMLI
(Grandcourt, 1917)

Surgeon J. McBean-Ross RN*
(Passchendaele, 1917)

Captain T.R. McCready RMLI

Lieutenant J.W. Middleton RMLI
(Spring Offensive, 1918)

Lieutenant Colonel A.St C. Morford
RMLI (Souchez, 1916)

Second Lieutenant G.A. Newling
RMLI* (Gavrelle Windmill, 1917,
bar Aveluy Wood, 1918)

Captain J. Pearson RMLI
(Miraumont, 1917)

Lieutenant F.A. Proffitt RMLI
(Aveluy Wood, 1918)

Lieutenant W. Russell RMA
(AA Brigade)

Lieutenant T.A. Ryder RMA
(Howitzer Brigade)

Lieutenant R.H. Sawyer RMA
(AA Brigade)

Lieutenant H.V. Scott-Willcox RMLI
(Beaumont Hamel, 1916)

Second Lieutenant H.C. Smith RMLI
(Staff)

Lieutenant R.W. Spraggett RMLI
(Logeast Wood, 1918)

Lieutenant T.G. Stewart RMLI
(Logeast Wood, 1918)

Second Lieutenant A.G. Stone RMLI
(Logeast Wood, 1918)

Captain H.B. Van Pragh RMLI
(Passchendaele, 1917)

Captain R.H. Vance RMLI (Logeast
Wood, 1918)

Lieutenant B.C.V. Weeks RMLI
(Souchez, 1916)

Captain R.H.P. West RMLI (Spring
Offensive, 1918)

Lieutenant G. Westby RMLI
(Passchendaele, 1917)

Lieutenant G.J. Wharf RMLI (Spring
Offensive, 1918)

Second Lieutenant W.A. Williamson
RMLI (Passchendaele, 1917)

Lieutenant S.H. Wood RMA
(Howitzer Brigade)

Lieutenant L.H. Wrangham RMLI
(Anneux, 1918)

Distinguished Conduct Medal

Sergeant Major A.J. Banks (1917)

Staff Sergeant D. Booth
(Medical unit)

Private W. Brindley (Grevillers,
1918)

Sergeant W.S. Carey (Niergnies,
1918)

Lance Corporal T.W. Childs
(Niergnies, 1918)

Corporal J.W. Coulthard (Anneux,
1918)

Corporal F. Cross (Howitzer Brigade)

Band Sergeant Major C. Dadd
(Howitzer Brigade)

Private G. Davies (Gavrelle, 1917)

Private J.L. Elliott (Souchez, 1916)

Sergeant Major H. Evans (Medical Unit)

Corporal T. Forsyth (Howitzer Brigade)

Sergeant G.H. Hastings (Logeast Wood, 1918)

Sergeant A.L. Hill (Logeast Wood, 1918)

Sergeant L. Insley MM (Niergnies, 1918)

Sergeant A. Paterson (Logeast Wood, 1918)

Corporal R.E. Payne (Howitzer Brigade)

Bombardier W. Pike (Howitzer Brigade)

Sergeant G.A. Priestly (Passchendaele, 1917)

Lance Corporal A. Sadd (Aveluy Wood, 1918)

Lance Corporal T. Salt (Gavrelle, 1917)

Company Sergeant Major A.H. Sands (1917)

Sergeant W.G. Scott (Miraumont, 1917)

Corporal T.W. Smith (1918)

Corporal W.J. Stone (AA Brigade)

Sergeant H.J. Trigg (Logeast Wood, 1918)

Sergeant E.C. Tye (Howitzer Brigade)

Corporal W.A. Watts (Souchez, 1916)

Staff Sergeant H. Williams (Howitzer Brigade)

Company Sergeant Major F. Windybank (Le Barque, 1918)

Sergeant A.C. Woodhouse (Howitzer Brigade)

Sergeant G.W. Woodward (Loupart Wood, 1918)

Distinguished Service Medal

Gunner W.R. Ash (RMA Heavy Siege Train)

Driver F. Baker (AA Brigade)

Sergeant B.P. Beale (RMA Heavy Siege Train)

Sapper W. Bottomley (Divisional Engineers)

Private M. Boyd (RMLC)

Gunner A.H. Bristow (AA Brigade)

Gunner H.J. Brookes (RMA Heavy Siege Train)

Sergeant G.H. Bruce (Antwerp, 1914)

Band Sergeant Major C. Bryan (AA Brigade)

Colour Sergeant W.R. Bryan (RMA Heavy Siege Train)

Sergeant S. Bull (AA Brigade)

Corporal H.C.B. Callaway (AA Brigade)

Gunner A. Campbell (RMA Heavy Siege Train)

Gunner E.G. Chamberlain (AA Brigade)

Sergeant F.S. Chapman (AA Brigade)

Acting Sergeant Major W.T. Clarke (AA Brigade)

Colour Sergeant W.J. Coen (RMA Heavy Siege Train)

Sergeant J.W. Cook (RMLC)

Lance Corporal W.J. Cook (Antwerp, 1914)

Sergeant B. Doull (RMLC)

Corporal J.B. Fathers (Divisional Engineers)

Private C.J. Fleet (Antwerp, 1914)

Lance Corporal T.C. Franks (Antwerp, 1914)

Sergeant Major J.T. Galliford (Antwerp, 1914)

Driver Glass (AA Brigade)

Private G.H. Hall (Antwerp, 1914)

Corporal G.E. Hanham (RMLC)

Gunner W. Jackman (RMA Heavy Siege Train)

Sergeant L.R. Jacobs (RMA Heavy Siege Train)

Quartermaster Sergeant S.J. Kenny (Antwerp, 1914)

Corporal J.E. Kersey (RMA Heavy Siege Train)

Private S. Lang (Antwerp, 1914)

Sick Berth Attendant J. Layland RN (Heavy Siege Train)

Sergeant E.S. Lewis (AA Brigade)

Sergeant J.W. Mace (RMLC)

Sergeant R. McIntosh (RMLC)

Gunner R.G. McCurrack (AA Brigade)

Acting Sergeant Major F. Merckel (AA Brigade)

Gunner J.H. Messum (AA Brigade)

Sick Berth Attendant F.E. Morse RN (RMA Heavy Siege Train)

Sapper J.H. Murray (Divisional Engineers)

Driver F.D.K. Newman (RMA Heavy Siege Train)

Private J.J. Rate (RMLC)

Sergeant W.H. Rogers (AA Brigade)

Sergeant E.C. Sessions (RMA Heavy Siege Train)

Gunner W.A. Sewell (RMA Heavy Siege Train)

Corporal F.R. Smith (Divisional Engineers)

Sapper H.S. Smith (Divisional Engineers)

Driver G.W. Stanton (RMA Heavy Siege Train)

Gunner J.A. Taylor (RMA Heavy Siege Train)

Sergeant W.H. Taylor (Zeebrugge, 1918)

Driver J.E. Thompson (AA Brigade)

Sergeant A.J.E. Thorburn (AA Brigade)

Company Sergeant Major C. Thornton (Divisional Engineers)

Corporal L.H. Tomlin (AA Brigade)

Sergeant H. Wright (Zeebrugge, 1918)

Chief Special Boat Service T. Young RN (RMA Heavy Siege Train)

Military Medal

Private W. Aldred (Beaumont Hamel, 1916)

Private W.C. Arnold (Drocourt-Quéant Line, 1918)

Private W. Artis (Aveluy Wood, 1918)

Private J. Baird (Gavrelle, 1917)

Lance Sergeant J.B. Bamber (Welsh Ridge, 1917)

Private A.E. Barker (Passchendaele, 1917)

Driver W. Barnes (Howitzer Brigade)

Private W.C. Beer (Drocourt-Quéant Line, 1918)

Private A.E. Bell (Drocourt- Quéant Line, 1918)

Private E.T. Bell (Aveluy Wood, 1918)

Private G.W. Bell (Aveluy Wood, 1918)

Sergeant W.N. Bennett (Miraumont, 1917)

Corporal E. Beresford (Aveluy Wood, 1918)

Private E. Berry (Miraumont, 1917)

Corporal S. Berry (Howitzer Brigade)

Gunner E.A. Bevan (Howitzer Brigade)

Private W. Blanchflower (Miraumont, 1917)

Corporal H. Bland (Howitzer Brigade)

Gunner W.G. Blundell (Howitzer Brigade)

Private F. Blythe (Logeast Wood, 1918)

Lance Corporal J.H. Bolan (Welsh Ridge, 1917)

Staff Sergeant D. Booth (Beaumont Hamel, 1916)

Private E. Booth (Gavrelle, 1917)

Private R.W. Booth (Passchendaele, 1917)

Bombardier F.J. Brighten (Howitzer Brigade)

Corporal N.F. Brown (Howitzer Brigade)

Private W.H. Bullen (Miraumont, 1917)

Corporal E.E. Burnett (Drocourt-Quéant Line, 1918)

Sergeant Major J. Bushnell (Gavrelle, 1917)

Gunner A.S. Butchers (Howitzer Brigade)

Lance Corporal J. Carlyle (Beaumont Hamel, 1916)

Sergeant J.H. Carter (Spring Offensive, 1918)

Private H. Castley (Gavrelle, 1917)

Sergeant A. Chatfield (Howitzer Brigade)

Private W.E. Clarke (Logeast Wood, 1918)

Company Sergeant Major F.T. Collins (Logeast Wood, 1918)

Private J. Collinson (Miraumont, 1917)

Private F. Cooper (Spring Offensive, 1918)

Sergeant E.G. Copland (Logeast Wood, 1918)

Private P. Coyne (Gavrelle, 1917)

Sergeant G.K. Craik (Divisional Train)

Private M. Crehan (Miraumont, 1917)

Sergeant W.D. Croke (Aveluy Wood, 1918)

Private A.E. Crook (Gavrelle area, 1917)

Corporal C.F. Cumiskey (Gavrelle, 1917)

Private R. Curry (Divisional Train)

Bombardier S.M. Curtis (Howitzer Brigade)

Private J. Davis (Beaumont Hamel, 1916)

Private C. Dean (Miraumont, 1917)

Corporal E. Dixon (Logeast Wood, 1918)

Lance Corporal F.H. Dobson (Passchendaele, 1917)

Private J. Donkin (Gavrelle, 1917)

Private G.H.W. Duckling (Souchez, 1916)

Private W.J. Duke (Miraumont, 1917)

Private D. Dutton (Beaumont Hamel, 1916)

Sergeant A.T. Eaves (Gavrelle, 1917)

Private D. Edmundson (Miraumont, 1917)

Private G.W. Elliott (Miraumont, 1917)

Staff Sergeant M. Elliot (Beaumont Hamel, 1916)

Lance Corporal G.H. Ellis (Logeast Wood, 1918)

Sergeant H.L. Evans (Drocourt-Quéant Line, 1918)

Private S.H. Feltham (Canal du Nord & Cambrai, 1918)

Private E.T. Felton (Miraumont, 1917)

Private E. Fitton (Miraumont, 1917)

Private C. Fletcher (Logeast Wood, 1918)

Gunner W. Frew (Howitzer Brigade)

Gunner R. Fulton (Howitzer Brigade)

Driver C.A. Gamble (Howitzer Brigade)

Corporal G.W. Gannon (Beaumont Hamel, 1916)

Corporal W.H. Gardner (Aveluy Wood, 1918)

Sergeant S.T. Gething (Beaumont Hamel, 1916)

Private C.F. Gilbert (Miraumont, 1917)

Private E. Gill (Beaumont Hamel, 1916)

Private H. Godfrey (Beaumont Hamel, 1916)

Gunner E.J. Goff (Howitzer Brigade)

Private D.L. Grant (Canal du Nord & Cambrai, 1918)

Private A.S. Green (Aveluy Wood, 1918)

Lance Corporal J.E. Green (Beaumont Hamel, 1916)

Private E.H. Greenwood (Beaumont Hamel, 1916)

Private J. Grimshaw (Spring Offensive, 1918)

Gunner J. Halden (Howitzer Brigade)

Private R. Hancock (Miraumont, 1917)

Private W. Hann (Canal du Nord & Cambrai, 1918)

Sergeant G.H. Hastings (Spring Offensive, 1918)

Sergeant J. Heaton (Howitzer Brigade)

Corporal A.W. Heselton (Beaumont Hamel, 1916)

Bombardier L. Hinchliffe (Howitzer Brigade)

Sergeant J. Hissock (Aveluy Wood, 1918)

Private E.V. Holden (Spring Offensive, 1918)

Lance Corporal E. Holway (Aveluy Wood, 1918)

Bombardier S. Hooper (Howitzer Brigade)

Gunner J. Howarth (Howitzer Brigade)

Private J.E. Hubbard (Miraumont, 1917)

Private R.J. Hulme (Souchez, 1916)

Gunner A. Hutchison (Howitzer Brigade)

Private A.F. Hutton (Gavrelle, 1917)

Corporal G. Ingram (Spring Offensive, 1918)

Sergeant C. Inman (Howitzer Brigade)

Corporal J.A. Innes (Miraumont, 1917)

Sergeant L. Insley (Welsh Ridge, 1917)

Private S. Jackson (Gavrelle, 1917)

Private A. James (Welsh Ridge, 1917)

Private D.J. James* (Souchez, 1916)

Private A.E. Janes (Miraumont, 1917)

Gunner H.H. Jarman (Howitzer Brigade)

APPENDIX

Private E. Jefferey (Logeast Wood, 1918)

Bombardier W.S. C.Jeffery (Howitzer Brigade)

Private F. Jones (Logeast Wood, 1918)

Private G.B. Jones (Canal du Nord & Cambrai, 1918)

Private T. Jones (Aveluy Wood, 1918)

Sergeant A.J. Kearslake (Gavrelle, 1917)

Private J. Keating (Logeast Wood, 1918)

Private C. Kibbler (Logeast Wood, 1918)

Sergeant W.O. Knight (Souchez, 1916)

Corporal J. Larter (Aveluy Wood, 1918)

Sergeant T.J. Lee (Howitzer Brigade)

Private C.A. Lock (Canal du Nord & Cambrai, 1918)

Pte J Lock (Drocourt-Quéant Line, 1918)

Sergeant W.J. Lock (Welsh Ridge, 1917)

Corporal T.C. Lockley (Howitzer Brigade)

Sergeant W.W. Love (Beaumont Hamel, 1916)

Sergeant E.R. Ludbrooke (Gavrelle, 1917)

Private J. Lyson (Welsh Ridge, 1917)

Private D. Mackenzie (Gavrelle, 1917)

Private H. Mangham (Miraumont, 1917)

Lance Corporal W. Marsden (Gavrelle area, 1917)

Private P. Marshall (Aveluy Wood, 1918)

Corporal J.S. Marston (Miraumont, 1917)

Private E. Martin (Spring Offensive, 1918)

Private J. Martin (Miraumont, 1917)

Private J.K. Matthews (Miraumont, 1917)

Corporal G.J. McCormack* (Aveluy Wood, 1918)

Sergeant W.S. McCullough (Aveluy Wood, 1918)

Private W.H. Meatyard (Beaumont Hamel, 1916)

Lance Corporal J. Meese* (Spring Offensive, 1918)

Lance Corporal W. Mills (Canal du Nord & Cambrai, 1918)

Company Sergeant Major R. Milne (Miraumont, 1917)

Private F.A. Morris (Welsh Ridge, 1917)

Bombardier J. Morris (Howitzer Brigade)

Corporal A. Morrison (Logeast Wood, 1918)

Sergeant R. Murray (Beaumont Hamel, 1916)

Private H.W. Nash (Passchendaele, 1917)

Colour Sergeant J.D. Ottignon (AA Brigade)

Gunner F. H. arkes (Howitzer Brigade)

Lance Sergeant G.W. Parkes (Spring Offensive, 1918)

Corporal D. Partington (Logeast Wood, 1918)

Private J. Partridge (Spring Offensive, 1918)

Sergeant F.A. Pearce (Miraumont, 1917)

Gunner S.E. Pearce (Howitzer Brigade)

Private F.G. Penny (Spring Offensive, 1918)

Private W.G. Phillips (Canal du Nord & Cambrai, 1918)

Corporal G. Pidduck (Beaumont Hamel, 1916)

Private J. Postin (Miraumont, 1917)

Lance Corporal J. Pullin (Miraumont, 1917)

Company Sergeant Major T.W. Read (Spring Offensive, 1918)

Bombardier E.J. Redman (Howitzer Brigade)

Sergeant C.S. Riman (Beaumont Hamel, 1916)

Sergeant J.C. Robson (Aveluy Wood, 1918)

Private K. Robson (Miraumont, 1917)

Private W. Rodger (Gavrelle, 1917)

Colour Sergeant R.C. Rogers (Gavrelle, 1917)

Corporal T. Salt DCM (Passchendaele, 1917)

Sergeant J.M. Sanders (Beaumont Hamel, 1916)

Sergeant C. Scott (Welsh Ridge, 1917)

Private E. Scott (Miraumont, 1917)

Private A. Senior (Beaumont Hamel, 1916)

Private H. Shepherd (Miraumont, 1917)

Bombardier A. Shepherdson (Howitzer Brigade)

Private J. Sherman (Miraumont, 1917)

Corporal F. Shuttleworth (Spring Offensive, 1918)

Private T. Simon (Miraumont, 1917)

Corporal G.W. Simpson (Logeast Wood, 1918)

Corporal V.G. Smeethe (Logeast Wood, 1918)

Private E. Smith (Spring Offensive, 1918)

Sergeant G. Smith (Spring Offensive, 1918)

Sergeant H.J. Smith (Drocourt-Quéant Line, 1918)

Private J. Smith (Beaumont Hamel, 1916)

Private P. Smith (Miraumont, 1917)

Corporal A.G. South (Beaumont Hamel, 1916)

Corporal G.K. Stanton (Welsh Ridge, 1917)

Sergeant W. Sullivan (Divisional Train)

Lance Corporal W.E. J.Sully (Passchendaele, 1917)

Private J. Sumner (Logeast Wood, 1918)

Sergeant H. Tarbottom (Howitzer Brigade)

Lance Sergeant H.D. Thomson (Beaumont Hamel, 1916)

Private A.W. Thorp (Beaumont Hamel, 1916)

Corporal W. Tildesley (Logeast Wood, 1918)

Private R.J. Tilley (Miraumont, 1917)

Sergeant W.T. Todd (Welsh Ridge, 1917)

Private J. Tomlinson (Spring Offensive, 1918)

Sergeant H. Trusler* (Aveluy Wood, 1918)

Private T. Urquhart (Welsh Ridge, 1917)

Private J. Vernon (Beaumont Hamel, 1916)

Sergeant E.A. Vinnell (Howitzer Brigade)

Sergeant L.B. Wagner (Beaumont Hamel, 1916)

APPENDIX

Private H.H. Waite (Welsh Ridge, 1917)

Private G.H. Warren (Miraumont, 1917)

Company Sergeant Major W.J. Waters (Spring Offensive, 1918)

Corporal W.H. Watts (Gavrelle area, 1917)

Sergeant D.O. West (Aveluy Wood, 1918)

Sergeant G. Wetton (Welsh Ridge, 1917)

Driver W. Wheeler (Howitzer Brigade)

Private R.E.F. Wild (Miraumont, 1917)

Private M.B. Wilkinson (Miraumont, 1917)

Private P.J. Willett (Beaumont Hamel, 1916)

Private G.W. Williams (Canal du Nord & Cambrai, 1918)

Gunner G.L. Willis (Howitzer Brigade)

Pte F. B. Wilson (Spring Offensive, 1918)

Corporal G.E. Wood (Howitzer Brigade)

Private W. Wood (Canal du Nord & Cambrai, 1918)

Gunner T.H. Woodrow (Howitzer Brigade)

Private J. Woosey

Private A. Wormold (Gavrelle area, 1917)

Gunner W. Wright (Howitzer Brigade)

Private A.W. Wyatt (Beaumont Hamel, 1916)

Meritorious Service Medal

Colour Sergeant J. Amos

Sergeant Major J.F.T. Ashton (Divisional Train)

Colour Sergeant G.W. Baker (Divisional Train)

Private F. Brown (RMLI att. RMLC)

Sergeant S.W. Buckle (RMLC)

Sergeant A.M. Butler

Quartermaster Sergeant J.B. Carr (Medical Unit)

Sergeant N.H. Chubb (Divisional Train)

Clerk F. Cook

Sergeant W. Davidson (Divisional Train)

Sergeant R. Dewhurst

Quartermaster Sergeant E. Diggle

Private A.H. Dowding

Private A.W. Dowding

Sergeant H.J. Eastaway (RMLI att. RMLC)

Company Sergeant Major D.E. Eccles (RMLI att. RMLC)

Company Sergeant Major E.E. Edwards (RMA Heavy Siege Train)

Acting Sergeant Major J. Edwards

Sergeant R. Fitton QM

Sergeant R. Gooding (RMLC)

Acting Sergeant Major F.R. Graham

Company Sergeant Major C.P. Hann (RMLI att. RMLC)

Driver A. Hicks (RMA Heavy Siege Train)

Private A.E. Howe

Quartermaster Sergeant S. Jones

Sergeant J.E. Lord QM (Medical Unit)

Company Quartermaster Sergeant G.G. Marks (Divisional Train)

Private F.A. Morris

Private J. Moore

Private B. Ortlieb

Sergeant Major D.J. Petit (Medical Unit)

Sergeant H.W. Pyne (Divisional Train)

Squadron Quartermaster Sergeant W.A. Read (Divisional Train)

Quartermaster Sergeant W.J. Saunders (RMA Heavy Siege Train)

Private A. Scott (RMLC)

Sergeant A. Sharp

Company Sergeant Major L. Smith (RMLC)

Private H. B. Spencer

Sergeant A.J. Spry

Sergeant B.L. Steed (RMLC)

Corporal Driver C. Sutton (RMA Heavy Siege Train)

Colour Sergeant B.G. Tomkins

Sergeant A.S. Traill (RMLC)

Colour Sergeant Major J.H. Wakeham (RMLI att. RMLC)

Private A.N. Waters

Colour Sergeant Major W. White

Quartermaster Sergeant F.G. Wright

Mentioned in Dispatches

Lieutenant J.E. Adam RM (Divisional Engineers)

Sergeant A. Ainsworth (Divisional Engineers)

Sergeant D. Alexander (RMLC)

Captain P. Allard RM (Divisional Train)

Second Lieutenant B.G. Andrews RMLI (France)

Sergeant S.B. Andrews (Divisional Engineers)

Sgt E. Annion (RMLC)

Gunner J.W. Arkill (Zeebrugge, 1918)

Lieutenant T.G. Atkinson RMA (Howitzer Brigade)

Lieutenant Colonel T.C. Aveling RM (Divisional Engineers)

Mechanic H.M. Avery (Howitzer Brigade)

Sergeant H. Bagge (RMLC)

Sergeant J.H. Bailey (Zeebrugge, 1918)

Captain A.E. Balfour RM (Divisional Train)

Driver J. Baker (RMA Heavy Siege Train)

Sergeant W.J. Baker (Zeebrugge, 1918)

Captain G. Barker RMLI (Antwerp, 1914)

Company Sergeant Major G. Barton (RMA Heavy Siege Train)

Driver Baverstock (Howitzer Brigade)

Sergeant E. Baxter (RMLC)

Sergeant J. Beatson (RMLC)

Lieutenant W. Beloe RM (Divisional Engineers)

Gunner E. Bennett (Howitzer Brigade)

Gunner J. Beresford (AA Brigade)

Sapper E. Best (Divisional Engineers)

Major A.E. Bewes RMLI (Antwerp, 1914)

Corporal C.S. Blake (Divisional Engineers)

Conductor L.A. Blake (Divisional Train)

Lieutenant H. Boffey RMA* (Howitzer Brigade)

Lieutenant C. Bollam RM (Divisional Engineers)

Lieutenant H. Borthwick RM (Divisional Train)

APPENDIX

Sergeant A.C. Branch (Divisional Engineers)

Lieutenant D. Broadwood RMLI (Zeebrugge, 1918)

Lieutenant A.H. Brownrigg RMA (Howitzer Brigade)

Sergeant P.S.W. Buckle (RMLC)

Sapper J.H.P. Burchell (Divisional Engineers)

Sergeant G.A. Burn* (Divisional Engineers)

Lieutenant A.W. Burns RMLC

Lieutenant G.E.M. Burnsside RMA (Howitzer Brigade)

Corporal A.M. Butler MSM* (France)

Major J.F. Cable RMLC

Lieutenant Colonel A.B. Carey RM (Divisional Engineers)

Captain (T/Maj) J.W. Carroll RMLI (att. RMLC)

Lieutenant Colonel F.J. Cartwright DSO RMLI (France)

Major J.B. Chancellor RMA (Heavy Siege Train)

Major C.L. Chapman RM (Divisional Train)

Sergeant J.G. Chapman (RMLC)

Colour Sergeant W. Chave (Howitzer Brigade)

Sergeant J. Church (RMLC)

Private C.B. Clark (RMLC)

Major N.S. Clutterbuck DSO (France)

Major W.E. Cook RM (Divisional Train)

Lance Corporal W.J. Cook (Antwerp, 1914)

Captain J. Cooper RMLC

Major A.A. Cordner RMLI (Zeebrugge, 1918)

Lance Corporal C. Cox (France)

Private F. Craig (France)

Corporal W. Craig (Zeebrugge, 1918)

Captain F.T. Connew RMA (Heavy Siege Train)

Private A. Cooper (France)

Captain T.C. Cuming RMA* (Howitzer Brigade)

Colour Sergeant T. Cunningham (Antwerp, 1914)

Lieutenant M. Curtin RMLI (Antwerp, 1914)

Lieutenant W.M. Curtis RMLI (France)

Sapper W.E. Curtis (Divisional Engineers)

Captain G.E. Cutcher RMLI (France)

Sapper E.L. Damant (Divisional Engineers)

Gunner W. Dance (Zeebrugge, 1918)

Corporal C. Davidson (RMLC)

Quartermaster & Hon. Lieutenant H.A. Day (Divisional Train)

Lieutenant H.A. de Berry RMLI (Zeebrugge, 1918)

Sergeant J. Dick (RMLC)

Corporal F.E. Donovan (France)

Lance Corporal J. Downie (France)

Sergeant A.B.L. Dutton (Divisional Engineers)

Major C.E. Eagles RMLI* (France, Zeebrugge, 1918)

Company Sergeant Major D.E. Eccles (RMLI att RMLC)

Lieutenant Colonel. F. Edwin RM (Divisional Engineers)

Lieutenant F.G. Eliot MC RMLI (France)

Gunner T.C. Englefield (Howitzer Brigade)

Corporal J. English (RMLC)

Major A.K. Evans MC OBE RMLI (France)

Private J. Evans (Zeebrugge, 1918)

Lieutenant Colonel E. G. Evelegh RMLI (Antwerp, 1914)

Sergeant Major C.J. Feeny (Divisional Engineers)

Sergeant H.N. Ferguson (RMLC)

Major M.C. Festing DSO RMLI*** (Antwerp, 1914, France)

Second Lieutenant J. Fielding RMLI (France)

Sergeant A.B. Fisher (RMLC)

Major E.K. Fletcher DSO RMLI (France)

Corporal A.R. Ford (France)

Corporal H.R.S. Frankland (France)

Sergeant Mechanic L.C. Freeman (RMA Heavy Siege Train)

Lieutenant C.G. Foote RMLI (Antwerp, 1914)

Captain L.L. Foster RMA (Howitzer Brigade)

Lieutenant Colonel R.F.C. Foster CMG DSO RMA*** (France)

Private R. Foster (France)

Major A.H. French (Antwerp, 1914)

Captain H.V. Fuller RMLC

Sergeant W. Fuller (RMLC)

Sergeant Major E.C. Gardner (France)

Sergeant W.F. Garnham (Divisional Engineers)

Driver E.W. Gellatly (Howitzer Brigade)

Captain T.H. Gill RMLC

Second Lieutenant F.W. Goldie RMLI (France)

Lieutenant G.R. Goldingham MC RMLI (France)

Private H.D. Gorringe (France)

Lieutenant D.J. Gowney RMLI (Antwerp, 1914)

Gunner J.H. Grady (Zeebrugge, 1918)

Captain R. Grierson RM (Divisional Engineers)

Pte G. W. Hall (Zeebrugge, 1918)

Lieutenant & Quartermaster J. Hammond RMLI (Antwerp, 1914)

Lieutenant Colonel G.H. Harrison RM* (Divisional Engineers)

Lieutenant W.D. Hart RMA (Howitzer Brigade)

Captain T.A. Harvey RMLC

Private J.F. Hawkesworth (Zeebrugge, 1918)

Private T. Hawthorn (RMLC)

Buglar C. Heffernan (Zeebrugge, 1918)

Acting Sergeant Major T. Henderson (RMLC)

Lieutenant G.F. Hilditch RM (Divisional Engineers)

Sergeant R. Hill (Antwerp, 1914)

Private H.W. Hoath (Zeebrugge, 1918)

Lieutenant R. Horn RMLC

Sergeant A.E. Howard (AA Brigade)

Gunner G. Howells (RMA Heavy Siege Train)

Corporal W. Hutchins (RMA Heavy Siege Train)

Lieutenant Colonel A R. Hutchison CB CMG DSO RMLI* (France)

Sergeant W.H. Jayne (Divisional Engineers)

Private N.S. Jeffery (Zeebrugge, 1918)

Major C.F. Jerram CMG DSO RMLI*** (France)

Gunner A. Jennings (Howitzer Brigade)

Driver G. Johnston (Howitzer Brigade)

APPENDIX

Quartermaster Sergeant S. Jones (France)

Colour Segeant E.E. Kirby (Zeebrugge, 1918)

Lieutenant A.G. Kyle RMLI (France)

Lieutenant E.H. Lamb RM (Divisional Engineers)

Sergeant R.H. Langdown (RMLC)

Captain J.H. Lawson RM (Divisional Engineers)

Captain W.R. Ledgard (Howitzer Brigade)

Lieutenant J.C. Lee RMLI (France)

Lieutenant T.W. Lewis RMA (Howitzer Brigade)

Quartermaster Sergeant J. Lintott (Divisional Engineers)

Major H.P. Liston Foulis RMA (Howitzer Brigade)

Second Lieutenant J.V. Lord (France)

Major R.H.D. Lough DSO OBE RMLI** (France)

Driver J.C. Lowe (Howitzer Brigade)

Major F.W. Lumsden RMA (Howitzer Brigade)

Corporal J. Macfarlane (RMLC)

Lieutenant P. Malarky RMLC

Private A.B. Mann (Zeebrugge, 1918)

Sergeant Major S.J. March (France)

Gunner E.J. Marshall (RMA Heavy Siege Train)

Captain J.S. Marshall RM (Divisional Engineers)

Lieutenant R.H. Marsland RMLI* (France)

Corporal E. Martin (Antwerp, 1914)

Gunner A.H. Mason (RMA Heavy Siege Train)

Major G. Matthew RMA

Captain C. Micklem RMA* (Howitzer Brigade)

Brigadier General G.E. Matthews CB CMG RMLI (France)

Lieutenant Colonel T R. McCready DSO MC RMLI* (France)

Captain W.K. McKay RMLC

Lieutenant (A/Captain) J. McKenzie RMA (att. RMLC)

Second Lieutenant J.W. Middleton MC RMLI (France)

Sergeant W.J. Millem (RMLC)

Colour Sergeant C.J. Miller (Howitzer Brigade)

Major L.W. Miller RMLI (France)

Private P. Mills (RMLC)

Quartermaster Sergeant J. Milne (France)

Sergeant A.C. Milson (Howitzer Brigade)

Captain C. Mitchell RMLC

Captain G.T. Monk RMLI (France)

Private J.J R. Montague (RMLC)

Corporal I. Moore (France)

Captain R. Morrison-Scott RMA* (Howitzer Brigade)

Private F.W. Munday (Zeebrugge, 1918)

Sapper J.H. Murray (Divisional Engineers)

Captain R.A. Neville RMLI (France)

Captain G.A. Newling MC RMLI (France)

Lieutenant R.H. Newton RMLC

Sergeant A. Nicholson (RMLC)

Sergeant J. Nimmo (RMLC)

Lieutenant & Quartermaster E. Nobbs RMLI (Antwerp, 1914)

Sapper R.S. Norrie (Divisional Engineers)

Second Lieutenant A.G. Norris RMLI (Zeebrugge, 1918)

Second Lieutenant H.P. Norris RMLC

Lieutenant A.M. Oakden RM (Divisional Engineers)
Private W.T. Osborne (France)
Major H. Ozanne RMLI* (France)
Private G.H. Page (France)
Major General A. Paris KCB CB RMLI* (Antwerp, 1914, Somme 1916)
Bombardier E. Parish (Howitzer Brigade)
Sergeant H.J. Parker (Zeebrugge, 1918)
Lieutenant Colonel C.M. Parsons RMLI (Antwerp, 1914)
Sergeant F.C. Parsons (RMLC)
Captain J.A. Paterson RMLC
Sapper J. Paton (Divisional Engineers)
Lieutenant Colonel P. Peacock CMG (RMA Heavy Siege Train)
Private L. Pearson (RMLC)
Company Sergeant Major H.J. Peck (RMLC)
Captain J.H. Percy RMA* (Howitzer Brigade)
Lieutenant J. Pettigrew RMLC
Lieutenant W.A. Pinkerton RMLI (France)
Lieutenant Colonel G.R. Poole RMA** (Howitzer Brigade)
Lieutenant J. Pordage RMA (AA Brigade)
Captain D. Primrose RMA (Heavy Siege Train)
Major W.H. Pryce-Browne RMLI (Antwerp, 1914)
Sergeant J.P. Purvis (RMLC)
Driver Puttock (AA Brigade)
Major G. L. Raikes RMA* (Howitzer Brigade)
Segeant W.H. Rann (RMA Heavy Train)

Gunner W. Ranson (Zeebrugge, 1918)
Sergeant G.W. Rayner (France)
Gunner E.W. Rayson (RMA Heavy Siege Train)
Captain J.W. Revell RM (Divisional Engineers)
Captain W.H.P. Richards RMLI (Antwerp, 1914)
Lieutenant C.N. Rigby RMA (Howitzer Brigade)
Lieutenant T.N. Riley RM (Divisional Engineers)
Corporal W.T. Robins (Howitzer Brigade)
Lieutenant F.L. Robinson RMA (Howitzer Brigade)
Lieutenant R.H. Roe RM (Divisional Engineers)
Corporal H. Ronald (RMLC)
Gunner E.H. Roxby (Howitzer Brigade)
Sergeant W.H. Ruffle (Howitzer Brigade)
Captain L.H. Rugg RM (Divisional Engineers)
Sergeant J.J. Russell (France)
Lieutenant G. Rutherford RMLI (Antwerp, 1914)
Major P. Sandilands DSO RMLI** (France)
Major F.J. Saunders DSO (France)
Corporal N. Sharrock (Zeebrugge, 1918)
Major C.L. Shubrick RMLI (Antwerp, 1914)
Major E.F.P. Sketchley DSO RMLI (France)
Sergeant W.H. Smee (RMLC)
Second Lieutenant H.C. Smith MC RMLI (France)
Corporal L. Smith (RMLC)

APPENDIX

Company Sergeant Major
P.E.A. Smith (France)

Corporal W.J. Smith (Divisional
Engineers)

Major G.H. Spittle RM (Divisional
Engineers)

Lieutenant A.B. Stewart RM
(Divisional Engineers)

Lieutenant C.A. Stock RMA
(Howitzer Brigade)

Sapper L.F. Summers (Divisional
Engineers)

Lieutenant E.S. Sutcliffe RMLC

Private G. Swire (RMLC)

Captain E.J.B. Tagg DSO RMLI**
(France)

Captain J. Tait RMLC

Company Sergeant Major E. Taylor
(Zeebrugge, 1918)

Major J.W. Teale RM (Divisional
Engineers)

Lieutenant Colonel A.S. Tetley (France)

Sergeant R.O.C. Thompson
(Divisional Engineers)

Lieutenant W. Thompson RMLC

Sergeant A.J.E. Thorburn (RMA
Heavy Siege Train)

Private J.T. Todd (France)

Brigadier General C.N. Trotman CB
RMLI (France)

Colour Sergeant J. Turnbull (France)

Sergeant J.H. Turner (Divisional
Engineers)

Lance Bombardier R.L. Turner
(RMA Heavy Siege Train)

Lieutenant Colonel J.A. Tupman
RMLI* (Antwerp, 1914. (France)

Driver A.B. Turner (Howitzer
Brigade)

Gunner W.A. Underwood (RMA
Heavy Siege Train)

Captain H. Vincent RMA (Howitzer
Brigade)

Sergeant E.A. Vinnell (Howitzer
Brigade)

Acting Sergeant Major J.H. Wakeham
(RMLC)

Captain W.W. Ward RMA (Howitzer
Brigade)

Company Sergeant Major C.J. Watts
(Zeebrugge, 1918)

Private F.J. Webb (France)

Lieutenant W.T. Webley RMA
(Howitzer Brigade)

Lieutenant T. Westby MC (France)

Sergeant F.P. Widdington (Divisional
Engineers)

Staff Sergeant H. Williams DCM
(RMA Heavy Siege Train)

Private H.J. Williams (RMLC)

Captain M. Williams RMA
(Howitzer Brigade)

Lieutenant G. Wilson RMA*
(Howitzer Brigade)

Lieutenant (A/Captain) R.H. Winne
RMLI (att. RMLC)

Company Sergeant Major J. Wishart
(RMLC)

Captain J. White RMLC

Captain W. Wood RMLC

Lieutenant T.G. Wright RMA
(Howitzer Brigade)

Major G.C. Woodcock RMA
(Howitzer Brigade)

Bibliography

BLUMBERG H.E., *Britain's Sea Soldiers*, 2006, Uckfield: Naval and Military Books.

BORASTON J.H. (Ed.), *Sir Douglas Haig's Despatches, December 1915-April 1919*, 1920, London: J.M. Dent.

BROOKS R. & LITTLE M., *Tracing Your Royal Marines Ancestors*, 2009, Barnsley: Pen & Sword.

BUXTON I., *Big Gun Monitors: The History of the Design, Construction and Operation of the Royal Navy's Monitors*, 1978, Windsor: World Ship Society.

CAVE N., *Beaumont Hamel: Newfoundland Park*, 2016, Barnsley: Pen and Sword Books.

COLEMAN E. C., *Khaki Jack: The Royal Naval Division in the First World War*, 2014, Stroud: Amberley Publishing.

CORBETT J. S., *Naval Operations Vol.1*, 1938, London, Longmans Green & Co.

CORRIGAN G., *Mud, Blood and Poppycock*, 2003, London: Cassell.

CRUTTWELL C.R.M.F., *A History of the Great War*, 1934, Oxford: Clarendon Press.

DAVIES F. & MADDOCKS G., *Blood Red Tabs: General Officer Casualties of the Great War 1914-1918,* 2014, Barnsley: Pen and Sword Books.

DONNELL C., *Breaking the Fortress Line 1914*, 2013, Barnsley: Pen & Sword.

DUNN S., *Securing the Narrow Sea: The Dover Patrol 1914-1918*, 2017, Barnsley: Seaforth Publishing.

EDMONDS J.E., *Military Operations France and Belgium 1914: Antwerp, Le Bassee, Armentieres, Messines and Ypres October-November 1914*, 1925, London: Macmillan.

EDMONDS J.E., *Military Operations: France and Belgium 1916*, 1932, London: Macmillan.

FITZGERALD C.C.P., *From Sail to Steam: Naval Recollections, 1878-1905*, 1916, London: E. Arnold.

FLETCHER D., *The Rolls-Royce Armoured Car*, 2012, London: Bloomsbury.

FOSTER H.C., *At Antwerp and the Dardanelles*, 1918, London: Mills & Boon.

FRASER E. & LAUGHTON L.G.C., *The Royal Marine Artillery 1804-1923*, 1923, London: Royal United Services Institution.

BIBLIOGRAPHY

FRENCH J.D.P., *Sir John French's Despatches*, 1918, London: The Graphic.

FUSSELL P., *The Great War and Modern Memory*, 1977, Oxford: Oxford University Press.

GIBSON W., *The Boat: Singapore Escape, Cannibalism at Sea*, 2007, Singapore: Monsoon Books.

GILBERT M., *Winston S. Churchill: The Challenge of War 1914-1916*, 2015, New York: Rosetta Books.

GLIDDON G., *The Battle of the Somme: A Topographical History*, 1994, Stroud: Sutton Publishing.

HARFIELD A.G., *Blandford and the Military*, 1984, Wincanton: Dorset Publishing Company.

HARRIS P., *The Men Who Planned the War: A Study of the Staff of the British Army on the Western Front, 1914-1918*, 2017, Abingdon: Taylor and Francis.

HART P., *The Last Shake on the Ancre,* 2005, London: Cassell.

HASTINGS M., *Catastrophe 1914: Europe Goes to War*, 2013, New York: Random House.

HERBERT A.P., *The Bomber Gypsy and Other Poems*, 1920, New York: Alfred Knopf.

HOGG I. V. & THURSTON L.F., *British Artillery Weapons & Ammunition 1914-1918*, 2019, Brighton: Firestep Publishing.

HOUGH R., *Winston and Clementine*, 1990, London: Bantam.

HUGHES E.A., *The Royal Naval College, Dartmouth*, 1950, London: Winchester Publications.

JERRAM C.F., *A Soldier Gone to Sea: Memoir of a Royal Marine in Both World Wars,* 2016, Jefferson: McFarland.

JERROLD D., *Hawke Battalion: Some Personal Records of Four Years, 1914-1918*, 2006, London: Naval and Military Press.

JERROLD D., *The Royal Naval Division*, 1923, London: Hutchinson & Co.

JONES R.M., *The Diary of a Royal Marine*, 2017, Bridlington: Lodge Books.

KENDALL P., *The Zeebrugge Raid 1918: The Finest Feat of Arms*, 2009, Stroud: The History Press.

KEYES R., *The Naval Memoirs of Admiral of the Fleet Sir Roger Keyes*, 1935, London: T. Butterworth.

LANGWORTH R.M., *Winston Churchill, Myth and Reality*, 2017, Jefferson N.C.: McFarland.

LIDDLE P., *Passchendaele in Perspective: The Third Battle of Ypres*, 2017, Barnsley: Pen & Sword.

LIVESEY J., *The Motor Bandits: The Royal Naval Air Service on the Western Front*, 2015, Oxford: Casemate.

LLOYD N., *Passchendaele: A New History*, 2017, London: Penguin.

MACDONALD J., *Supplying the British Army in the First World War*, 2019, Barnsley: Pen & Sword.

MASON F. K. & WINDROW M., *Air Facts and Feats: A Record of Aerospace Achievement*, 1970, New York: Doubleday.

MCCARTHY C. & SIMKINS P., *The Somme: The Day by Day Account*, 2016, London: Unicorn Publishing Group.

MESSENGER C., *Call to Arms: The British Army 1914-18*, 2015, London: Hachette.

MIDDLEBROOK M. (Ed.), *The Diaries of Pte. Horace Bruckshaw Royal Marine Light Infantry 1915-1916,* 1979, London: Scholar Press.

MURRAY J., *Call to Arms: From Gallipoli to the Western Front*, 1980, London: W. Kimber.

MYERS A.W., *Captain Anthony Wilding*, 1916, London: Hodder & Staughton.

NICOLAS P.H., *Historical Record of the Royal Marine Forces Vol.1.*, 1845, London: Thomas & William Boone.

OLIVER J.J., *Samson and the Dunkirk Circus*, 2017, Createspace Independent Publishing Platform.

PAGE C., *Command in the Royal Naval Division,* 1999, Michigan: Spellmount.

PAUWELS J.R., *The Great Class War 1914-1918*, 2016, Halifax: Formac Publishing.

PELLING H., *Winston Churchill,* 1989, New York: Springer.

PEVSNER N., *The Buildings of England: Hampshire and the Isle of Wight*, 2002, New Haven: Yale University Press.

RAWSON A., *British Expeditionary Force: The 1914 Campaign*, 2008, Barnsley: Pen & Sword.

RINALDI R.A., *Order of Battle of the British Army 1914*, 2008, Delhi: Ravi Rikhye.

ROBBINS G.J. & ATKINSON J.B., *The London B-Type Motor Omnibus,* 1970, The World of Transport.

ROBERTS M., *T. E. Hulme*, 1971, New York: Haskell House.

ROSS, J.N.M., With a Royal Marine Battalion in France in *Journal of the Royal Naval Medical Service*, Vol.3, 1917.

SELLERS L., *The Hood Battalion*, 1995, Barnsley: Pen & Sword.

SMITH P.C., *Per Mare Per Terram: A History of the Royal Marines*, 1974, London: Balfour Books.

SPARROW G & ROSS J.N.M., *On Four Fronts with the Royal Naval Division*, 1918, London: Hodder & Staughton.

STARLING J. & LEE I., *No Labour, No Battle: Military Labour During the First World War*, 2014, Cheltenham: The History Press.

STEEL D., *Steel's Original and Correct List of the Royal Navy, Hired Armed Vessels, Packets, Excise and Revenue Cutters, &c,* 1802, London: Steel.

STRACHAN H., *The First World War: Volume I: To Arms*, 2003, Oxford: OUP.

SWALES R., *Nelson at War 1914-1918*, 2004, Barnsley: Pen & Sword.

BIBLIOGRAPHY

TALLETT K. & TASKER T., *Gavrelle*, 2016, Barnsley: Pen and Sword Books.

TUCKER J.S., *Admiral the Right Hon The Earl of St Vincent GCB &C, Memoirs*, 1844, London: Richard Bentley.

TUCKER S.C., *World War 1, The Essential Reference Guide*, 2016, Santa Barbara: ABC-CLIO.

VANACKER L., *The British on the Belgian Coast in the Great War*, 2018, Ghent: Academia Press.

WARD W.D., *Ole Bill: London Buses and the First World War*, 2014, London: London Transport Museum.

WARNER P., *The Zeebrugge Raid*, 1978, London: William Kimber.

WINTON J., *The Victoria Cross at Sea: The Sailors, Marines and Naval Airmen Awarded Britain's Highest Honour*, 2016, Barnsley: Frontline Books.

ZERBE B., *The Birth of the Royal Marines*, 2013, Woodbridge: Boydell Press.

Archive Documents

ADM 1/8412/51 (Despatch of personnel of Royal Marine Artillery and two howitzers to France).

ADM 137/3065 (RMLI Battalions Aug 1916-Apr 1918).

ADM 137/3072-3 (Royal Marine Artillery Howitzer Brigade).

ADM 137/3925 (Royal Marine Artillery Anti-Aircraft Brigade, Departure for Dunkirk).

ADM 157 (Royal Marine Attestation Forms).

ADM 183 (RMLI Chatham Division Records).

ADM 184 (RMLI Plymouth Division Records).

ADM 185 (RMLI Portsmouth Division Records).

ADM 193 (Records of RMLI Detached Units).

ADM 1 8527/162 (Provision of a Distinctive Badge for Royal Marine Labour Corps).

WO/95/3110 (RMLI War Diaries).

WO 95/327 (Army Troops. Heavy Howitzer Royal Marine Artillery).

WO 95/483/1 (Army Troops. 1 Gun, Heavy Howitzer Royal Marine Artillery).

WO 95/3108/2 (Royal Marine Brigade Chatham Battalion Aug-Oct 1914).

Private letters of 2Lt Louis M. Stokes RMLI, Rugby School Archive.

Endnotes

Introduction

1. NICOLAS P. H., *Historical Record of the Royal Marine Forces Vol.1.*, 1845, London: Thomas and William Boone, p1.
2. ZERBE B., *The Birth of the Royal Marines*, 2013, Woodbridge: Boydell Press, p43.
3. STEEL D., *Steel's Original and Correct List of the Royal Navy, Hired Armed Vessels, Packets, Excise and Revenue Cutters, &c*, 1802, London: Steel, p43.
4. *Reports from Committees 1847-8*, Vol.15, Pt.II, Navy, Army and Ordnance Estimates, p.1045.
5. House of Commons Debate 7 March 1956, *Hansard* vol.549, cc.2080-1.
6. PEVSNER N., *The Buildings of England: Hampshire and the Isle of Wight*, 2002, New Haven: Yale University Press.
7. *Mexborough & Swinton Times*, 21 August 1915.
8. FITZGERALD C.C.P., *From Sail to Steam: Naval Recollections, 1878-1905*, 1916, London: E. Arnold, p262.
9. HANKEY M., *The Supreme Command, Vol.1*, 2014, London: Routledge, p167.
10. BLUMBERG H.E., *Britain's Sea Soldiers*, 2006, Uckfield: Naval and Military Books, p472.
11. HARFIELD A.G., *Blandford and the Military: Including the History of Blandford Camp*, 1984, Bridport: Dorset Publishing Company, p33.
12. SELLERS L. *The Hood Battalion*, 1995, Barnsley: Pen & Sword, p38.
13. *The Statutes of the United Kingdom of Great Britain and Ireland, 10 & 11 Victoria,* 1847, HM Statute & Law Printers, p495.
14. *The Public General Statutes: With a List of the Local and Private Acts Passed in the Fifth and Sixth Years of the Reign of King George V, Vol. 53*, 1916, London: The Council of Law Reporting, p38.

Chapter 1: Belgium 1914

1. BLUMBERG H.E., 2006, p109.
2. *The London Gazette*, Issue 28765, 17 October 1913, p7237.

3. FRENCH J.D.P., *Sir John French's Despatches*, 1918, *The Graphic*, pp10-12.
4. MASON F.K. & WINDROW M., Air Facts and Feats: A Record of Aerospace Achievement, 1970, New York: Doubleday, p101.
5. CORBETT J.S., *Naval Operations Vol.1*, 1938, London, Longmans Green & Co, p124.
6. FLETCHER D., *The Rolls-Royce Armoured Car*, 2012, London: Bloomsbury, pp1-4.
7. RAWSON A., *British Expeditionary Force: The 1914 Campaign*, 2008, Barnsley: Pen & Sword.
8. LANGWORTH R.M., *Winston Churchill, Myth and Reality*, 2017, Jefferson N.C.: McFarland, p58.
9. PELLING H., *Winston Churchill,* 1989, New York: Springer, p184.
10. GILBERT M., *Winston S. Churchill: The Challenge of War 1914-1916*, 2015, New York: Rosetta Books, p14.
11. GILBERT M., 2015, p15.

Chapter 2: France 1916

1. MIDDLEBROOK M. (Ed.), *The Diaries of Pte. Horace Bruckshaw Royal Marine Light Infantry 1915-1916,* 1979, London: Scholar Press, p143.
2. SELLERS L., 1995, p118.
3. MIDDLEBROOK M. (Ed.) 1979, p154.
4. HERBERT A.P., *The Bomber Gypsy and Other Poems*, 1920, New York: Alfred Knopf, pp18-19
5. Private letters of 2Lt Louis M. Stokes RMLI, Rugby School Archive.
6. PAUWELS J. R., *The Great Class War 1914-1918*, 2016, Halifax: Formac Publishing, p303.
7. CAVE N., Beaumont Hamel: Newfoundland Park, 2016, Barnsley: Pen and Sword Books.
8. ROSS, J.N.M. With a Royal Marine Battalion in France in *Journal of the Royal Naval Medical Service*, Vol.3, 1917, p468.
9. CAVE N., 2016.

Chapter 3: France and Belgium 1917

1. BLUMBERG H.E., 2006, p325.
2. *The Blue*, Vol.XLV, No.7, June 1918, p148.
3. COLEMAN E.C., *Khaki Jack: The Royal Naval Division in the First World War*, 2014, Stroud: Amberley Publishing.
4. JERROLD D., *The Royal Naval Division*, 1923, London: Hutchinson & Co, p269.

Chapter 4: France and Belgium 1918

1. 2/RMLI War Diary 1 February 1918.
2. TUCKER S.C., *World War 1, The Essential Reference Guide*, 2016, Santa Barbara: ABC-CLIO, p307.
3. BLUMBERG H.E., 2006, p363.
4. SELLERS L., 1995, p275.
5. JERROLD D., 1923, p326.
6. BLUMBERG H.E., 2006, p381.
7. SELLERS L., 1995, pp118-119.

Chapter 5: The Royal Marine Artillery

1. ADM137/3072. ADM 137/3925.
2. ROBERTS M., T.E. Hulme, 1971, New York: Haskell House, pp30-1.
3. BLUMBERG H.E., 2006, p180.

Chapter 6: The Raid on Zeebrugge

1. KEYES R., The Naval Memoirs of Admiral of the Fleet Sir Roger Keyes, 1935, London: T. Butterworth, p249.
2. *The London Gazette*, Issue 30807, 23 July 1918, p8586.
3. *The Marine Corps Gazette*, Vol.3, 1917, p156.

Chapter 8: Miscellaneous Units

1. WARD W.D., *Ole Bill: London Buses and the First World War*, 2014, London: London Transport Museum.
2. ROBBINS G.J., & ATKINSON J.B., *The London B-Type Motor Omnibus*, 1970, The World of Transport.
3. MYERS A.W., *Captain Anthony Wilding*, 1916, London: Hodder & Staughton.
4. BLUMBERG H.E., 2006, p452.
5. ADM 1 8527/162.

Chapter 9: Notable Personalities

1. See GIBSON W., *The Boat: Singapore Escape, Cannibalism at Sea*, 2007, Singapore: Monsoon Books.
2. *The London Gazette, Issue 29940, 13 February 1917.*

Index

INDEX